BEWILDERED TRAVEL

Bewildered

STUDIES IN RELIGION AND CULTURE
Frank Burch Brown, Gary L. Ebersole, and Edith Wyschogrod, Editors

Travel

The Sacred Quest for Confusion

FREDERICK J. RUF

University of Virginia Press • Charlottesville and London

University of Virginia Press
© 2007 by the Rector and Visitors of the University of Virginia
All rights reserved
Printed in the United States of America on acid-free paper
First published 2007

9 8 7 6 5 4 3 2 1

Library of Congress Cataloging-in-Publication Data
Ruf, Frederick J., 1950–
    Bewildered travel : the sacred quest for confusion / Frederick J. Ruf.
        p.   cm. — (Studies in religion and culture)
    Includes bibliographical references and index.
    ISBN 978-0-8139-2667-4 (cloth : alk. paper) — ISBN 978-0-8139-2674-2
(pbk. : alk. paper)
    1. Pilgrims and pilgrimages. 2. Travel—Religious aspects. I. Title.
BL619.P5R84 2007
910.4—dc22   2007007499

Excerpts from "Going There," "On Stone," "Beyond Beginnings," and "The Edge
of the World" from *The Great Fires Poems, 1982–1992* by Jack Gilbert, copyright
© 1994 by Jack Gilbert, used by permission of Alfred Knopf, a division of Random House, Inc.

To Natalie Kontakos, who shows me new destinations

Contents

Acknowledgments

TO SAY THIS BOOK WAS YEARS IN THE MAKING IS NO EXAGGERA-
tion. It began when I boarded a TWA flight for the Netherlands
in August 1968, and it only ends now arbitrarily. I've spoken with
a lot of people about travel in those decades, so this list of names
is partial and inadequate, but it is, more or less, chronological:
My thanks go to Jack Perfect, Erik Thunnissen, Norton Rosenthal,
Randy Perry, Jim Clemons, Danny Lesny, Rick Reckman, Chris-
tine Ruf, Lew Rosenbluth, Tom Walker, Steve Forrest, Josie Pat-
terson, Ben Lynch, Joe Murphy, Theresa Sanders, Jim Donahue,
Reni Ovadia, Charlie Winquist, the Syracuse University Religion
Department, Corrine Dempsey, Alessandra Farkas, Nancy Good-
man, Ariel Glucklich, Susanna Thomas, Muriam Davis, Jen Val-
lon, Brent Plate, Heath Atchley, Yasemin Congar, Julia Forrester,
Naomi Keller, Matt Lewis, and Natalie Kontakos. A particular
thanks to Joanna and Jesse Ruf: home and away my best compan-

ions. It always seemed gratuitous when authors thanked their students, but now I understand: thanks to all of you. The research and writing were supported by a Karl F. Landegger Faculty Development Grant at Georgetown University, by a Georgetown Graduate School Grant-in-Aid, and by the daily stimulation of my colleagues in the Theology Department of Georgetown University.

See his eyes darken in bewilderment—
No, in joy—and his lips part
To greet the perfect stranger.

James Merrill, "The Friend of the Fourth Decade"

Introduction

AS I WAS FINISHING THIS BOOK, I WAS MUGGED. IT WAS NOTH-ing terrible, a two-inch bruise on my upper arm was the only physical effect. The teenager who robbed me shouted that his friend had a gun, which caused the strongest emotional effects, fear and intimidation. I surrendered what he wanted, my cell phone and some cash. I offered no resistance when he hit me several times, just bending to shield my head. I surrendered any ability to question, to object, to challenge, to resist. I became a victim. But as such things go, it was a mild incident. He was so preoccupied with the cell phone, fishing it out of my pants' pocket, that I was able to protect my wallet, taking two bills out from among the mess inside. Maybe he got forty dollars, maybe he got two. He didn't seem to look. He wanted the cell. I got away more or less unscathed.

I begin this book with the incident for a number of reasons. It happened eight-tenths of a mile from my home, as I walked to catch the Washington Metro, and so, in a way, it took place traveling. No one is mugged at home. But as soon as we walk out of our front doors, the journey begins, and travel means mischance. It means misfortune. It means the safety and protection of home are gone. Home is where there are walls and doors and locks, and the people there mostly don't steal from us. Leaving home means taking risks, whether it's eight-tenths of a mile away or a thousand. Our homes are on streets and not far are other streets. They lead us to misfortunes.

I bring it up, too, because of an odd feeling I have had through the years of writing this book. In the chapters ahead I recount travels by Paul Bowles in Morocco, by Henry Miller and Jack Gilbert in Greece, by Susan Brind Morrow in Egypt, by Alphonso Lingis in Thailand, Nicaragua, and the Philippines, as well as my own in Mexico, Ghana, India, Israel, Turkey, Iran, the Netherlands, and the Czech Republic—and there are many other foreign places discussed. But I have had the feeling throughout that I didn't need to go so far. Of the seventeen thousand people in my town, a close-in Washington suburb, nearly a third were born outside the United States, half of them in Latin America and most of the rest in Africa. There is a neighborhood a mile away that is predominantly Latin and West African, and when I go shopping for food there, I am among Salvadorans, Guatemalans, Hondurans, Dominicans, Ethiopians, Nigerians, and Eritreans, and I could as easily buy foods that puzzle me as foods called normal in much of America. When I walk into the tiny shop where I get my hair cut, there are chairs staffed by women from Cambodia and a man from Vietnam. I am the outsider.

Why travel abroad? Why cross the border of the town, not to mention the state or nation? I say again, once we step across the threshold, we are abroad. As soon as we step into the street, we are about to encounter everything I describe in this book. In some ways it could be much more fascinating to study travel near home, the travel that is not home though it seems to be, as going into our own attics, basements, and garages—even into the cabinets and under the sink—is leaving home, too. But "abroad" is where we have gone. We have felt the need to step across the border, to fly across the ocean, to go "far" away, and yet we should not feel at home while we are still "here." Bewilderment with all of its values is here, too.

Two more reasons why I bring up the mugging. As I look back at the description I have of it, I notice all the sentences that begin with "I." We are taught not to use the first-person pronoun when we write academic prose. Our high school English teachers sternly warned us. The style manuals for journals discourage it. If our analysis is to be persuasive, the impersonal voice is crucial. Reason is speaking in academic prose, not a person, as much in the humanities as in the sciences. This book is not authoritative, I'm afraid. *I* am writing it. *I* am speaking in it. *I* am a particular person—male, white, born in New York in 1950 of a native New Yorker who taught music in the public school system and a South Carolinian, exiled from the South by a World War II romance. This study is idiosyncratic. It relies on experiences I have had, on books I have loved, on intellectual theories that have been persuasive to me. My task in this book is not to reveal how "we" ought to think about travel, but to pass some ideas along on the chance that "you" will find them interesting. I often say "we" in this book, not because I presume to know but in order to suggest, gently. My "we" will no doubt fail as often as it succeeds. How could it be otherwise? I am listening to a song as I write this. David Gray is singing, "Tell me something I don't already know."[1] All I want to do is tell you something you might not already know.

The final reason for citing the mugging is the real point of the book. As I have been suggesting, leaving home is risky. In the title of the book, it risks bewilderment, and bewilderment is not usually fun. Confusion is what we don't want. Knowledge, information, clarity, and good sense are what we cling to and seek . . . and yet. That is a two-word quote from Wallace Stevens that I have long loved and that I find myself repeating to myself as I travel, "and yet." We believe that we have it right, and how could we possibly have it wrong? Knowledge, information, clarity, and good sense! And yet. And yet we leave home, we step into the street, street carries us to street, and within eight-tenths of a mile we are mugged, perhaps physically, certainly emotionally. The intimidating assaults us, confusion confronts us, and we bend our heads down to shoulder the beating of our clarity and good sense. And this is the strangest part: we submit to it willingly. It is why we have left home. Not to be mugged, of course. Not to become the victims of crime—please don't misunderstand. But we go to where we are strangers, unable to make sense of what is going on, unable to understand the local language or customs adequately. We are stunned by sights and encounters. We lose our moorings. We get lost. It is difficult, very difficult. And yet. And yet, we are glad we went. It's not the only way to see travel, but it's what this book will urge: that what travel means is not just misfortune but seeking misfortune. In some sense, wanting it. And it is of such crucial importance to us that we must call it religious.

Leaving home, stepping into the way that will lead us away, far away, walking among strangers, being stunned, getting lost— those are religious behaviors. William James defines the religious as what enables us to "front life." It is a nautical metaphor, I believe, one that suggests pointing the craft into the wind, into the storm, into life, not fleeing it, but heading right into it. However valuable clear sailing might be, religious value results from going out into the deep seas and the powerful winds and fronting them. Pilgrimage (in the idiosyncratic view of this book) is the epitome of religion.

The following chapters contain nothing else. Henry Miller, Paul Bowles, Jack Gilbert, Alphonso Lingis, Susan Brind Morrow, Diane Johnson, Walt Whitman, Ralph Waldo Emerson, and many others. And me. Fronting life. Looking for a beating. Wanting to be robbed. Craving the sacred.

ONE Love of Ruptures

I WAS ONCE IN AGRA, IN INDIA, AND WALKING NOT FAR FROM my small hotel, the deep crimson of the Red Fort looming less than a quarter mile away. I'd only been in Agra for a few hours, and I wanted to get a feel for the place. Ahead I saw a crowd of people, and I walked over to see what they found so compelling. I easily looked through the people to what was on the ground in the center of the crowd—a woman with no hands and no feet, trying to eat. The light from that sight etched into my retina for a fraction of a second before I reeled away into the crowded streets, hoping that other sights would rub it away. They didn't. Nothing has. The sight of such deprivation has lain like a wound in my memory. Every day in India had experiences that ruptured my accustomed surfaces, many of astonishing beauty or kindness and others like that corrosive sight, and yet I loved them all. And wherever I travel, I am seeking more disruption. What is there to love? That is the subject of this chapter and ultimately of this book.

At the beginning of one of his books of travel, Paul Bowles declares, "Each time I go to a place I have not seen before, I hope it will be as different as possible from the places I already know."[1] I wonder if everyone who reads that statement feels the same mixture of alarm and excitement as I do. I suspect that most people are as attached to the familiar as I am, as glad to arrive home in the afternoon or evening, and as happy that "home" is still homelike, with nothing radically changed.

I have moved many times in my life, and each time it was fairly wrenching. The most recent move was to the Washington suburbs, and it took at least two years before I felt like it was my town and that I was part of it. For those two years I felt that the neighbors were sizing me up, deciding whether to be neighborly, after all. I felt wary in the stores and on the streets, unable to let down my guard. Today it seems foolish because this town now feels so thoroughly like my home, but I've also been here seventeen years now. Bowles wants to be in an unfamiliar place? Not I. I want to be on friendly ground, among family, and in a town that I know. I want to live in a place that's as familiar as possible, not ever more foreign, as seems to be true for Bowles.

That's why I feel alarmed by Bowles's statement—because the familiar is so hard to establish and can be taken away so easily. Soon after my family and I arrived in our town, a house a few streets away developed a gas leak that exploded. I drove past that house several times, horrified by the walls that had buckled out and fallen off the foundation. A year or two later, Washington was struck by violent thunderstorms with vertical winds of such power that hundreds of very large trees were blown down. When I finally reached home that day, I saw dozens of enormous oaks leaning on neighbors' houses. They looked a bit as though they'd fainted and required some brief support, but for the splintered eaves and gaping roots displaying what opens up or rips when the familiar loses its stability.

For those reasons and more, as soon as my car clears the top of the hill across from my home, I check for the signs of whatever might have disturbed the familiar—gas or lightning, the collapse of a chestnut oak, or the bursting of a pipe. Yes, I want home to be as familiar as possible. I want the kids to run and give me a hug. I want to be able to find the book I'm currently reading. I want the usual schedule of soccer games and maybe a drink with friends on my porch. But Paul Bowles appears to want none of it.

So why does Paul Bowles want a place to be as different as possible—and why does that prospect paradoxically attract me?

Consider this story: Three young Americans arrive in North Africa just after the end of World War II. It's an odd time to travel, just as millions of others around the globe are heading home after years of being refugees or combatants. These three wandered in South America during the war, and now, as though in search of landscapes that are even farther away as well as desolate and scarred, they arrive at the North African port. They seem determined to be refugees and to be ever more homeless. They travel, they say, in order to reject what's not to their liking, and they quickly shun nearly all they encounter, people and places. They stay in no town long, but quickly move on.

One, of course, is the leader, the instigator, and his name, ironically, is Port. Even he hesitates as soon as they stand on the dock. He finds himself wanting to stay on the ship and go on to Istanbul, a place less remote, but he doesn't. With a kind of fatality, they travel into the interior, into greater and greater emptiness and strangeness until Port is dead and his wife, Kit, is enslaved, and one alone, as the saying goes, returns to tell the tale. "The difference between something and nothing is nothing," Port remarks enigmatically but ominously.[2] They have insisted on leaving any place that resembles "something" and moving on toward a very inhospitable nothing.

These are the events in *The Sheltering Sky,* a book that has attracted readers by the millions. Bernardo Bertolucci made it into a very successful film. Why? Why don't readers reject it outright—shun it, ignore it? It has sold millions of copies and been translated into dozens of languages. It has been called the greatest novel of the postwar period. What is its attraction?

Why, in fact, is there an entire tradition of American travel writers who try to get lost and who seek the strange? I should make my grandest claim clear from the start: in spite of what I have said—quite sincerely—about the importance of home and of the familiar, bewilderment has a powerful fascination for us. It's in Bowles and Henry Miller, in Mark Twain and Walt Whitman, in the poets Mary Oliver, James Merrill, and Jack Gilbert, in such present-day travelers as Susan Brind Morrow, Mary Morris, and Diane Johnson, and in the philosopher Alphonso Lingis. But most importantly, it has been pervasive among Americans generally over the past hundred-odd years. It's in most of us. Just like Bowles, we are fascinated with the quest for higher and higher degrees of strangeness, for the circles farther and farther from home. And we search for bewilderment ourselves. I think we crave it. I call it the love of ruptures.

Orientation

This book about travel and its love of ruptures is a religious study, and since that may be an odd perspective for many, I want to explain it. To put it simply, if we want to understand how travel functions so crucially for us, we need to look at its role in our lives. We need to see how travel and our love of its ruptures provide us with orientation in our lives, and that is a topic for a religious study.

We are accustomed to two attitudes toward religion: advocacy and avoidance. If we are religious, our attitude is seldom lukewarm or dispassionate. Religion is said to present ultimates, and those ultimates are demanding. They are thought to be absolutes so they ground, they justify and require. The religious position against abortion or capital punishment, or against racism, or for justice or sexual purity tolerates little if any compromise. Religion is thought of not as a mere surface phenomenon; it comes from the depths, and depths are commanding. We sacrifice to the deeps, casting in the superficial, letting it fall and break, even

bleed if it is living. Mere tempor‸
or even reason must be sacrificed ‸
we value most must be sacrificed: lo
really God, then even Isaac, our own ch
great-great-grandfather Rev. Samuel Moc
"command and compel." He was a man wh‸
rishioners out of a tavern or denounce them
dared to walk out of his church.[3]

Such strong and often single-minded determi‸   ‸kes
others uneasy. We've all been at social gatherings wh‸ ‸ the easy
conversation hits a rock of religious conviction, and we try to
move on past without anything being bruised and some roll
their eyes. We look elsewhere in the room for conviviality for
there is none on that unshifting place. Political values, artistic
ones, community—everything can break against religious conviction and, hence, it is avoided. If we have religious convictions
ourselves, then rock knocks against rock. Ancient truths echo to
equally ancient ones.

The religious depths are thought to be something extraordinary, the arduous and rare, the supernatural, the transcendent.
Poet Mary Oliver says that the spiritual and artistic take place
only in the extraordinary, never indoors, never among comforts.[4]
We think it must involve a God beyond all thought or an event of
transhistorical value or a place that is the absolute center.
Uniqueness, "beyond-ness," "utter-ness" are thought to be where
the really religious lies.

I would like to suggest that we step back and focus on what
these absolutes *do*—and to suggest that their function is not so
extraordinary at all but extremely common: they provide humans
with orientation in their lives. In fact, that function is so basic
that all humans have it. Orientation is so ordinary that we don't
realize how crucial it is, like gravity, and like gravity it keeps us
on the ground.

Its value became vivid to me when I taught high school and
had a student who seemed to be chronically disoriented in the
spatial sense. We go to the supermarket—or to the kitchen, for

...nd it without needing to search because we ...orientation. We don't even need to think. And if ...s a more difficult place to find, a place we go to less commonly, our orientation gets us there, too. Where's Joanna's basketball game this evening? How do I get to Sligo Middle School? Oh, yes, out University and then, somewhere past Colesville Road, a left, then a ways beyond Sligo Creek Parkway on the right. We do it with compass directions—north, south, east, west—or with landmarks or major routes. However it is done, orientation in our surroundings is crucial to our functioning. Ultimately, it keeps us alive since we need to find not only basketball games but our dinners and our homes.

My student, David, was tall, awkward, slightly befuddled, somewhat unkempt, utterly sincere—and quite thoroughly disoriented. He could not manage to find my PE class from the locker room—a sixty-second walk down a driveway, across a field, and through some trees to the football field. Twenty minutes into the PE period, David would wander up. He'd found us, I think, by trial and error. It's possible, I'm sure, that David spent the twenty minutes hanging out by the parking lot, smoking cigarettes, or that he hated playing touch football and just stayed in the locker room as long as he could, but I don't think so. He was just chronically lost.

On a field trip to Amish Country, the ninth grade and I sat on a bus outside the hotel for a long time, waiting for David. I went upstairs—not a complicated route—and found him between his door and the elevator, walking in circles, unable to begin the journey of just sixty feet. I think he lacked the critical ability to imagine how to move from here to there. I sometimes wonder what's become of him. I hope there's someone who helps him find his way to work and then back home. For without spatial orientation—well, potentially we could die. Without it, we don't eat and don't have shelter. Without it, we can't move far from home, and our physical surroundings are constantly foreign and strange.

But far more crucial than spatial orientation is orientation in our lives—is having a sense of how we get where we're going in our lives. For we're going somewhere in our lives, and we require a sense of direction to move there, wherever "there" is. I think back to when I was about five, the middle child of three, living in a borough of New York, my father a teacher of music and my mother exiled from the South. What brought me from there to here? How did I find my way to the courses I teach every week, to the family in the Washington suburbs, to the PC on which I'm writing this book? There are numberless external factors, of course—just as there were for David those mornings in Connecticut—but there is also a sense of orientation that I possessed that helped direct my choices and bring me here.

In order to be oriented either in the spatial or the "life" sense, we need to have an answer to three questions: Who are we? Where are we? And where are we going? The answers to those questions will determine our orientation. Each of them is a vast question with no single answer for any individual. We never formulate answers explicitly. But we do have a complex of senses of who and where we are and where we're going, complexes that are in constant motion, just as a gyroscope is, and that, perhaps, provide us with direction in a similar way.

I had a student once who was raised by her family to think that she was the nice one and her brother was the smart one. There's quite an orientation provided by such a sense of identity. Many of us are told something similar, and it strongly influences us to make the "nice" choices, to choose the nice friends, to pursue a nice career. The effect on our orientation is subtle and pervasive. This particular student was involved in an awful tragedy. Her parents were zealous members of a religious sect and, in a test of faith, barricaded themselves in their home and fasted. After a number of days, my student realized that her brother was dying and insisted on getting help. Her parents asked her if she had faith in God. So she stayed—and her brother died. She was the nice one, she told me.

And what of the child who is told that he always screws up? The child who senses that it is up to her to keep her family happy?

What of the child who is physically or sexually abused? The possibilities are endless, but everyone develops a sense—a number of senses—of who they are, and their movement through life is powerfully affected by that aspect of their orientation.

I had another student who wrote an essay about his mother's devotion to a younger brother who lay dying of cancer over several years. The subtext of his essay was his own deprivation, as caring for the other son completely absorbed his mother, and my student's own nourishment dried up. What became of his orientation in life? "Where" is he? In a world where mothers must leave their own sons for a more important commitment, a place without complaint, for who could begrudge a dying brother? Where is he going in his life? What decisions will he make? Who will he fall in love with? What sort of work will he do? Where will he be in five years, in ten, in twenty? I'm not suggesting a rigid determinism. There is not one orientation that results from a brother's death. He might see all women as likely to withdraw their care, or he might realize how much care matters and pursue it instead of other attributes in a woman. But the orientation that is composed, in part, of his sense of "where" he is will shape where he "goes" in his life. It will create his orientation.

❖ • ❖

Religions have formed our orientations traditionally and historically. In fact, shaping orientation has been the most important function of a religion. It is religion that has told humans not only who they are but who they really are. They are children of God. They are made in God's image. They are sinners. Religions talk of souls or the atman or about no atman. Religions have told humans where they are really: in a place of trial, a fallen world, a vale of tears. And religions have told humans where they are really going: the kingdom of God, the afterlife, salvation, damnation. As Jacques Barzun puts it, it made about as much sense in the European Middle Ages to ask what your faith was as asking today what your physics is.[5] Faith—and its definite sense of who you were, where you were, and where you were going—determined a person's orientation until recent centuries.

But at least for the past four centuries and perhaps for far
longer, our orientations have been formed not simply from religions. And that is the importance of "ordinary" religion and what
is sometimes called "implicit" religion. We need to be oriented
no less today than previously, and what composes that orientation is more likely to be quite ordinary and often not even no-
ticed. I'm reminded of what T. S. Eliot considered the religiously
significant aspects of culture: he listed "Derby Day, Henley Re-
gatta, Cowes, the twelfth of August, a cup final, the dog races, the
pin table, the dart board, Wensleydale cheese, boiled cabbage cut
into sections, beetroot in vinegar, nineteenth-century gothic
churches and the music of Elgar."[6] The boiled cabbage is what I
love, for there's certainly nothing arduous or rare about it, nothing elevated, nothing ethereal, nothing transcendent. We are oriented by what's on our table. Is it vegan? Venison we hunted ourselves? The meatloaf my mother perfected? What we take into
our mouths may be religiously crucial. So might be a song, a pho-
tograph, a film. A ninth-grade English teacher invited to dinner
who praised my sense of humor. My father's strong defense of
my mother when she was insulted by a store clerk. My sister lying
in a St. Vincent's Hospital and dying of leukemia. Those events
orient me, telling me who I really am or really ought to be, and
they function more powerfully than reciting the Baltimore Cate-
chism in Saint Boniface Elementary School or Father Fee lifting
the host at 9 a.m. Mass or the Stations of the Cross lining the
little stone church in Sea Cliff, New York.

◆ ● ◆

Needing and finding orientation is not remarkable. What constantly surprises me is how often we want to be disoriented, often
when we leave home. Diane Johnson tells a story of tobogganing
down an icy slope in Switzerland—at night. It's incredibly stupid,
of course, and she knows it but hurtles down that mountain anyway. It's Europe—"cozy old Europe," she calls it—so as close to
home as Johnson can be without actually being home. Yet the
place is still eerily strange (there are window displays of "sinister
steel dental implements" and mock-stalkings by people in Mickey

Mouse masks), and Johnson suggests that has something to do with her taking part in the crazy sledding adventure, very much against her better judgment. In the strange we do the strange. She and her husband push off into the darkness down an icy track with nothing but its rising side and their very uncertain control of the toboggan protecting them from a precipitous drop. They can't see where they're going, and they're moving very fast. Trees don't come with foam padding or toboggans with airbags. As soon as they build up speed they are out of control and unable to see well enough to steer. Naturally enough, people get hurt. She knows it's stupid, but she does it anyway. It's what we do when we travel, she says.

But all of us have similar stories—tales of wandering too far from home and finding the very unhomelike. When we return, we love to tell the stories of danger and distress. I wonder if we don't, in fact, seek them.

Disorientation: The Love of Ruptures

I would like to call this craving for disorientation the "love of ruptures," with full acknowledgment of how puzzling and perhaps even perverse that love may seem to be. I'm afraid it will take this entire chapter to make it sensible. I will try to keep one foot on the ground in describing this love of ruptures by citing a stunning example of it, from the poet Mary Oliver, and by telling a few anecdotes of my own from time to time.

Mary Oliver is a Pulitzer Prize–winning poet and not usually considered a travel writer. In fact, her first volume was bluntly titled No Voyage and Other Poems (1965). She says in the title poem that she doesn't travel because travel seems like a means to escape the turmoil that she finds at home, and she's determined to face those domestic conflicts. But as the years and volumes pass, she does travel, after all—not abroad (usually) but out into the bogs, seashores, and forests of Ohio, New York, Vermont, and Cape Cod, her homes. She has, in fact, discovered that turmoil is not avoided but discovered in those trampings: "All my life," she writes, "I have been restless—I have felt there is something more wonderful than gloss—than wholesomeness—than staying at home."[7] In nature she searches for the "dazzling darkness" that will startle, alarm, and amaze her there—owls, foxes, bears, snakes, and egrets (the last animal she calls, memorably, a "dark death that opens like a white door"). So home won't do for Oliver, any more than it will for Bowles—or us. "Wholesomeness," "glossing over" won't do. She, too, seeks the disruptions of travel.

In the early 1980s, she also travels abroad. In a poem she titles "Magellan," she urges, "Let us risk the wildest places, Lest we go down in comfort, and despair." She does risk those places in three poems ("Singapore," "Indonesia," and "Acid") that resulted from a U.S. Information Services–sponsored trip to Asia in 1984. The poems are probably not among her best for she does not achieve the almost mystical acceptance of the "dazzling darkness" that we discover in her walks into the marsh or woods. There is, instead, principally disturbance.

The poem called "Acid" finds her in Jakarta, where she happens across something wilder than she'd bargained for. In the Indonesian capital she is "among the vendors of flowers and soft drinks," but that appealing image is broken when she encounters a child "with a hideous mouth," intentionally deformed to make him a more effective beggar. It's a horrible encounter, enough to make us yearn for home and wholesomeness. What do we do when we feel that we have the strength to leave home, the strength to encounter "wildness," and we encounter, instead, a still more terrible home—a home where deforming the child's mouth is, perhaps, a shrewd financial move or a necessary one?

Oliver gave the boy a small coin, and he gave her "a look of cunning." It's a chilling statement of an extremely disruptive encounter. In a phrase that epitomizes the ruptures that I wish to discuss in this book, she describes his look as "a bead of acid." The very tissues of her mind have been burned, not just by a deformity and not just by an intentional one, but by one addressed directly to her—"a look of cunning." The woman who is glad to encounter the "dark death" of the egret has gone too far into the wild. Maybe it's time for Magellan to sail on home (though Magellan, of course, dies on his return voyage). She's traveled six thousand miles to encounter something that she simply cannot assimilate—something, in fact, that burns instead of dazzles.

But Mary Oliver does not simply fly on home. As far as I can tell, she took no more distant journeys, just those into the local natural wilds, but she does not flee, as one might if one had been burned. In fact, she says that she carries the bead of acid with her—as a reminder of how "you can creep out of your own life and become someone else." She wants to remember. She wants to continue to see the "look of cunning," becoming both that boy and the woman who has been burned by his look. Common sense tells us not to carry acid, even if it's just a bead, and if we must, to carry it in a sturdy Pyrex flask. But Mary Oliver carries it in the tissues of her mind, and I am fascinated by that recklessness. I see the paradoxical love of ruptures in it. Some years earlier Oliver wrote that she envied a grandmother who was able to "[pour] confusion out" when she canned fruit in her kitchen. When she is in the Cape Cod forests she is able to encounter and transform confusion (the egret, for example), but in Jakarta, Oliver cannot. The "painful and irrational scene" is what she finds in Jakarta. And, crucially, it is what she has sought in all her travels, of whatever distance from home, and we need to understand why.

I would like to hold onto that poem and the experience it presents and spin out a way of imagining the role of disruptions in our lives generally. It's a theory—one that is fairly commonplace in postmodern thought—that may help us understand the importance of ruptures in our lives, and, as a result, our puzzling love of them.

Exploring Surfaces

In 1936, William Butler Yeats wrote that "All things fall and are built again / And those that build them again are gay."[8] His generation had witnessed intense disruptions in wars and economic depression, and they felt that civilization itself was in danger of collapse. In fact, the entire twentieth century seems to have been preoccupied with the falling, breaking, shattering, dissolving, fracturing, and fissuring that took place everywhere it looked: in atoms, tectonic plates, personalities, scientific theories, political coalitions, ethical absolutes, national boundaries, and religious icons. Was there ever a century as focused on the fracturing of what had seemed solid? But it isn't only a factual matter that "things fall apart." As has often been pointed out, other centuries have had their cataclysms, too. But throughout the last century it was actually satisfying to us, for whatever reasons, to view breaking and tearing as integral to nearly everything around and inside us, and that is a tendency that is still strong as the century has ended and a new one begun. In fact, I believe that we can say that it is deeply satisfying to see ruptures wherever we look. It is an odd and fascinating idea that ruptures should be so satisfying, and perhaps it is exactly that which makes some call us "postmodern" and religious.

❖ ● ❖

But before we can have ruptures, we need to have surfaces for they are what rupture. "We live among surfaces," Ralph Waldo Emerson declared, "and the true art of life is to skate well on them."[9] Emerson is a writer claimed by philosophers, religious thinkers, and literary critics, and for good reason: he said what Americans felt and said it extremely well. To read Emerson is still to read a powerful voice within many. He was trying to make the most of a terrible situation when he declared that we live on surfaces, for his son Waldo had died, and Emerson had lost his optimistic sense that he (and we) could soar beyond all surfaces into the divine itself. His fear was that we live in a spiraling fall. No, he declared grimly, we live only on surfaces—mere surfaces—not falling but also not standing solidly on the divine or the real or the true. If we are upon a solid foundation, no ruptures are possible for what could change? Either in the absolutist religious world or in the realist scientific world of facts, and even in our commonsense world, there is no breaking for there is nothing to be broken.

The contemporary world has adopted Emerson's view: there are only surfaces. The Romantic period might have been the last time people in the West felt they could leap off the surface into the infinite, be it through a blade of grass or a grain of sand or the Word of God. That era faded, brought to earth by industrialism, wars, the encounter with other cultures, and the compelling notion that even the most impressively divine being was another mere surface. That we are dealing with the way things appear and not how they "are"; that we live in language and not directly among the things language speaks of; that we can never lose the cultural orderings and know what is "natural"—this is by no means the only view in the early twenty-first century, but it is a powerful one. We live among surfaces.

Yet what surfaces they are. Emerson might have imagined our surfaces as ice, frozen and lifeless and made for skating when compared with the mystical regions he had lost (and I have been terming them "mere" surfaces for contrast), but today we're as likely to see the abundance of life on our surfaces. Everything that we have—our meanings, our values, our facts, and our emotions, our promises and our ambitions, our accomplishments and our despair—all are surfaces. Not mere surfaces, but the surfaces upon which we live. They function well for us, providing not only support but nourishment. They are crucial to us; they are our lives. Every aspect of all of our meanings is a surface.

So Mary Oliver travels with her surfaces. In fact, as a poet her sensibility is unusually acute, so that she is aware of the flowers and soft drinks in Jakarta, carrying her sense and taste for them from Ohio, New York, Vermont, and Cape Cod. She carries, too, her notions of what a child is and a parent—they are in the "nest of wires" in her mind that is exploded by the boy. Without those surfaces, we have no experiences, no way to order and make sense of the data from our eyes and hands and lips. A parent cares and protects, and a child trusts and grows.

We all travel with our understandings, with our sense of what's what—what smells "good" (or exotic or putrid), what feels "right" (or off or disgusting), or what we judge to be "just" (or shady or reprehensible). In fact, we often discover what our surfaces are when we travel, not having realized that there could be other surfaces until we leave home.

I was eighteen when I became an exchange student in the Netherlands. Of course, it's a country where many people speak English, and speak it very well, but the aim of "exchange" was to pass into the culture, fitting into the spot, I suppose, that the Dutch student vacated when he was traded for me. So the other twenty Americans and I were trained for our roles, attending language classes in a vaguely art deco yellow-brick building in The Hague owned by Dutch Shell.

I discovered how cumbersome it was to fit Dutch into my mouth, the gutturals feeling like oversized dentures, and, then, how difficult it was to communicate. I had to search around for the right words as laboriously as though they were kept in a warehouse, and I had to dash back there and take many words off a shelf and examine them until I found the right one. Even when I became somewhat proficient, the words I chose and the phrasing and the groups of sentences were only roughly apt, like those occasional times now when I've forgotten a pencil and straightedge and have to mark a board freehand with a nail before I cut it. My parents shipped me books—Shakespeare, James Baldwin, e. e. cummings, John Hersey, Hemingway—and I discovered (with a delight that I still feel, over thirty years later) that English flowed through my mouth with infinite fluidity. I hadn't realized just how many thousands of flavors of words I knew. It was as though those Dutch dentures had revealed to me (once they were out) how perfectly English fit my mouth, bringing with it all the subtle tastes of meaning. The deconstructionists tell us that words are only signs—and signs of signs—not, as we like to think, evidence of bedrock or the opening of deep vents into the core, but how varied and wonderful those surface signs taste. Those signs are aesthetic, lovely, erotic. Our surfaces enable us to think, communicate, and live.

Yet the surface is not all. Surfaces crack. Holes open. No surface, no meaning is impervious. Whether it is made of wood or metal or stone or even diamond, every surface can break—be they scientific facts (that are always mere theories) or ethical imperatives (that are dependent on circumstances) or aesthetic judgments (that the first sight of a cubist shatters) or a sense of who I am (as Mary Oliver discovers). If we consider our meanings from the perspective of eons, the surfaces simply flake and fly away. If our view is microscopic, there is nothing level; all is pitted and cracked. And in the scale of ordinary space and time, all of our meanings are vulnerable. Breakings are everywhere.

That afternoon in Agra my comfortable sense of what we may see in life was shattered. At home if I see a crowd and I join it, I expect to see a juggler or a magician. I might see a person ranting about a cause. At the worst I might see a bicyclist who has fallen, a bloody leg, and someone holding a cloth to the wound. None is especially the rupturing of a surface. Our surfaces are very elastic. In Agra, mine broke.

And when Mary Oliver saw the deformed boy, it wasn't merely a matter of identifying a "son" or "child." Those surfaces failed. We see a boy, and we know what a boy is. We see a scarred mouth, and our compassion rises. There is a cracking of the surface possible because we feel helpless. How can we respond to this boy? But when we glimpse the fact that the deformity is intentional and the boy looks at us with cunning—which of our meanings is intact? Child? Victim? Manipulator? The meanings all collapse. The adequacy of our surfaces is always at issue: can we stand on them or not? Will the surface hold? What she discovers in "Acid" is that her sense of a parent and child was inadequate. They burned, they exploded. She experienced ruptures.

The cracks and ruptures take place at home, too, for our surfaces are subject to pressures, the pressures of our experiences. A student walks into my office and tells me about his depression. A space empties under the term "depression," and I know the inadequacy of the term. I feel it break apart. His desperately earnest planning, the weariness of his voice, his need of a shave, the reference to a past semester off—all seem like tidal forces on the mere word, the mere surface, "depression." He may struggle to hold his experiences together with that term. I try to make sense of what I see with that casual diagnosis. But I feel the poor surface crack under the strain of new words and sights and sounds. Travel means exposing our surfaces to other forces. It means leaving our piece of earth and moving to strange shores upon which we walk uneasily. If we love to travel, we love the experience of our surfaces being broken.

The history of pilgrimage, by the way, also involves the breaking of old surfaces, and another book could be written of the continuities of pilgrimage with modern travel. In their classic study of pilgrimage, Victor and Edith Turner focus on the necessity of departure, of leaving what is known, as well as on the liminality of the journey, usually through quite arduous terrain for extended periods of time. Pilgrimage has been seen as a fascinating phenomenon because it suggests that the most valuable religious experiences must involve leaving the usual and the known.

"Everything good is on the highway" wrote Emerson, but when we travel there are few roads without pits. I was in Accra, Ghana, wandering through the city and not realizing it had gotten late. A friend knew a priest at the cathedral, and I was trying to find him—to maintain the line of friendships, I suppose. But then it became dark, and as I walked in the streets that were entirely lacking streetlights I realized my peril—there were potholes that were huge and trench gutters beside the roads. Both could break my leg, I suddenly realized, if I stepped into one. And I could see nothing. I took shuffling steps until a car would pass and light up the next twenty yards, but my memory of the clear path faded about as quickly as the light. Another day I took a bus from Accra to Cape Coast, the road broken widely along the edge, sometimes giving a grudging shoulder but then suddenly a deep pit halfway to the center of the lane. A bicyclist was up ahead, timing (by hearing, I suppose) the approach of the racing bus before the pavement ran out. Being crushed was the price of being wrong. And every few miles an accident—an overturned truck and a small crowd around someone on the ground. Another time I was driving in Mexico with my daughter and nephew and suddenly found myself forced between an enormous hole and an oncoming car, both certain car wrecks—and I had to dare to split the difference. And for days and days I felt the adrenaline in my arms and hands. To travel is to meet holes of all kinds, and the literal holes are not the only dangerous ones. This book attempts to bring some of those holes to our attention.

Discord and Disruption: Seeking Ruptures

What then of the value of ruptures? What of the love of ruptures?

Our ordinary inclination is to judge that ruptures are harmful. After all, a woman with no arms and legs, a boy with a deformed mouth—who could see them as valuable? Our line is clear: clarity, order, integrity, peacefulness are valuable and certainly preferable to confusion, disorder, disintegration, discord, pain. To a considerable extent, our task in life becomes the pursuit of the first and avoidance of the second. And I can hardly disagree. Except that there are so many instances where the choice is less clear, and instances where we choose discord and disruption.

In Flannery O'Connor's short stories, for instance, moments of emotional or even physical violence are usually presented as preeminently valuable. The self-satisfied Ruby Turpin is waiting in a doctor's office, silently pitying all the other patients for not being as fine as she is when a college girl with a bad complexion and a bad disposition strikes her with a book, then chokes and curses her: "Go back to hell where you came from, you old wart hog."[10] Surprisingly, the woman comes to see the deeply disturbing event as "abysmal life-giving knowledge." Or when John Donne beseeches his God to "batter" his heart: "That I may rise, and stand, o'erthrow mee, and bend / Your force, to breake, blowe, burn and make me new."[11] The highly religious Donne wants to be broken by his God. To be rebuked and reproved would be the highest good. The Book of Job presents readers with a God who is divine by utterly silencing not only human voices but all pretensions to knowledge or justice. Job's friends think they understand God, and so they assume that Job must be guilty since he is being punished, his children and his animals destroyed. Job believes he understands God, as well, insisting that God explain Job's punishment. God's answer is an utter silencing of all human understanding. No one understands God. The annihilation of wisdom is divine. As all these instances show, the rupturing of our religious surfaces can be seen as extremely valuable.

But the ruptures needn't be so extreme or given divine validation to be valuable. A student sees the blue, tattooed number under her math teacher's arm and loses all pleasure in ridiculing the teacher; a woman whispers to her professor before an exam that she may not perform well that day because she has just been diagnosed with cancer, and suddenly the professor feels that "final exam" has lost its importance. Death in general may be a topic that can never be considered without a rupture of our usual surfaces, and while we may wish there were no death, facing its terrors frankly and feeling the rupture it causes constitute a part of human profundity.

On the other hand, laughter is an activity that indicates that a rupture is taking place, as well, and there is no doubt that we treasure laughter. It's well known that talking about humor is a pointless exercise, pathetic in its inappropriate seriousness, in its attempt to pull the incongruous, the absurd into the realm of the sensible. To laugh we have to crack up. It's mocking, it's fractured. Some surface we have been comfortable with is ridiculed, and our bodies shake, noises erupt from us. Any explanation (even this one) is an attempt to make a rupture back into a surface. We laugh at the attempt.

Tears, too, are a sign of rupture. I have often thought that a wedding hasn't really taken place until someone cries, which is a way of saying, I suppose, that we need tears because there is no bonding without a rupture. In fact, we might say that all emotions are a sign of rupture, as they break through our composure. Aren't there times when we both welcome and value the disturbances of strong emotions, however ambivalent our welcome might be? In his *Confessions,* Augustine tells of his despair when one of his friends dies, and many find it chilling when he regrets that he loved the friend too much. The anguish of the friend's death, he says, was too extreme, and he resolves never to love a human so deeply again. Yet don't we take our despair in that situation as a sign of the depth of our humanity? Would we really wish to mourn no more? Would we want to be so composed, so unresponsive, so cold? Don't we value the disruption of our composure, even of our life?

The situation is simply more complex than our common sense may tell us. The rupturing of our surfaces is something we can both need and love.

I would suggest five reasons for the love of ruptures. First, if we love leaving the surface, it may be to escape harm. Second, we may also love ruptures simply to get to still more surfaces—to multiply our surfaces—even if the place we leave involved no harm at all. Third, by leaving our own worlds through a rupture, we may experience our vitality, or the wider dimensions of our resources. Fourth, we may love the plunge into the rupture because of the test or ordeal it affords us, and passing that ordeal may promise us success in the future, more serious ones back home. Finally, we may bring treasures of some sort from the ruptures.

If we love our ruptures, it may be because of a desire (or need) to escape our surfaces. There seem to be two possibilities. First, our surfaces can be harmful, as with Mrs. Cotter. An elderly Irish woman who lived down the street from me when I was a child, she had been told by her parish priest that she had one purpose in life, to have children. I like children, and I love being a parent, but the only purpose in life? It is not a bad surface to shatter. Some surfaces imprison, restrict, suppress, and their rupture is a liberation. Paul Bowles left the United States in 1929 to escape an abusive father. The hostility between them had dated, perhaps, from when Bowles was four and his father had savagely accused him of making his mother ill. Years later his grandmother had told him, dramatically, "your father wanted to kill you." Bowles finally flipped a coin when he was a student at the University of Virginia and thereby decided upon leaving America instead of suicide.[12] It was a rupture that he critically needed.

A more difficult and challenging possibility is the rupturing of surfaces that are not harmful, surfaces that really do sustain us, working well. We leave our happy homes. Our sense of right and wrong, of what is valuable or harmful, of who we are and where we are. Those surfaces also break, and yet I think we can love those ruptures, too, though it is an excruciating paradox. At the university, I serve on boards that hear disciplinary cases, usually of violent incidents: a student who has died in what may be a shoving match, falling back and striking his head on a curb; a young man who has entered a woman's room at night and performed oral sex on her, perhaps without consent; unwanted fondling; a student raced after and punched. The cases go on and on. Sitting on a board to judge whether an assault has indeed taken place, entering the world where students are not students but victims or victimizers—and even that is not a distinction that is at all clear—is fracturing a very useful surface of academic (or any) life. We see them in the classroom and they are intellectually very capable and distinguished only by the kind of smart, the degree of insight, the power of analysis, or the aptness of expression. Enter the disciplinary boards, and it is as if a lens has been twisted in the scope, yielding an entirely new view. They are now people who are hurt and who harm others. They assault and are assaulted. They rape and are raped. I wish none of it had ever taken place. I wish I could continue to see them puzzling over Kant or Nietzsche or Tillich. Those usual surfaces are in ruins—and, oddly, I am glad to have been there to see past the collapsed heaps to the new and terrible landscape. Why? This is not being witness to the falling of the oppressive surface but the rupture of the beneficial. What is the value of that agony? What is that love of ruptures? Why would we leave home to travel when our homes are happy ones?

One answer is that there are simply more worlds to see, more surfaces to walk on, more selves to witness. If they are there, we need to see them. My students are students but they also have other lives, often terrible ones and those lives need to be seen. The self and the world are larger places, and we cannot get "outside" without leaving. We might as well stay satisfied with the smile of someone we encounter as stay only with the accomplished student. There are more surfaces, more selves, and to get to them we often need to see the prior ones shatter. This is the love of rupturing the old to get to the new.

The third reason we love ruptures is because we are able then to experience our own vitality. Our surfaces define us. They make us who we are, and whether that definition is gentle or authoritative, beneficial or harmful, we need to say "no." To be able to say "no," even to what we love, carries the same benefit as fasting does to an ascetic. It isn't just being willful, and it isn't just being world-denying. Saying "no" to food and comforts, saying "no" to home or to all we know is saying we are able to throw off the essential, the very ground upon which we walk, that which provides us with the air we breathe, the nutrition that sustains us. In this sense, the love of ruptures is a measure of our vitality. We can say "no" because of how much life we have. This value of rupture resonates most powerfully for me.

Alphonso Lingis is a philosophy professor in Pennsylvania and a man who takes the most difficult trips that I know of, trips that involve an insistent "no" to his usual surfaces. In 1983, during the Contra uprising against the leftist Sandinista government in Nicaragua, he went to Managua.[13] He calls it "the enemy capital," and, to the Reagan administration and much of America, it was. It is also still a scene of devastation because of the earthquake of 1972 so this place of the enemy is also one of "shanties and rubble." As though that weren't enough, Lake Managua, in the capital itself, is teeming with sharks. Why go to such a place?

Characteristically, Lingis takes a hotel right on the edge of the earthquake zone and then, as though that weren't close enough to the scene of disruption, drives off into the mountains where the Contras are active. He is stopped by a Sandinista with a rifle— Augusto—asking for a ride, and, astonishingly, Lingis gives it to him, changing his own destination to go on to where Augusto wants to go. That night the Contras come, and Augusto saves Lingis's life, leading him for miles through the forest, but finally leaving him alone in the dark. When dawn breaks and the philosophy professor is able to walk back to his hotel in the mountains, he finds the Sandinista—Augusto—lying dead on a rug, his face "a muck of blood and flies."[14]

There are few who say "no" to the culture, politics, and identity of their homes as emphatically and dangerously as Lingis does. He makes a point of mentioning that when Augusto looks at him, he does *not* see him or his places—the classroom, the offices, the American streets, and the shopping malls: places and roles that are both harmful and beneficial. Lingis is leaving not only a Reagan-era America he detests but a university life that (one trusts) he values, too. His identity and his placement are "not" for the Sandinista. Lingis seems to have chosen to go where he and his are "not." He has left the surface and fallen. No, he has leaped. He has sufficient life to leap.

The love of ruptures is a way of saying we're more. We can live even without what's absolutely essential—and not only can we survive, we can thrive. We're larger. We're other. We're denizens, too, of the desert or the deep. We can still be even through terrors. Take away the very ground, the very air. I still am.

I believe this is a crucial aspect of the love of ruptures, so please indulge another example—Henry Miller, who has far too much exuberance to be held by any nation or border. His famous lust is expansive, not restricting, and his hunger for more travel and more experiences is omnivorous. As much as he comes to love France, he disparages its walls and seeks the wilder landscapes of Greece and its more tumultuous history.[15] I wish I were the traveler that Henry Miller was, but I am not. I rarely speak to strangers, not to the American beside me on the plane and not to the professors I could easily connect with abroad. Miller not only speaks to everyone, but he especially seeks out those who are most challenging, those most unlike "home." He wants more than home. He's delighted to discover that the caretaker of a castle in Nafplio had spent years in prison for murder. He's gleeful that a taxi driver has tried to cheat him. Miller befriends a Greek named Katsimbalis and makes him the central character—indeed the colossus—of *The Colossus of Maroussi*. Katsimbalis is a man with an enormous personality, able, even, to mesmerize the considerable personality of Miller himself. "More," Miller seems to say. The familiar is not enough. "Give me more."

Sometimes, instead of desiring to break the surface, we can desire the rupture itself, desiring the tumult, the chaos, the confusion, the violence, the fear, and the excitement. We don't love leaving the shore as much as entering the surf. We love it when the earth opens up, and we love the something that is there. My favorite movie as a child was *Journey to the Center of the Earth*, the 1959 version of the Jules Verne adventure. What mattered was that a very dreary northern surface in Iceland could lead to an exciting world of brilliant gems and minerals, ferocious dinosaurs, and an ocean that became a whirling maelstrom at the very center of the earth. All that's needed is a crack in the surface, a hole to descend into, and we enter a world that's much more fantastic, much more fascinating, and much more dangerous than our ordinary landscape. We should all find a rupture and begin climbing down.

Paul Bowles seeks just such a world. On his first trip to Istanbul, he describes the city as a "roller coaster in motion" because it is so strange, incongruous, and disorienting.[16] He gets lost in the souk and is besieged by merchants, but he only loves the place the more. Minarets sprout like mushrooms, the buildings appear never to have been painted, and the people seem a mixture in every possible way, with no unifying characteristics. Being in the city is like being in a dream, and Bowles craves just that otherworldliness.

One reason to value the incongruous world of the rupture is because it is a test, an ordeal. I love Diane Johnson's travel essays because she is so frank and cranky about the dangers and inconveniences.[17] More than most, she's aware that there are dangers. She claims that she is merely accompanying her husband, a doctor, on various professional trips, but she recognizes a tight spot when she sees one—far more than most travelers do—and is vividly relieved when she lives through it. "I have survived," she says, "therefore I will survive," as though it is a sign that one will also have the luck to survive the paltry dangers of home—failing to get the kids on the school bus, forgetting to pay the phone bill, neglecting the fish until they're floating on the top of the tank.[18] It also may be a sign that we will survive the great existential dangers that eventually fell us—cancers, accidents, heart disease. We put ourselves, as Johnson does, on a Swiss mountain slope in a toboggan at midnight, knowing that it is foolhardy and dangerous and stupid, but doing it anyway because we're not home, because it's part of being away, part of travel, like jumping off a mountain in a dream. And passing the ordeal will prove something about our courage or our luck, or it will earn us credits in the future tests that count, at home.

Diane Johnson knows that tobogganing into the dark on a steep, icy slope is reckless, as I knew in 1974 that piling into an old Ford minivan with twenty-odd tribesmen at the edge of the Baluchistani desert at the borders of Iran, Pakistan, and Afghanistan was reckless or that telling aggressive "guides" to fuck off in the middle of the Marrakesh souk was reckless. But stepping into an object made of metal and weighing hundreds of tons and expecting it to fly you across a measureless ocean is reckless, too. Let's jump off the edge of the land straight into the rupture—and then survive. The benefit of surviving such an ordeal would seem to be measureless.

The final value of a rupture is what emerges from it. What comes out of those fissures in the earth, the ones that break open our surfaces and into which we reach or leap? Treasures. But treasures can be of many different kinds, some of them valuable even though they look very ugly. I'm risking becoming a Joseph Campbell or a Bruno Bettelheim, mining myths and fairy tales for symbols, but I'm taken with the notion that we can go below the earth, as fine an image for the foreign as there is, perhaps, and emerge with objects that we value nearly above all others—

gold, diamonds, rubies, emeralds, or the hard-won wisdom of an Orpheus, a Persephone, or a Herakles, or of a Milton or a Dante, for that matter, the ones who tell those travel stories.

I've mentioned a lot of people—myself included—and claimed that they had a love of ruptures. Did we bring anything out of the underworld? Did we really find rubies or gold? Mary Oliver goes below. What does she bring out? It sounds awfully trite, perhaps, to say that self-awareness is gained from our disruptions, but what better gain is there?

And perhaps that's why I appreciate the disruptions of the sexual assault hearings: they crack open my sense of what a person is and of who I am, and I come to realize that it's beneficial to leave the lucidity of stereotyped roles (innocent and guilty, victim and victimizer, judge and judged), to become immersed in the fogging that is all of us, and, still, to navigate. We can, after all, find our way in those baffling circumstances, as Thoreau is said (by Emerson) to be able to follow a trail in the dark.[19] But it isn't because of any greater clarity or broader sight. We've thrown away our customary guides, the terrain is far, far trickier, but still we manage, somehow. We are the bafflement and the bewilderment and the confusion, and we're also the walker of those woods.

Alphonso Lingis's "treasure" is the touch and collision of bodies, the feeling of others' bodies on his own. It's an unusual and wonderful souvenir. He seems to believe that the real strangeness of strangers is best preserved in sensations and not in words or ideas, so he collects touchings that are sometimes ordinary and sometimes extreme. He writes of being on a bus in Peru and feeling the sensation of a man's leg resting against his. He writes, too, of an old woman's hand touching his when she hands him a cup of maté or of another old woman reaching out for his arm when she stumbles.[20]

On the other hand is the body sensation brought away by Jack Gilbert, a poet. His collection *The Great Fires* presents us with many travels, to Greece, mostly, but also to Denmark and Italy. The travels are searches—for his dead wife, for love or passion, for the spirits he hears singing inside a cathedral's huge doors. One poem concerns a married woman that he loved and their love-making while her husband was away and while her baby slept—and then awoke and cried—nearby. Gilbert goes and gets the baby, and they hold him as they finish, and then Gilbert and baby, both, "nursed at her, our heads / nudging each other blindly in the brilliant dark."[21] Gilbert searches in the rupture of Anna's marriage and in the rupture of his own aloneness and desire, and what he finds is an especially nourishing and very physical treasure.

We don't pay enough attention to the bodies we bring back from the ruptured surface: not only the memory or impact in our bodies, but the parasites and viruses, the fungus. The man who began a program of travel for credit in my college later died, and in my imagination it was because of a long-dormant microbe he brought back from India. My first cross-country hitchhike ended in a warehouse in San Francisco where my friend Danny and I slept on old mattresses. I brought back a fungus under my arms that I kept with me (wherever else I went) for years. The treasure that comes from the rupture can be an impact or a touch, or it can be a foreign body that refuses to be domesticated. It can be a fixed idea, an obsession, an image that erupts from time to time. I'm thinking of the look of cunning on the boy's face that becomes Mary Oliver's bead of acid or my vision of the woman with no arms or legs who was surrounded by a crowd watching her try to eat in Agra. If nothing else, these foreign bodies are indelible marks, like passport stamps, saying, "I have been elsewhere, and now I am not the same."

Above all, we bring back stories, and we all act like Samuel Taylor Coleridge's Ancient Mariner, fixing friends and acquaintances with our bright-eyed stare as we startle and amaze. It's the best souvenir, the most negotiable rock carried out of the earth. "How I spent my summer vacation" becomes virtually every travel book ever written, a very large collection. I spent my last two years in college listening to my friends who had spent a semester in India telling their stories, night after night after night (after night). Those stories seemed in no way inferior to those I read for courses by Coleridge or Milton or Conrad. I decided that I wanted some stories of my own, something to startle and amaze, so I set off to travel, too, and in one way or another it's become a career.

◆•◆

I am told of a woman who compulsively cut her skin with a knife, rupturing the integrity of her own skin. "I need to see if I am still alive" was her explanation. I do not intend to search for balance in the love of ruptures, but to proclaim my fascination with those who figuratively cut their skin. I simply seem to observe a lot of people—virtually all of us—in such pursuit, and I want to bring it to our attention. We like to think of ourselves as leading balanced and stable lives, seeking order and avoiding disorder. But our behavior says otherwise. We value ruptures, even severe ones, to the point of actively seeking them.

My fascination with the quest for confusion may strike some as worse than imbalanced. What of further orientation, reorientation? What of ethics, what of our political responses to the challenges we encounter? What of our responsibility to others and to ourselves? Am I simply suggesting that we throw ourselves out there to our own moral and mortal peril? Can I say that I am chiefly interested in discussing the value of bewilderment? I know that is not the end of the matter, and I hope that readers find ways to respond, incorporating disruption into the mix of their various orientations.

I could choose any number of areas to explore in support of my notion: music, film, the use of drugs and alcohol, our emotional lives, our pursuit of love, our "leisure" pursuits (hurtling down frozen slopes on skis or running far past the point where our bodies have beseeched us to halt), our involvements in violence, religion. The deconstructionists insist that language itself involves a fundamental rupture: an "absence" made present. Vice alone would be an apt topic, the shadowy realm of our often quite delighted entanglement with rupture. And in none of these cases are we in the realm of the clearly or solely harmful. In all, we seem as surrounded by ruptures as we are by the gaps between objects;

they are as common, as important, and as desirable as our meanings themselves.

But of this large realm of ruptures, it's travel that attracts my attention in this book. It's there—going "there" and being "there," in fact—that we quite strongly show our need for, our craving for experiences that break the notions of ourselves, our fellow humans, and our world that function quite well for us "at home." More of us than we might suspect would agree with Paul Bowles when he declared, "Each time I go to a place I have not seen before, I hope it will be as different as possible from the places I already know." Perhaps it is a little clearer why I agree with him and why that is not so strange. We love the surfaces of the familiar, but we love our ruptures, too, and need them. We all do.

TWO

Commerce with the Ancients

I'D HAD DISCUSSIONS WITH A LOT OF PEOPLE ABOUT MY NOTION that we travel in order to become confused before I realized why the idea was so unconvincing to some. It is perfectly obvious to most of us why we travel, and confusion has nothing to do with it. We travel to learn, to broaden our minds, to lessen our provinciality, to become cultivated. Travel, in fact, has the precise opposite of confusion as its aim; travel enlightens, it educates.

Henry Wadsworth Longfellow, for instance, declares: "I shall never forget the delightful feelings awakened within me on approaching Venice, and entering its principal canal. It was a bright and moonlight night, and a thousand lamps glimmered in the distance along the water's edge."[1] Where is the confusion? Where is the bewilderment? And where does Longfellow go in Venice? To the Doge's Palace, where he is led through the dungeons and reads on a wall, "Confide in no one; think and be silent, if thou wishest to escape the snare and treachery of spies."[2] He sketches the Bridge of Sighs, and observes the house where Byron stayed. In short, he goes exactly where we would go today: touristic pilgrimage sites of historical, literary, or artistic merit. In each of the countries he visits (France, Spain, Italy, Germany), language study is his first emphasis. He had been hired by Bowdoin College to be their first professor of modern languages, and toured Europe for three years to gain mastery of those languages, a task he largely accomplished.

What could be more different from my notion that we travel to experience the disruption of our surfaces? Longfellow travels to learn, immersing himself in the cultures of those four countries in order to absorb the languages as a way of life, and to expand himself culturally. As Longfellow's 1963 biographer puts it, Longfellow became a great teacher both at Bowdoin and then later at Harvard because he had "stored up" an "inexhaustible fund" of experiential knowledge.[3] Longfellow extended his surfaces; he did not travel to feel them break.

Even though he wrote that "traveling is a fool's paradise," the same desire to expand the self through travel is true of Emerson, though he is more unabashedly interested in himself than places.[4] As with many Romantics, it is the self and not the world that is a vast place, so, Emerson writes in his journal, "wherever we go, whatever we do, self is the sole subject we study and learn."[5] Emerson's first wife, Ellen, had died in 1831, and on Christmas of the following year Emerson embarked for Europe, using the money she had left him. He landed in Malta and traveled to Sicily, then the rest of Italy, Switzerland, France, and Britain.

He seeks out his literary heroes—Coleridge, Wordsworth, Carlyle, and another writer less known to us today, Walter Savage Landor. Throughout his travels, Emerson tours people, far more than monuments or palaces or artistic sites. It is human beings that Emerson travels to see. He concludes that "the singular position of the American traveller" is to be able to observe that a moral human is always the same, regardless of extreme changes in places and customs.[6] He concludes, in other words, that one need not leave home in order to travel within the Self, but that travel is expansive and expanding, not confounding and confusing.

Emerson, like Longfellow, describes Venice on a moonlit night, saying that "St Mark's piazza showed like a world's wonder," but he proceeds to contemplate his own self-worth. What does it matter where we are, he notes, "as long as all of us are estranged from truth & love." "One act of benevolence," he writes in Milan, "is better than a cathedral."[7] All the travel one needs can be accomplished through self-reflection. One should voyage in the limitless self.

In 1969, I arrived in Venice myself, with two fellow exchange students in a limping Ford. The car would break down, beyond repair, several hundred miles farther, and I would break down, too, felled by sunstroke as I tried (and failed) to hitchhike to Paris to rendezvous with a young woman. But first was the eleventh-century St. Mark's Basilica and the famous piazza, as well as vaporettos, the Academia Bridge, and the Doge's Palace. It was a city of water and stone, two substances that could not be more incompatible and yet barely kept their places, water breaking through the stone streets in small canals or flooding them (as happened one morning), and stone rising from the pewter gray, arching over it, and, elsewhere, visible just beneath the slight ripples. We camped outside the city, and I memorized speeches from *The Merchant of Venice* out of a little hardbound volume titled *Great Shakespearean Soliloquies* (what could the other campers have thought of the American teen murmuring, "The quality of mercy is not strained. It falls like a gentle rain from heaven" as I walked between the tents? Do Italians roll their eyes or is there a hand gesture to communicate the same message?) My friends and I talked to Italian campers and drank beer with them out of tiny glasses, and then visited museums to see the Renaissance art.

Becoming Modern: The Big, Broad Self

Just a few months off I would read the masterpieces of modernism in college—Eliot and Pound and Woolf and others—without realizing that I had been enacting modernism myself, seeing an Italian city as a section of the great mosaic of high culture, with its Titians and Tintorettos and Vivaldi and references in Shakespeare. I was there not to expand my experiential knowledge, like Longfellow, or to reflect on the essential self, like Emerson, but to see some of the elements of timeless art. In the cultural theory of the time, the great works were assembled with the same assurance that collected the laws of physics, and the purpose of our stop in Venice, though we were not conscious of it, was to see another few meters of the mosaic of high culture. The pieces fit together flawlessly, it was thought, just as they did in Pound's *Cantos,* which might be near-impossible to read but— damn it all—still connected Odysseus, Circe, Tiresias, Proteus, and a boatload of other Greeks to Picasso, Robert Browning, Li Po, Irish legend, Frank Lloyd Wright, Eleanor of Aquitaine, Provencal poetry, and Dante, in an exhilarating tour de force that was nearly intoxicating. "So it all fits!" we think on reading it, though we might be a bit unclear just how.

To change the metaphor, culture was like the spreading water in Venice itself, eventually wetting everything in sight, and giving me the sense that I could not only sail that water to any piece of stone but somehow be part of it all myself. Odysseus, Browning, Dante . . . me!?! It is hard to underestimate what such a sense of belonging meant to an adolescent. It was 1969, and already travel was coming to mean the student revolt in Paris, tanks in Prague, and pot in Amsterdam. In two weeks I would be desperate to get from Spain to Paris and that young woman, Rosemarie. Cultural expansion would come to an end, and conflict would take its place. But for the time being, I wanted the seamless "more" of high culture. I wanted to feel a part of all that history and music and literature and art by reciting Shakespeare and seeing the Venice of literature. I wanted to be that large. That aim, I believe, is religious. It is like being "part or parcel of God," in Emerson's mystical expression.[8]

Like Longfellow, Emerson does not travel to meet disturbance, and he has no particular love of rupture. He travels to explore the "colossal dimensions" of his inner self, a limitless surface for his exploration.[9] His aim proves to be religious. It is on his return that Emerson resigns the pulpit and commences on the vast expansion of transcendentalism, feeling himself "an inlet into the deeps of Reason," by which he means the limitless reaches of the soul.[10] It always seems a sign of Emerson's hubris that he meets Coleridge, Carlyle, Wordsworth, and Landor in order to realize their limits—"so," he seems to say, "is that all?" He learns to trust to no others to give him access to religious deeps. It is still expansion that he wants—to the dimensions of divinity, in fact— but through his own efforts and his own original insight. No tour groups for Emerson. There are no guides. Standing on the "bare Common" in Cambridge one day, he expands to the illimitable, "part or parcel of God." But the religious epiphany is one of continuity with the universe, one that happens instantly through the feelings, "without mediator or veil."[11]

And this, too, is how we consider travel, isn't it? We travel to "broaden" ourselves, either by the knowledge we accumulate, like merchants buying goods, or by the self-awareness we gather, as though we were going into the desert to contemplate and purify our souls. In this model, we travel to become larger, to expand, not to bend or break.

Such modern journeys of expansion began with the "Grand Tour" in the eighteenth century with young Englishmen going to Rome, Venice, Florence, Naples, and then Paris, occasionally adding a tour of German cities. The constant theme in the letters, journals, and books of these travelers is the improvement of their understanding. Their travel seems like a kind of natural history, as we might expect from a century that had learned so much of the world by the experimental method. The natural and human sciences had matured in the century because of the strict use of the understanding (memorably disparaged as the "hand of the mind" by Emerson), limited to comparison and measurement rather than the sometimes wild intuitive leaps of the previous century and the following. How better to put together exact and reliable notions of human societies than to gather more data? So the Grand Tour gathered data to expand human understanding.

Matthew Arnold represents especially well the view that travel is educational. We know his photographs, as those of the other Victorians—Tennyson, Ruskin, Disraeli, Newman, Carlyle, Darwin, Dickens, George Eliot. They are the first poets, novelists, essayists, philosophers, politicians, and religious thinkers we can see in photographs, and that fact makes them both unusually actual and extremely old-fashioned. Arnold has muttonchops that appear to be three inches thick, hair parted in the middle, deep-set eyes, and a long, worried face. It is the face of a schoolmaster, and that, essentially, is what Arnold is. He wants to educate us, and when we travel to broaden ourselves, we are taking part in his ambitious Victorian program of banishing philistinism and promoting what he liked to call our "best selves."[12]

Arnold was perhaps the most important British literary and social critic of the second half of the nineteenth century. The combination of those two—literary and social—is apt in Arnold's case because he felt that literature played such a crucial social role. To put it briefly, literature could save us, socially, politically, morally, and religiously. He'd been a bit of a wayward youth, surprising everyone when he came out with a book of poetry—*The Strayed Reveler,* appropriately; no one thought he'd amount to much. As a poet, he was a generation or more younger than the great Romantics such as Coleridge, Wordsworth, and Keats, and he envied and to some degree emulated their worship of nature as a solution to all ills. But as he matured, the influence of his father, a renowned master of Rugby, a prominent secondary school, came to the fore, and nature was no longer our savior; character was. He comes to admire those who are "cheerful, and helpful, and firm," that is, teachers.[13] In his essays and books of the following decades, he attempted to be one of the "helpers and friends of mankind," like a kindly Mr. Chips of a worldwide private school. Even on a day-to-day basis, social edification was his aim for he served as an inspector of schools throughout Britain and toured educational systems on the continent, as well.

So Arnold was concerned with our self-improvement, much like Ben Franklin, though living in the age of the great engineering projects—the Eiffel Tower, the Suez and Panama Canals, and the Brooklyn Bridge (begun in 1869 when Arnold published *Culture and Anarchy,* his major work, and finished in 1883, just before Arnold's final book of essays)—Arnold had a stronger sense of the tools that could be wielded to construct a "best self." Franklin's "Poor Richard" had aphorisms ("The heart of a fool is in his mouth, but the mouth of a wise man is in his heart"; "Men & melons are hard to know"; "He's the best physician that knows the worthlessness of the most medicines"; "Beware of meat twice boil'd, and an old Foe reconcil'd"), but the second half of the nineteenth century had iron and the principles of John Roebling, Gustave Eiffel, and the Count Ferdinand de Lesseps. It had more ambition, building character.

We remember Arnold today for his attack on philistinism, above all else. As the stern schoolmaster, he cast his eye over the class and condemned what he saw. Character, he felt, was deplorable. First there was the middle class, self-satisfied, "stiff-necked," and damnably resistant to improvement. Philistines. Sure, it may have had the vigorous energy that helped create the British Industrial Revolution, but it was also complacent, and aimed at nothing better.[14] The highest ambition of the middle class was merely "business, chapels, [and] tea-meetings."[15] That was the narrowness that required broadening.

As schoolmaster Arnold looked out over the class (a class of social classes), he was equally critical of the upper class, whom he called "Barbarians," surely an insulting epithet for this the most cultivated of all social classes. Yet their vigor and "staunch individualism" made them no better in his view than Visigoths dressed in animal skins. It was the common feeling, the social feeling that Arnold required of his British pupils, and an intellectual strength. The narcissism and excessive self-confidence of the upper-class "Barbarians" earned his scorn, for "unawakened [was] a whole range of powers of thought and feeling." Like a noble Barbarian, theirs was an outward nobility only, displayed in "worldly splendor, security, power, and pleasure."[16]

Arnold revealed real anxiety about and fear of the working

class. He described them as lurking beasts, low on the evolutionary scale, only partly human, and ready to pounce. This "Populace" (the benign term itself may reveal Arnold's anxiety) was, he cautioned us, "raw and half-developed and has lain half-hidden amidst its poverty and squalor." The working class was now "issuing from its hiding place" like some rough beast, and we could almost hear the screams of terror. They were not only the ignorant, mumbling, ill-dressed members of Arnold's imagined classroom; they also earned the schoolmaster's rebukes for being prone to intolerance, envy, and violence and were in the strongest need of improvement.[17]

Is Arnold's diagnosis, however full of stereotypes, all that different from how we see our own deficiencies? Something is lacking in us, something needs development or refinement. We are spending our time involved in worthy activities—"business, chapels, tea-meetings"—but they seem narrow. We feel narrow and in need of broadening. In fact, these activities feel at times like dead-ends, and we hope that travel will awaken new sensibilities, even new selves. We need to be larger than the narrow roles of work and social activities. And it certainly isn't only the respectable and responsible middle-class activities of job, community, and church that feel too small to us, but the narcissistic preoccupations Arnold spies in the upper class, cultivating "the manly exercises [in] vigor, good looks, and fine complexion."[18] Much as we value them, we still feel that our devotion to health clubs, golf, tennis, mountain biking, and running forty miles a week is superficial—not really our "best self" (one of Arnold's favorite terms). Finally, like Arnold's working class, we like "bawling, hustling, . . . smashing . . . [and] beer," which is to say we have our emotional rages and our vices, and they certainly feel like a "smaller," less valuable part of ourselves.[19] We are mundane, superficial, and destructive—all British social classes rolled into one—and something must be done about it.

Arnold's concern is religious, with who we are—sinful beings, it seems—and who we must become to be saved. His interest is in social redemption. Education is not just important; it is absolutely critical. "Doing as one wants" is his catchall for the root evil, something like Augustinian cupidity or desire. Humans are flawed in being selfish, narrow, superficial, and destructive. He is seeking to address flawed humanity and save it. I have argued that any meaning that provides us with a sense of who and where we are is a religious surface. I would also say that any action that stems from who we are and makes who we ought to be is religious, too, as we "ascend" from surface to surface. Arnold, in fact, recognizes the religious scope for he sees his role on that large a scale. *Culture and Anarchy* is his great work, but we might rename it "Redemption and Damnation" for that is what is at stake. In fact, Arnold's analysis is an attempt to provide us with orientation by peering into our souls and proclaiming us Philistines, Barbarians, or Populace. "Arise sinners!" he might be saying. "Cast out thy superficiality, narcissism, and violence!" might be his demand if he'd used Jonathan Edwards's rhetoric. Arnold wants to save us.

Arnold's redemption comes through travel, though not literally. He wants self-improvement through figurative travel: reading, looking at art, listening to music. It's the sort of figurative travel that the West had been involved in since the Renaissance: going to Greece and Rome by coming under the influence of its works and thus its values. If we are exposed to the great classical works, Arnold preached, we can acquire human perfection through our "endless expansion [and] endless growth in wisdom and beauty."[20] Arnold actually uses the term "perfection." His aim is by no means modest. Such perfection is accessible through the Hellenic virtue of "thinking clearly, seeing things in their essence and beauty," and thereby getting "rid of one's ignorance."[21] Once one is able to "[see] things as they are," there results "the touch of life, and there is a stir and growth everywhere."[22] What we require, in short, is the famous Arnoldian "sweetness and light," and the result is not just the improvement of the self through the elimination of our flaws but its perfection. What could be more religious? And yet that perfection is perfectly secular. It takes place right on the surface—the perfect surface of high Western culture.

Again, when we believe that travel improves us, that it educates and broadens, are we so far from Arnold? "Thinking clearly," "seeing things as they are," "wisdom and beauty"—don't these appeal to the "best self" that will be brought out by travel? The Louvre, the Concertgebouw, the Royal Shakespeare Theatre, the Acropolis, the remnants of the Berlin Wall, Hadrian's Wall, the Prado, the Anne Frank House. They are why we travel, and it is in those shrines that our pilgrimage reaches its end, rising above the Friday morning conference call, or the Thursday afternoon hoops game, or our too-frequent tempers. In seeing "the best that has been thought or known in the world," we feel enlarged by feeling equal to it.[23]

Arnoldian travel is religious by improving and correcting. Disturbances are quelled, flaws are repaired, and ignorance is allayed. Clarity, wisdom, and beauty are the ideals that heal and perfect. That which corrects and improves is enormously powerful for the sight of it alone is effective, like a Christian relic. We see it and are healed. These cultural sacraments impart their benefit directly to us, without a great deal of work on our part and without error. Their value is religious.

I was in Oaxaca, the capital of the southern Mexican state of the same name, with a beautiful colonial center (yet, radiating from it, miles of proliferating and much more deteriorated city). When I think of Oaxaca, I get images of reds, yellows, and greens, bright colors—colors that seem to be oddly restoring, regenerating, and maybe even redemptive. I went to Oaxaca after the stresses of the end of semester. Worse, I was getting divorced, feeling guilty, my life seeming torn into small scraps, worrying about my children. I was in need of restoration. It seems an odd choice to fly to a foreign culture in that situation. Why not stay put? When the personal world has become so strange and estranged, why go somewhere strange?

Upon arrival at the airport, a *colectivo* heads directly to the colonial square of Oaxaca, the zocalo, softly lit at night, lined with calm cafés, and available only to feet, not wheels. Without any traffic there is only the sound of many voices, and a few musicians. Tall trees fill the air above the zocalo, along with huge clutches of bright Mylar balloons. On the paths are men shining the shoes of very important-looking people, politicians, perhaps, or businessmen. Indigenous women sell handicrafts in front of the cathedral, children play, and farmers in straw hats wander in a group of six or eight, looking around themselves with some amazement.

Thick-walled and high-ceilinged colonial buildings surround the zocalo, and it is in those streets, with their restaurants, museums, galleries, cafés, handicraft shops, and hotels that most visitors—Mexican as well as foreign—walk, up and down, up and down. I did, too, in the following days. I took photos of the elegant facades, their muted colors so appealing in the early or late sun. I visited the Museo de Arte Contemporaneo, where there was a biennial exhibit of local artists. "Jorge de Boa," I wrote in my notebook, while looking at his wooden sculpture in a small bare courtyard. "Pilar Bordes, 'Obituario,'" I wrote as I stood in front of a panel of dozens of tiny dark scenes, the final notice of a life. In the museum, there are bold abstractions by Rudolfo Nieto, paintings, I say to myself, worth the entire trip.

Was it distraction that I got from the strolls around the zocalo and the museum trips? Did I get to forget about the painful loss of one life and the anxious making of another? Arnold and the others who believe in the religious value of "wide" travel, the travel that makes us larger and better, would say both yes and no. We do lose our narrow selves, but only as we "spread" into a wider and better life, they would say. Being in an important culture, among all that architecture and art, among all those textures and colors is simply and impersonally improving. Beautiful art, culture itself is better than we are, and we become better—better, also, in the sense of "healed"—by seeing it. The colonial buildings had withstood earthquakes in 1834 and 1931. Like they, I could withstand some major tremors, too, but only by being a part of that bigger and better whole.

Outside Oaxaca are the Mesoamerican cities of Monte Alban

and Mitla, and they have an Arnoldian religious value, as well. On a flattened mountaintop and hundreds of yards long, Monte Alban is pool-table flat but broken with tall, high-stepped structures—temples, palaces, tombs, observatories: the functions mentioned in the guidebooks seem like guesses, attempts to tame the astonishing stones. Mitla is smaller and slightly more recent, but also with structures that enlarge our notion of civilization, history, culture, city, religion.

Busloads of people—Mexican, European, American, and Canadian—visit both Mesoamerican cities, coming from the colonial Oaxaca, moving centuries back in time. And the movement is largely what Arnold would have recommended, had he been less narrow-minded and Eurocentric. Both there and near the zocalo, we became larger people, expanded now not just to the limits of European culture but to Mesoamerican culture, too.

Arnold wrote that our lives are mundane, superficial, and, in many ways, destructive, but that sounds so abstract and formulaic. This book largely disagrees with the "educational" view of travel, but it's important to give that view its due. We need to be "bettered" by what's larger, more valuable, and more permanent. We're self-centered, living as though walled by our offices, our cities, our countries, and our civilizations, and we walk down the Calle Alcala for some perspective. The beauty of those buildings, of the handicrafts, and of the art supplement and correct the neoclassical architecture of Washington, the wares available in the Gap, Restoration Hardware, and the Pottery Barn, and the art of the National Gallery. We're impressed and amazed by the sheer aesthetic beauty of the Spanish and Mesoamerican stones, designs, and textures. But we're also corrected ethically. We are destructive, ignoring those small news items in the *Washington Post* that mention accidents, prison killings, and hurricanes in Latin America. We don't mind the regimes, or the living conditions. I had a very talented student in a recent semester who declared the superiority of Western civilization with neoconservative fervor. What I found most distressing was that he wasn't immature, pampered, and affluent like so many student conservatives. He was hip, sensitive, well-read. He had long hair and idiosyncratic taste in clothes. And yet he declared loudly in class that the West has a "superior civilization," his actual words. He doesn't include Mexico in the West, either. He means Europe and the United States. But many of us are more like my student than we might admit. It does us good to walk down the Calle Alcala and climb the structures at Monte Alban. My student is a Philistine, and so are we all, to one degree or another, Philistines, Barbarians, and Populace. We need to see. We are better for having been "there."

And yet what's most surprising is the boundary we don't pass—the boundary that lies around the colonial city or the Mesoamerican ruins. Travelers don't go to the dilapidated, worn Mexican city of Oaxaca. As the colonial buildings diminish, the foreign visitors stop. Arnold's "best that has been thought or known in the world" ends there, and now there is "the worst": broken masonry, barefoot children, very ordinary architecture, lives that do not seem at all extraordinary. My friend and I walk the dozen blocks to the second-class bus station through those ordinary streets. We take an eight-hour local bus to get to the coast. There is no "broadening," no art, nothing restorative or redemptive there. A Canadian couple warns us about the bus ride. They call it harrowing. But I think that bus ride was the most valuable part of our trip.

Arnoldian benefits can be seen in any current travel magazine. I have before me the January 2003 issue of *Condé Nast Traveler* (but it could be virtually any travel magazine). If Arnold wanted us to pursue our best selves by encountering "the best which has been reached in the world" (one of his favorite catchphrases), this magazine is there to help. Its monthly departments are dedicated to revealing the notable architecture (Federation Square in Melbourne, "like a Cubist sculpture writ large"), music (Habib Koite from Mali), museum exhibits (Leonardo da Vinci, Master Draftsman, at the Metropolitan in New York; Ellsworth Kelly: Red Green Blue, in San Diego), and food (a guide to food stands in Salvadore de Bahia, Seoul, Singapore, Budapest,

Florence that "seasoned epicures" recognize as "authentic regional cuisine").[24] The issue's "Gold List of the World's Best Places to Stay" ranks proximity to museums, concert halls, and opera houses nearly as high as luxurious decor and attentive service. The magazine knows that Arnold's "wisdom and beauty" is the purpose of travel.

The issue's features aim to produce enlightened and enlightening travel, as well. "Arabian Iberia" by Jeffrey Tayler provides a historical and cultural account of Moorish Spain and Portugal. Banished is the stereotype of Islam as backwards or violent. The Moorish rule and legacy is characterized by harmony and beauty: "Iberian poets writing in Arabic were legendary throughout the Muslim world; architectural masterpieces were renowned as among the finest on earth; the religiously diverse population lived in peace under enlightened caliphal rule."[25] The magazine helps to "know and express the best which has been reached in the world."

Does the magazine oppose what Arnold does—the selfish, narrow, superficial, or destructive self, philistinism and narcissism and intolerance? There is absolutely no criticism of its readers, and certainly no scolding or moralistic tone, as in Arnold. Instead, as with Arnold, beauty, wisdom, and clarity are simply presented, as though the sight of them alone were sufficient for their benefits to take hold. It is amusing, for instance, how often a "view" is praised. There are "saloons with a view" in Los Angeles, New York, Shanghai, Rome, and Tokyo, for instance, and a significant number of the "Gold List" hotels have a "beautiful view." One wonders about the value of a "view"—it would be a topic worthy of extended discussion. But what is implied is that merely casting one's eyes on a sight is sufficient for benefit, even for personal improvement. Certainly that is what takes place commonly in a museum. Few are there to study, few to learn the techniques of painting. Museumgoers are there to look. Simply seeing a Vermeer is culturally valuable, as though the beauty of the painting becomes part of the viewer. There is some Arnold in that belief, as in the magazine's praise of view.

If the foreground of *Condé Nast Traveler* is the personal better-ment that comes from travel, becoming larger and better humans as we extend our cultivated selves in a one-to-one ratio to the amount of the earth's surface we have covered, in the background of the magazine lie a number of threats. Post–September 11, those threats are especially vivid in travel magazines, but they have in fact always been there. Travel is dangerous, the magazine ac-knowledges, but if one follows Wendy Perrin's tips on "How to Travel in an Uncertain World," then the dangers can be contained. David Kaufman writes on how to avoid "common crime," and the magazine offers attractively illustrated products to prevent the dangers of sunburn and insect bites ("sun smoothers"). The mag-azine ombudsman addresses reader complaints about the "mis-ery," "nightmare," and "despair" of a misadvised bicycle tour in France ("Two-Wheel Ordeal") and being mischarged by a credit card company. There are risks and dangers, the magazine ac-knowledges, but they can and ought to be remedied.

Traveling "Lite"

It might be hard to imagine, but Henry Miller takes delight in being cheated by taxi drivers and guides in Greece, Alfonso Lingis feels he benefits from being thrown in jail in Bangkok, and Albert Camus states that the "value of travel is fear." And Mary Oliver, of course, does not write about the scent of flowers and spices in Jakarta but about being burned by an acid sight. Educational travel, the travel that seeks to broaden and cultivate, like *Condé Nast Traveler,* sees those as problems to be avoided or solved.

It is interesting that Arnold didn't travel, except to tour Euro-pean schools as part of his work. He had no need to since he could see clearly and knew, already, "the best that has been thought and known in the world" from his travels in literature. But he does present his view of one foreign culture, America, and there indicates his estimation of the value of the foreign. The United States, first, is not especially different from Britain in his view. It is simply "the English on the other side of the Atlantic."[26] So much for any challenging sense of otherness. And if America is to have a value for Britons, it is to be the improvement of British civilization. He has been told that in America there are "people of good taste, good manners, good education, peers of any people in the world, reading the best books, interpreting the best music, and interested in themes world-wide."[27] Such love of intellect and beauty—if it exists—can help cure Britain of its philistinism, he hopes. It is not anything new or surprising that Arnold hopes to discover in America, but a civilizing tonic of "better selves" useful in his educational project. Unfortunately, Arnold discovers too little cultivation in America: "All that we hear from America . . . points as far as I can see, to a great presence and power of these middle-class misgrowths there as here."[28]

The conventional end of travel is a perfectly Arnoldian education: not to encounter anything truly strange, but to see a better version of what we have at home and so to improve ourselves. Why else do so many universities include travel in their curricula? A brochure describing my own university's "summer sessions abroad" makes it clear that part of what we do in universities is to import a culture, much as Arnold imported Hellenism. Courses on French literature, German philosophy, the history of Indochina, African ideas of God. Thus, it's a logical step—in fact, it's an improvement—to travel to the culture itself and combine "in-class instruction and on-site observation and participation . . . to increase [our] knowledge and understanding of French [German, Spanish, Chinese, Japanese] language and culture," as well as of "the French [German, Spanish, Chinese, Japanese] way of life."[29]

But such a firm link between travel and education is not restricted to college students. Why else do so many universities offer trips to alumni, trips complete with university professors on board to elucidate the literary and archeological aspects of the Greek isles, for example? Those trips only make explicit what is implicit in much casual travel, for what is in our travel itineraries but museums, historical sites, concert halls, architectural marvels?

Viewed as the proverbial Martian anthropologist might view

us while we travel, our behavior is truly bizarre. While we might visit cultural sites at home on occasion, once we leave home they are our exclusive concern, perhaps our obsession. We behave as though we had an insatiable craving for paintings and historical artifacts, devoting time, money, and effort to putting ourselves in front of as many as possible. What is this peculiar passion that sees us spending thousands of dollars in order to examine something as obscure as the armaments collections in the Vesting Museum in Naarden, the Netherlands, as I once did? Why pay even more to walk shoulder to shoulder with hundreds of other tourists back and forth across the fourteenth-century Charles Bridge in Prague? We know something culturally important is going on when a people spends enormous amounts of money and devotes inordinate amounts of time and effort simply to place themselves in front of buildings or objects. That is precisely what we do in travel, and all in order to "augment the excellence of our nature."[30]

Arnoldian travel involves no rupture at all. Its aim, in fact, is to combat the social and personal rupture in "anarchy." Arnold's major book is *Culture and Anarchy,* and that alternative, culture versus anarchy, is Arnold's overarching project. It presents, as Lionel Trilling says, a "grim alternative."[31] Arnold wanted to strengthen our fabric, not rip it, by demonstrating the excellence of our heritage, extending the "surface" of our "best" meanings back 2,500 years. Continuity is Arnold's message, and it is ours, too, when we travel for education. The Turners in the Tate Gallery expand our acquaintance with and knowledge of art history or aesthetics, providing us with greater intellectual or personal continuity. Visiting Kafka's house behind Prague Castle is a pilgrimage to a cultural shrine, whereby our actions and our presence bond with our memories of *The Trial* and *The Castle* and its importance to us culturally and personally. We do not need to overcome an abyss in encountering the Elgin marbles, do not have to feel a recalcitrant self shatter in listening to Mozart in Salzburg, or need to experience an eruption of disturbing passion in a production of *Oedipus at Colonus* in Epidaurus. The "perfection" that is involved is the fruition of that which was already sewn back home.

If the religious life takes place wherever the self is formed, Arnoldian travel is as religiously significant as any pilgrimage that sought to enlarge the geography of the faith to Lourdes or Jerusalem or Santiago de Compostela. The Divine Order it is called, not the divine disorder, and pilgrimage demonstrated that the faith had a geographical dimension, site linked up to site, saint linked up to saint. As each place was visited, spiritual merit accrued and enlarged, and the order of the soul approached the order of the sainted and the order of the divine. Arnoldian travel, the travel that "augments the excellence of our nature," is a secular pilgrimage, but one that does not merely mimic the religious. It is religious by forming the self in a similarly expansive order.

So "confusion," "bafflement," "ignorance" are strictly opponents for Arnold. "Commerce with the ancients" is to provide us, he says, with a "stay." It's a revealing metaphor. In a world in which we are "sick and sorry," in which "the shock of accident is unceasing," and in which we waste away in a superficial philistinism, we need "an ever surer and surer stay."[32] It's the nautical term that I hear, suggesting the threat of a storm that will require the mast to be supported. Travel is support and stability. But the other meaning of "stay" is unavoidable: the "ancients" can "console us [and] sustain us" only if we do not move, if we stay.[33] We need to remain right where we are in the great tradition of "the best that has been written and thought" and not wander from it. If we are to travel, then, we must stay within the compass of that which is not strange. Only then we can "educe and cultivate what is best and noblest" in ourselves.[34]

Perhaps that is why the sustenance that Arnold finds in cultural travel is—paradoxically—so "lite." Hellenism gives us "sweetness and light," surely as insubstantial a buttress against anarchy as we might imagine. Even honey has more heft than the mere quality of sweetness. And its operation is nearly automatic: Arnold suggests over and over that merely to see the "best" is to move toward it. It is hard to avoid the conclusion that Arnold's notion of culture and of its enemies lacks seriousness and heft. As Stanley Kauffmann noted, "Victorian pessimism of the 'Dover Beach' kind . . . always suggests that there is a comforting cup of tea waiting somewhere in the cosmic void."[35] Anarchy is not more serious than trampling the flowerbeds in Hyde Park, and the greatest disruptiveness coming from ourselves is an over-earnest involvement in tea meetings or from "bawling [and] hustling." Is there anything more than troublesome schoolboys here? Thus the resources of culture needn't be very potent, either. We're all of good stock, and all we really need is to be reminded of that—to see and, thereby, be.

Educational travel is "lite," too, designed to reinforce, not force. It has no real awe, no intensity. It is no accident that most educational travel is within the West, and to the cultural shrines of museums, concert halls, opera houses, public squares, historical monuments, architectural sites, universities, government buildings. These shrines are monuments, that is, institutionally established places, sanctioned by the culture as valuable, where a visitor can gain access to the values of the culture in a manageable way. As Lynda Sexson, a religious scholar of contemporary experience, puts it, the monumental "puffs . . . seals . . . codifies" the values of the culture. They are usually clean, usually stone, usually easy to find, and it is usually easy to feel their significance.[36] We navigate about a city in relation to them: they are our landmarks. We navigate about our cultures and about our lives in relation to them, too.

For years I have sent students to these sites in Washington—the Lincoln Memorial, the National Gallery of Art, the Capitol, the National Archives, the Supreme Court, the Vietnam Memorial, and the Holocaust Memorial and Museum. As those last two show, it isn't that memorials only "augment the excellence of our nature." They can compel an encounter with evil, not to mention with confusion. That possibility was embodied well in a student who, with an anguish that didn't diminish through repetition, read her father's name on the Wall of the Vietnam Memorial. It was also evident in a Polish student who recognized, to his acute distress, how much he looked like some of the Nazi guards pictured in the Holocaust Museum. I would like to claim these experiences for the sort of travel that this book will present, for travel that leads to rupture. Rupture can happen in many places, West or East, slums or palace. What matters is the way in which the site functions: "augmenting," "enlarging," "sustaining," "explaining," "inspiring," "improving," "civilizing," and "curing" are indications that Arnoldian and Victorian education are taking place. I would be very narrow-minded to insist that those gerunds are merely superficial or of negligible importance. I send my students to those sites because they are powerful and important. I would be a fool to claim that educational travel is nonexistent or superficial. What I insist upon is that it is only half the story, perhaps less.

"Commerce with the ancients"—Arnoldian travel—means maintaining in several senses the integrity of our surfaces. The reason why we travel is to grow, but while that growth must take into account three crucial aspects of our distress—which I've called (in somewhat Arnoldian fashion) the mundane, the superficial, and the destructive—it is not a frank, which is to say, not a potentially rupturing encounter with them. Instead, we assume that they are there, and that merely "seeing" the great achievements of our culture through the glass will eradicate them. We needn't break through the surface to encounter them; nothing, in fact, need be broken. Beauty and truth are healing, painlessly. I have no doubt that educational travel is immensely valuable. We are isolated within our routines and our cultures, and we do feel ourselves broadening, feel new sensibilities awakening when we stand on the Academia Bridge in Venice at dusk or view a sunrise over the Dutch bulb fields of Sassenheim or witness a performance of *The Marriage of Figaro* and discover that opera is—who would have guessed?—enormously moving. Arnold's language is stilted, but the experience is genuine: they "educe and cultivate what is best and noblest" within us. But for this kind of education to take place, we must remain separated from what resists within us and from what is harshly offered to us from without. The sort of travel that I will discuss in the remainder of this book is characterized by encountering those barriers, perhaps even breaking through them.

Arnold finally came to America in 1883, and Walt Whitman had a telling response: "Arnold always gives you the notion that he hates to touch the dirt—the dirt is so dirty! But everything comes out of the dirt—everything."[37] The chief difficulty with educational travel, with "commerce with the ancients," is that so little dirt is encountered. In Arnold, we are "seeing" or "knowing" with our hands on books, sitting in our parlors or libraries. One is reading, not touching, not even walking. And when travel is involved, museums, concert halls, and monuments are exceedingly pristine.

As it happens, there is a tradition of travel that explicitly scorned Victorian, educational travel, and that sought the "dirt." It is travel outside Oaxaca's zocalo, travel on the local buses with people hauling crates of produce, travel where there is nothing of high cultural value. By accident (or not), it is strongly an American style of travel, inaugurated by Whitman himself, as well as by a writer mocked by Arnold as an exemplar of philistinism, Mark Twain. It is continued by two writers who insisted upon the dirt, Paul Bowles and Henry Miller, as well as dozens of others. It is in these writers that we find the literary expression of the journey to bewilderment—which is to say, the journey to dirt.

THREE The Pilgrim's Progress

THERE'S SOMETHING ABOUT THE HUGE CRUISE SHIPS, ANCHORED out in the harbor, that makes some insistent on drawing a firm line between "tourists" (on the ship) and "travelers" (in the streets). The ships are so aggressively modern, so sleek, so gleaming that they seem a Hollywood version of the affluent world, being shown on the dirty screen of a developing nation's coast. It is a cliché of writing on travel, as well as of being a traveler, that there is a vast difference between being a mere tourist, on one of those ships (or any equivalent—on a tour bus, in a tour group, or in a luxury hotel, for instance) and being a real traveler. And that distinction has to do with confusion: travelers risk it, tourists shun it.

Two images come to mind. In Federico Fellini's autobiographical *Amarcord,* a passenger ship floats past the quiet Italian town of his youth. It is glamour and style and affluence and it is going . . . elsewhere. The ship is obscured in the fog, so we follow it with difficulty. Cruise ships do not land. They remain off the coast. They are a message to those on shore that the advances of affluent modernity may be near but not very near. As I watch the huge ships from the beachless waterfront in Ensenada, Mexico, I yearn for them, too. What incredible pleasures seem to be on board. They are a message to all of us—the beautiful life of music, romance, and fine cuisine is there, floating effortlessly by.

The other image is from *Heart of Darkness*. When Marlow sails along the coast of Africa, on his way to that utterly disruptive heart, he sees a French man-of-war firing into the jungle. "There wasn't even a shed there, and she was shelling the bush." It seems incomprehensible to Marlow, "firing into a continent."[1] Conrad is a fine counterpoint to Matthew Arnold's self-building, for while Arnold was confident of our ability to see and consume what we visit, as we can read and absorb the great literature of the West, Conrad presents so great a gap between "off the coast" and "in the interior" that not even violence has effect. Maybe that is because of the clichéd "unbridgeable gap" between "West" and "East," but it may also have to do with all travel: there is simply no getting "there." There is no moving from ship to shore, and the utter disparity between the hypermodern cruise ship and the dusty town proves it.

It is images like those from Fellini and Conrad that lead many fine writers to draw a very hard line between tourists and travelers. Tourists come in ships that are exaggerations of home, and while the tourist may venture off ship, they are always able to return to the ship—and will. They are safe, protected, risking nothing. Travelers, on the other hand, go to the "jungle" or the winding streets and remain there, giving up their homes for the duration of the trip. Travelers risk discomfort, illness, foul odors, beds with bugs, and maybe even insanity. And they scorn those who do not.

And it's not only about vacation trips, of course; it's about the religious import of travel. In the religious quest for disruption, too, we tend to separate the tourists and the travelers: those who take it easy and those who take it hard; those who maintain the comfort of their selves and of their lives and those who crawl on their knees for miles, who endure the worst discomfort and pain, and who travel as a scourge or as an ordeal in order to effect the most profound changes in their selves and their lives, the most challenging test, and the most extreme results. The travelers, it is claimed, risk most rupture. They tolerate it, seek it, value it, while the tourists never leave the ship or the surfaces they depend upon and so avoid rupture. Pilgrimage had its rankings. For medieval Christians, it was the pilgrimage to Jerusalem that was the apex of spiritual value, although it could easily involve many months and considerable danger. Historically some argued that pilgrimage was not necessary, God being as present in the home as in Jerusalem, but soon pilgrimage took firm hold, and there was, in fact, more merit in traveling to Jerusalem or other pilgrimage sites than in visiting the village shrine. We have a bias toward suffering when it comes to religion, and a bias toward rarity. If it's down the street, it can't be of as much value as if it's around the world. If it takes place once in a lifetime, it's of more religious value than if it takes place every afternoon. Religiously we tend to value travel and prefer the "true" pilgrim to the mere religious tourist.

Scorn is flung at both travelers and tourists—and anyone else who moves into other cultural worlds—by those who see a virtually inevitable colonialism still taking place in any contact, and they condemn the very literal killings, enslavements, and rapes, as well as the savage physical and emotional sufferings inflicted historically by the European nations (and their extensions, the United States, Canada, Australia, New Zealand, and the rest) upon the non-West. In the present day, such violence continues in the destruction of cultures, economic exploitation, diseases allowed to ravage, and political subjugation. These critics are angry and zealous in rooting out every evidence of continuing colonialism. Traveler or tourist—what matters such a distinction when both are perpetuating such harm?

I find myself wanting to defend the tourist against the condescending traveler and both against the politically and ethically enraged postcolonial critic. It isn't because both criticisms aren't valid—the postcolonial one especially. Yet both are too extreme, and too much is lost in the loud denunciations. Even the principal postcolonial critic, Edward Said, praises traveling because it abandons mastery and subjects itself to "motion [and the] willingness to go into different worlds, use different idioms, and understand a variety of disguises, masks, and rhetorics."[2] Couldn't that apply to all who leave home? But first let us look at the traveler's condemnation of the tourist.

Beyond the Stigma: Tourists as Pilgrims

The foremost contemporary proponent of this self-congratulatory view is Paul Fussell. His *Abroad* is an enormously popular analysis of travel after World War I—you'll find it in every bookstore's travel section; what Carole King's *Tapestry* once was to record collections, *Abroad* is to travel books: it's always there. With academic authority, it perpetuates the snobbish condescension toward tourism that we are probably all susceptible to as we are susceptible to many biases. As Evelyn Waugh famously said, "the tourist is the other fellow." Fussell yearns for the "great age" of travel when the mammoth ocean liners carried those of independent wealth to exotic places where they needn't encounter the riffraff from home. Alas, the Industrial Revolution meant that even the uneducated were given vacations and possessed the means to go abroad, and soon there were packaged tours to even the remotest places. The work of travel is lost, Fussell says—the difficulty of learning about a foreign place, of subsisting without reservations and learning customs the hard way, by making costly mistakes. "The tourist moves toward the security of pure cliché," he says—where nothing is uncertain, nothing is surprising, nothing takes shape.[3] But not "us"; "we" are travelers.

It might be thought that this book would sympathize with Fussell's view. If we strip his view of its economic elitism, class snobbery, and sense of his own superiority, it might appear that he criticizes tourism precisely for its loss of the risks of disruption, the risks that I insist are so important. In fact, he quotes a fine observation by Lawrence Durrell, "Let the tourist be cushioned against misadventure, your true traveler will not feel he has had his money's worth unless he brings back a few scars."[4] It's a wonderful notion, and it reminds me of what a friend told me—that she loves coming back from a hike and not knowing how she got the scratches. That has long seemed to me to be an epitome of the quest for confusion, both mental and physical: we're willing to throw ourselves into powerful encounters and do not emerge unscathed. Even more, our lives as we travel are beyond us, beyond recollection and recall: where did we get those scratches? And tourists, we often think, acquire no scratches.

I certainly confess distaste for those cruise ships and for tour buses, as well. I've spent too many afternoons at a table next to people fresh off the ship, laughing and drinking as though they were still in L.A., their conversation seemingly unaffected by the oblique beauty or desperate poverty of a city like Ensenada, Mexico. Outside the Bab Bou Jeloud in Fez, there was a fat new bus of Europeans every half hour, and I certainly found their ten-minute tour of the souk and rush back to the bus amusing. I've even made a tour of the best hotel in town a standard aspect of my travel, admiring the way plastic automatically sheathes the toilets in the Intercontinental Hotel in Prague or watching deals being cut in the Novotel in Accra, Ghana.

I think it's a vast mistake to label "us" travelers and "them" mere tourists, as though we could divide the authentic from the false so easily and recognize full encounter with confusion from none at all. It's just more complicated than the neat tourist versus traveler divide would indicate. Fussell sees a lamentable historical decline, as explorers became travelers and travelers became tourists, the golden age eventually becoming bronze and then tin. I wonder if the encounter with bewilderment hasn't, instead, become egalitarian. I wonder if tourists aren't, at least in part, in search of confusion, as well. I wonder if there aren't surfaces put at risk for everyone who travels. I think all travel may have religious value.

The beautiful Greek island of Santorini may be as tourist-infested as any place on earth. On the stunning lip of the crater, dropping into the Aegean, tourists shop for souvenirs, sit with a glass of retsina, or snap photos of the donkeys that brought them up from the landing. It's shoulder-to-shoulder with folks right off the tour boat. Just a bit inland, it's Fort Lauderdale at spring break—hundreds of college-age kids from all over Europe walking up and down the street called 25 Martiou, drinking, and looking to hook up for the night. And at the end of the day, crammed buses bring both groups up to the northernmost town of Oia to watch what's actually billed as the most beautiful sunset on earth. A dozen or so streets that are too narrow for cars are absolutely full, people sitting on every pastel wall, even standing on the roofs of low buildings and turned toward the west, their faces burnished by the low sun, like worshipers awaiting the live sacrament, or like the hillside believers in Spielberg's *Close Encounters of the Third Kind*. It was a nice sunset—a real nice one—as it's a terrific cauldron and there are some fine bars, but worth such a pilgrimage? Is it in fact a pilgrimage for these tourists? Are surfaces ruptured? Is the self remade?

Yes. But not because shopping, drinking, and sunsets are so valuable and utterly different from what takes place at home. What's missing when we give tourism nothing but our disdain is the fuller context. The shopping, drinking, and sunset watching are ordinary activities of home, but they are not taking place at home. Isn't an ordinary activity transformed by taking place in the middle of the Aegean, thousands of miles from home? Isn't it deformed, even undermined? In fact, the rupturing that I discussed in the first chapter may be strongest in our most ordinary travel activities—the often violent rupturing of the meaningful activities that ordinarily structure our lives—and tourists by definition engage in the most ordinary activities.

As I have been saying from the start, we can understand travel and its disruptions best if we take it most seriously, that is, not as a vacation or a holiday or a lark but as an activity that serves the same powerful function as pilgrimage did historically and still does for a great many people, providing us with orientation.

Travel taken seriously is a religious activity. A common religious distinction is between the devout adept and the casual believer, the priesthood and the laity, the true devotee and the weak adherent, those who dedicate their lives, utterly renounce the world, and, therefore, dive most deeply into the divine realities. Travelers, then, are the true devotees and tourists merely casual. But that view underestimates how subtle and broad religious orientation is: all people have orientations, not just the most energetic or well-focused. In the metaphor I used in chapter 1, we all live on surfaces whether they are composed of *People Magazine* or the *Parisian Review,* collecting bits of twine or string theory. Possessing a powerful devotion to one surface—to cell biology, like my sister-in-law, or to Democratic politics, like my neighbor, one in the National Academy of Sciences and the other frequently quoted in the *Washington Post*—does not make one more oriented and thus more religious than the rest of us. It isn't just the professionals, it's the amateurs and even the utter failures. We are all religious, all oriented, all living on surfaces. And when we travel we expose our surfaces to the weather, and they are inevitably worn and scored, etched and warped, dented and pocked. All travelers are pious pilgrims, putting their faith—that is, their orientations as humans—to the test.

My own exposed surface is seen where I choose to have a meal. I make my table a habit. A hundred or so yards down from my hotel in the medina of Tangier was a restaurant I initially hated. When I first walked in I was starving after the long bus and ferry trip from Spain, so I tolerated the TV, broadcasting the World Cup, and a couple of Westerners, but I intended never to return once I finished that first tajine. I wanted to be away and did my best to avoid looking at the screen or the European couple. Yet I returned to that restaurant—and the TV and assorted Westerners—the following day and then the next, eating at least one meal there a day for my entire stay. The same was true of the tight, dark, art nouveau café in the rainy winding streets of Prague; the blue plywood table, curtained from the kitchen in a sunny dirt street of Accra; the breezy open-air café in the marble-tiled square of Nafplio, Greece; and the two-tabled restaurant hidden behind a bright limestone wall just inside Jerusalem's Damascus Gate. In part, it's the opposite of any search for confusion—it's a routine, a familiar waiter or cook, a nod and a greeting. The same table. The same people to eat with. It's the connection with those familiar Westerners and the familiar sport. But it was also a rude reminder of just how far away my own dining room table and family were. The routine was the same every day at home—sitting in my seat at the dining room table, covered with the *Post,* while my daughter rushed through her oatmeal before the bus and my son ate an Eggo waffle, studying his Pokemon cards. Fall, winter, spring, and summer. And in the evening, each dinner was a family meal, no exceptions, to occasional loud protests. And across the oceans I keep a meal routine, too, but it impresses the fact even more powerfully that my family isn't seated there, that the food isn't familiar and possibly not healthy. There are a few archetypal places that denote home, and certainly bed and table are among them. So I go to the same bed and the same table, but I discover nothing familiar at all. Necessary surfaces, crucial surfaces, are ripped. And isn't that part of tourism generally?

In a way, travel is both antiritualistic and ritualistic. It involves leaving, breaking, and violating. It means not doing what we usually, habitually do. We leave home. It means the loss of routines and habits, even those that most sustain us, perhaps especially those. But it also means both continuing old habits and routines and establishing new ones. When we travel we discover what we need—food, companionship, intellectual or artistic engagement, rest—and we ritualize those, filling them with meaning, making them into the significant surfaces that will support us as we travel. Sleep, eat, talk, think: those become ritualized. We depend upon them more than ever. We live upon them more acutely and consciously. We seek a place to sleep and want it to be right. We seek a place to eat, people to talk to, matters to consider, and they all become far more pent than they were at home. Travel is religiously significant because we are so ordinary when we leave home, because we strip our activities down to the most fundamental and we rely upon those with an acuteness that we never experience at home. Our most basic activities are ritualized—and then exposed to harm. For the newly ritualized is constantly de-ritualized, challenged, questioned, and disrupted, as though we took this fresh and newly made practice and placed it immediately out in the weather. We need it to help us live in the elements, but the elements themselves tear at it.

We scorn tourists because to be a tourist is synonymous with two things: superficiality and a leisured affluence. Six countries in six days. Comfortable hotels, not the fleabags of true travelers. Big tour buses. Those sleek cruise ships. In *Amarcord,* the ship represents the good life, and the locals look longingly after it. Developing countries don't have tourists, except among the rising middle classes and economic elites. Instead there are pilgrims and migrant workers, one an ancient form of travel and the other more ancient than we might think. We tend to think more highly of both than we do of tourism since they seem to be validated by ancient cultural imperatives or severe economic necessity. Tourism, on the other hand, is precisely the opposite: a dilettantish tasting and a flaunting of excess cash. And, of course, it is. But just as there is a hidden ripping in all of tourism's ordinary activities, there is also distress in superficiality and affluence. To be a tourist is to be appealing and to be distant.[5]

It may sound vapid to speak of the distress of affluence, something like the Who singing about how tough it is to be Aryan in "Behind Blue Eyes": "No one knows what it's like / To be the bad man / To be the sad man / Behind blue eyes / No one knows what it's like/ To be hated / To be fated / To telling only lies." Certainly there's much more distress in malaria or malnutrition or torture or much else than in being a tourist. But I'm not interested in a contest of ills. What I'd like to point out is that even to be a tourist is to be confused, that "travelers" have no monopoly on "travail," and that one aspect of the tourist malaise is to feel envy without a remedy, to feel desired at an unalterable distance, a distance that the tourist cannot—and not just will not—cross. When Henry Miller traveled in Greece he was frequently accosted by

Greek Americans who saw him as a way of reaffirming their Americanness, which is to say how up-to-date and affluent they were in comparison with their backward countrymen. Miller hated it and scorned and rebuked them. Miller, who tolerated so much, hated being envied. On the boat from France to Greece, one of them insisted on hanging onto Miller, but "I apologized to my fellow passengers for the presence of this idiot; I explained to them that that's what America does to its adopted sons."[6] Still they came, using Miller as an exclamation of their difference. He was modernity, affluence. He was the cruise ship. And they wanted on. Who could blame them, of course? And who could envy Miller for being seen as a mere vessel?

To insist on being a traveler and never, no, never a tourist, is to pretend to avoid this particular distress, to pretend that one can walk through the streets without being this appealing foreigner, the symbol of affluence. But we're all gringos whether we came by cruise ship or rickety bus, whether our hotel has superb air-conditioning or a weary ceiling fan that threatens to fall and mangle our feet. To acknowledge that one is just a tourist is to be humbled.

The predicament of the tourist goes even further. Since I live in Washington, D.C., I see lots of tourists. They're on the Mall, in the museums, on the streets of Georgetown, and even on my campus, snapping photos of the large statue of Georgetown's founder, John Carroll. These ridiculous-looking men and women, in their vacation clothes, with cameras and fanny packs and children, are probably far from ridiculous at home. They're lawyers and doctors, pharmacists, computer programmers. Where they belong I might well admire them or feel pleased by their attention. I might be intimidated by them or hope they speak well of me. They might have much I would envy—a way of being with their children or a talent for friendship. But as soon as they become tourists—as soon as any of us become tourists—we become hapless. We're stripped of what's made us formidable, competent, and admirable, and like ludicrous clowns we're objects of ridicule and scorn. And what may be worse, we have no recourse. What could we do? Can we say, "Hey, if you saw me in my office, you'd have a little respect!"? No. There's no redress. To be a tourist is to be unable to set anything straight, to be unable to speak—both because tourists don't speak the language and because no one would listen even if they could.

I heard a new term the other day from a colleague, "contempt for the world." She used it in describing a nun she knew who intentionally wore unattractive clothes, did not bathe regularly, and was careless about her hair. There is a Christian tradition, my friend explained, called contempt for the world: the religious person shows their rejection of worldly values not just by ignoring them but by flagrantly violating them. Tourism and travel seem to belong in the same tradition, oddly enough. They seem a kind of asceticism. One chooses to be ill-adept, to mis-fit, to misunderstand. One abandons one's standing in the world, and one moves through the world stripped of accustomed status and privileges. Touristic asceticism is hardly living off of alms and dressing in the proverbial sackcloth. Tourists may, in fact, dress better, eat better, and sleep better than most inhabitants of the city they visit. But they have left most of what makes them admirable and accomplished and submit themselves to the nakedness of tourism.

Struggle and Encounter

A better contrast than that between tourist and traveler may be that between the one who has no trouble speaking and the one who struggles. Henry Miller is, as always, instructive here. He has no troubling speaking, of course, but his speaking is a manner of wandering, of exploring, of alternately being lost and getting found, then plunging off into more conversational dark alleys. In *The Colossus of Maroussi,* his account of travels in Greece just before World War II, he has special scorn for the English—even more than he has for Greek Americans. It's the dogmatism of their opinion of the Greeks that he most objects to: "The Englishman is lymphatic, made for the arm-chair, the fireside, the dingy tavern, the didactic tread-mill. . . . They seem to think that the Greeks ought to be eternally grateful to them because they have a powerful fleet."[7] Arrogance, condescension, and smugness are all ways to remain in the "arm-chair" instead of taking the risks of confusion. Tourists may be smug, but so are many travelers, and there are many tourists who arrive on the cruise ship because their threshold is very low and the impact of that single child reaching for coins before she's shooed off the waterfront is quite powerful enough. Such sensitivity is not, I think, ridiculous.

Travelers' arrogance is what Paul Bowles finds objectionable in the Lyles, a mother and son in *The Sheltering Sky*. They are contemptuous of the people in Morocco, as well as insulting. The Arabs, says Mrs. Lyle, are a "stinking, low race of people," as are Jews and most others among whom she travels.[8] She announces that she has found a beautiful mosque, "but it's all covered with brats, all shrieking like demons."[9] Fortunately she has learned how to behave with foreigners: "The ruder you are to them the more they admire you."[10] And the wonderful irony is that Mrs. Lyle writes guidebooks, showing other visitors just how to despise and insult, I imagine. And yet Fussell might have a hard time categorizing the Lyles as tourists since they have been in Africa for five years and in India for three before that. They travel not to the tourist sites but to inaccessible places "without reservations," and encounter them so thoroughly that they have acquired "an astonishing list of diseases."[11] What makes the Lyles so objectionable is the rigidity and superiority of their judgments. Eric Lyle speaks with the pedantry of an old professor, and his mother's conversations consist entirely of bitter, often ludicrous arguments.

Wouldn't a better distinction than that between tourist and traveler be that between those who allow themselves to encounter and be affected by another culture so that they are required to suspend their usual understandings and those who do not? Those who know exactly what's going on (as the Lyles or Miller's British do) and those who are caught off guard—as Miller, Bowles, Twain, and many tourists are?

Friedrich Nietzsche was a traveler, wandering through Switzerland and Italy in self-imposed exile from his native Germany (and much like Miller and Bowles in that). He's the origin of the wonderful advice that might be the motto of travelers and tourists alike: don't trust thoughts unless they come to you while you're walking.[12] He views life as unmoored and chaotic, with no God or science to anchor it. It's not that things are (as my father thought when he warned me about Nietzsche) meaningless. Instead, our role in the meanings of things is paramount so the weight of responsibility on human beings is tremendous. In one of his aphorisms he (typically) harangues his readers, telling them that they live in a formless universe and that he despises them if they don't tremble at the thought—tremble with fear and with delight for the news and responsibility are momentous. At the very least, he says, they should hate him for giving them the news. Fear and hatred show that at least they're aware of formlessness, aware enough to try to deny it, and that, at least, earns Nietzsche's respect. We may not be especially concerned about earning Nietzsche's respect (though I have to confess that I am), but something that I do respect about tourists—about all of us when we're tourists—is their fear and denial. Staying on the ship is recognition that the shore is a threat to them, and that seems better than being oblivious to risk.[13]

The religious value of fear is nothing new. We may think of people cowering before gods as a crass and destructive superstition, but that criticism is an Enlightenment flattening of an important aspect of religion. If religious objects really are "wholly other"—if God really is God—then there is something terrifying and intense, something that would cause humans to pause or stand stock still. The definition of religion as "absolute interruption" suggests that we are halted and even intimidated. Encountering the divine is often presented in this way, while being oblivious to such power and fear is sheer superficiality.

If we look at travel as Nietzsche might, then many travelers to places that are very, very foreign could simply be impervious to extreme differences and dangers. We might call this the "harlequin phenomenon," after the simpleton in *Heart of Darkness* who dances through the same regions as the intellectual and mad Kurtz but is completely unaffected. He had "a light heart and no more idea of what would happen to him than a baby."[14] My favorite "harlequin" is Eric Hansen, a remarkable traveler who walked across Borneo, a virtually unequaled accomplishment, even by native peoples. Immense heat, forest so dense that becoming lost was a constant danger, the threat of being hurt and of small injuries becoming infected—all that and much more make his journey fascinating and impressive.

But the theme of Hansen's book is his naiveté. It makes him seem something more like a guy crossing town than a man taking extreme risks with his life. His first encounter with Borneo was marked by a Gawai Antu, a ceremony for the dead, and it remains in his memory as a kind of spectacular frat party, with a great deal of drinking and rude pranks. Years later he returns to relive the fantasy of "wonderfully strange events" that take place off the known map.[15] Unfortunately, as he laments time and again, "I had no idea what I was doing."[16] He is refreshingly frank about his innocence and illusions—wasting money on impractical trade items, twisting his ankle and being forced to return to his starting point, being unable to find appropriate guides. "I anticipated the 'Lost World' of Sir Arthur Conan Doyle, and in doing so I made a thorough job of setting myself up for some breathtaking surprises in the jungle when it had long become too late to turn back."[17]

Such frankness about his naiveté would seem to set the stage for a growth in wisdom, but while Hansen learns a great deal—how to speak languages, how to manage the customs of conversation, how to walk for weeks on end through an extremely harsh environment of heat and leeches, and impossibly rough trails—his failure is one of imagination. He really does not grasp that he is elsewhere.

The climax of his story is a solitary journey between two isolated villages, four months after his arrival in Borneo and deep in the interior of the island. Though the inhabitants warn him in the strongest terms not to set out on his own, astonishingly he ignores them. After several hours of extremely difficult hiking, he meets a group of frightened people and realizes only much later that he is the cause of their alarm. He has been taken for a spirit—a *bali saleng* who wanders alone through the forest to kill people and collect their blood. Through the following days he ignores the fear and hostility of those he encounters because "it was too farfetched for me to take seriously." Finally he is attacked, confronted, and accused—and tries to persuade his attackers that they are being superstitious![18]

Hansen travels, he says, for reasons that fit my theory well. He wants to go to the "blank places" on the map, beyond all Western influence.[19] "Travel," he says "is the act of leaving familiarity behind," and what he wants is to leave the world he understands. "What I wanted from my journey was a unique experience, something so far beyond my comprehension that I would have to step completely out of my skin to understand and become a part of my surroundings."[20] He certainly makes one of the most remarkable journeys in my acquaintance, but it's also a remarkably ignorant one. I believe I have greater respect for the tourist who can not walk any farther into Ensenada than Avenida Lopez Mateos, lined with craft shops, because he feels afraid. He has felt more fear than Eric Hansen and therefore has a much greater sense that he is at the margin of his world. He has come to the very frontier of the strange and looks across—though at nothing more than at auto repair shops and an *aesthetica* and, far down, the spire of the cathedral. Eric Hansen walks through rain forests where, perhaps, no Westerner has ever been, and he does so for months, but I wonder if he does it with any more "loss of familiarity" than he would crossing from one side of his hometown to the other. Give me tourists. At least their timidity reveals their awareness of how close bewilderment is.

Threshold anxiety is taking place for these tourists, as for any religious initiate. When someone is being initiated into a religion, there is a tremendous change that must take place. One is moving from a profane to a sacred state, from the outside to the inside of a more genuine way of being, from falsehood to truth, from indifference to commitment, from being at risk to being saved. One might well pause at that threshold. Mircea Eliade, the historian of religions, uses travel metaphors in his description of a religious threshold, calling it "a limit, a boundary, a frontier."[21] There is one state here and another there, and moving across that boundary is like changing one's very molecules. One ought to halt, to have one's identity checked by the guards, to be searched for objects hostile to the new state. One ought to be prepared by looking across that border and by asking: "Do I really want to cross? Can I really accept that new state? Can I really be in that state?" At the religious border, the initiate is questioned by representatives of both states, the old and the new. One's family bids one good-bye, and one has to ask if she really wants to leave. She has to mourn what she is leaving. And one is greeted by the members of the new orientation, after the scrutiny, after the testing. Passing into a religion has been compared to undergoing a rebirth, not just because of the degree of change that is involved, but because of the labor that is not, as we know, easy. Is there any wonder why there is threshold anxiety as tourists approach the land?

The sense that there is an elsewhere, that there is a difference between ship and shore and that you can look but you can't cross—that is the sense that shows up in fear or anxiety, in silence, in dread, or maybe simply in awe, and it is what matters in travel, not how many months one is gone, how few have been there before, how many diseases one has caught, or how many insects creep out of the bed.

But what of another kind of tourism—traveling to swim in a gorgeous pool or lagoon, to play golf in a beautiful setting, to eat some fabulous food? The trip may be for a vacation rather than traveling, and the point may be pleasure and not bewilderment. That sort of holiday may seek to reduce stress, to eliminate a sense of disproportion, and to induce a kind of deep relaxation that is more like dreamless sleep and yet not near the yawning lip of oblivion.

But even a pleasure trip may be colored with a great deal that is darker than pleasure. I recently heard a radio report that tourists are flocking to the beaches of Gabon, West Africa. Is it really the same as Europeans going to the south of France or the Adriatic coast of Italy or to the Costa del Sol or Americans to the Florida Keys, the Outer Banks, Cape Cod, or Malibu? I have never been to Gabon, but I suspect that traveling to its beaches is not unlike traveling to the beaches of Morocco, and one doesn't simply "go to the beach" in Morocco. One might begin on a train whose air-conditioning has failed and consequently is as hot as the diesel engine pulling it, and sitting across from you is a man who wants you to visit him—or, at least, that's what he seems to be saying, but your command of French is poor (and your knowledge of Arabic nonexistent). And after an hour's conversation it seems more and more likely that it isn't hospitality that he's offering but carpets. And when the train arrives in Agadir and taxi drivers offer—or, should I say, insist—on carrying you to your hotel, are you about to be cheated? Have they really heard of your hotel? Where will you be going if you put yourself into their hands? And once you are on the beach, what shall we eat and drink? If we buy some food from a stand, will we be ill for weeks? Where exactly was that water bottled? What parasite lurks in it?

"Going to the sun," like all pleasure trips that take place elsewhere, is just not as simple as it sounds because it is altered by the context and by being away, far away. Going to the sun may also be going to the edge of the surface upon which we live.

Packing Preconceptions: The Awareness of Postcolonial Travel

The most serious and influential criticism of travel today applies to travelers and tourists alike, a criticism for the harm that they all can do, regardless of how far they get from the cruise ship or how "deeply" they travel. According to this criticism, many travelers, including anthropologists, Peace Corps volunteers, businesspeople, diplomats, ex-patriots, and relief workers are informed by a way of seeing the world established by colonialism. The group even includes those who never go but only turn their imaginations to the East or South and write, speak, paint, or even daydream. None of them is able to look around themselves and simply see what's there. Instead they see what they're prepared to see, what culture has prepared them to see. They participate in a discourse that was established during colonialism and unknowingly perpetuate it. In many cases, Western travelers use the non-West to benefit themselves. They exercise a kind of neocolonial power over the non-West and the nondeveloped, controlling it, dominating it, and manipulating it for their own purposes. Much as diamonds, silver, slaves, and spices were once brought out of the colonized East for European enrichment, so the contemporary colonialists bring out images. Intrigue, eroticism, cruelty, and mystery are mined today for the benefit of Westerners and without regard to the effects on those among whom they travel.

These postcolonial critics make a powerful case, and make it impossible to see travelers and tourists (among all the others) as innocents abroad. The process is actually a great deal like what we saw in Matthew Arnold, for just as he sought "the best that has been thought or known in the world" solely for his own edification, so we also may engage with our images of the non-West for our own benefit. Those images may, in fact, result in acts of violence of both literal and figurative kinds.

At core, the criticism is that we need to maintain stable stereotypes of others to maintain our sense of self. The need comes from what I discussed in the first chapter, the fluidity of our sense of self. "Who are you?" I often ask my students, and there's simply no "factual" answer that's at all satisfying. Am I my name? Am I my gender or my height and weight? I'm a loose and constantly shifting collection of adjectives—gnats in a net, to use an image from Virginia Woolf. And while that can be an exciting notion to someone like Nietzsche, for others it can be extremely unsettling. They need to use others for their own stability—*we* need to use those others, for are any of us entirely innocent of that colonial discourse?

The influential critic Edward Said provides several full listings of the European and American "knowledge" of "Orientals": they are "gullible, 'devoid of energy and initiative,' much given to 'fulsome flattery,' intrigue, cunning, and unkindness to animals."[22] They are also "irrational, depraved (fallen), childlike."[23] They are not "rational, peaceful, liberal, logical, capable of holding real values."[24] How useful it is for us in the West, lacking selves that simply are in the ways we would them to be (like rational, peaceful, logical, and ethical) to know so clearly what (and who) we are not. It's a fine instance of gliding in on the sleek Western ship, spotting the heathens on the shore, and feeling pretty damn good about our common sense and fine sanitary systems.

Said has several points to make about these stereotypes. First they are limited and they limit the ways in which we can think—and act. There is nothing nuanced or pluralistic about them. As a result, they dehumanize, making others into what we might call caricatures if the consequences weren't so harsh, if people didn't suffer and die as a result. And that is the third aspect: we can justify our own mistreatment of these others because of the images we have of them. We can kill a hundred thousand Iraqis in the first Gulf War and then starve their children in years of sanctions because we don't think of them as fully human. Contrast our reaction when a hundred of "us" die in a plane crash, these critics say.

The core difficulty is the otherness of these others. They are not familiar—they have other religions that challenge (and contradict) our own. They have faces with other features. Their way of going about the everyday may be in strong contrast to our own. We attempt to make them familiar, but we can only do so with a concise list of clichés that controls their otherness.

I was exploring the various ways to leave Accra, Ghana, for other cities along the coast or up into the interior. There is a train station, built when the British ruled and, seemingly, in steady decline since then. It is worn, pale, falling apart—a ghost of a train station—and there are few trains, and my guidebook says that they're very slow. Most Ghanaians take the bus, but there is a multitude of bus companies, one run by the government and many other private lines. There are also tro-tros, dilapidated minivans, often with religious slogans on the back ("And because he so loved the world . . . "; "Jesus is Lord"; "The meek shall inherit the earth!"), and bush (that is, shared) taxis. Which to take? How to go about finding out the destination, the departure time, the cost, buying a ticket? It's like being a child again, in a bewildering world, with almost no clue.

I admire those who can deal with such situations with confidence, brushing through all confusions that I usually feel to be intimidating. My response is to scout out the situation, to wander through the dusty parking lot full of buses and people (and stands selling food, toiletries, canned goods, etc.) in a turmoil that I just cannot resolve into sensible patterns. Ticket stand? Schedule? Bus company personnel? I wander through the crowd, trying not to call too much attention to myself and to my confusion. I study the situation, hoping to get those sensible patterns. I move on, frustrated.

I realize that I should simply give myself over to someone, to ask for help. The Ghanaians are extremely friendly and helpful, but I've only been in the country for a few days, and I don't know that yet. And I'm just naturally reticent. Shy, even. Shy people have no business traveling. We tend to be swept along without ever speaking up and requesting a hand. One would probably be extended and would pull us easily to shore, but we never ask.

I've made two forays through the teeming area, slowly walking and intensely studying, and on the return trip I pass, again, an old man, his hand out to me. And this time, his call resolves into words I understand, the same call, I realize, I had heard after last passing him. "Many are called . . . !" he shouts, just those three words, lingering for a long time on the last syllable. "Many are called . . . !" wailing through the din of late afternoon, through the wood smoke, and the dusty street. Walking on, I turn his call over and over in my mind, beginning to see the religious allusion (". . . but few are chosen") and the wonderful matter-of-factness of it. The man called many. Few answered. And the subtle threat to those not answering his call, those who will not be chosen: the chosen, the generous will achieve salvation while the others will be damned. It's poetry, and it charms me as I wander back to my hotel, still confused about the buses, and wishing I could have my call answered, too. But I call silently, so who can answer?

What are our clichés about Africans? Happy, childish, disorganized, careless, and then liable to murderous tribal frenzies. The traveler is provided with these ways to see and hear, and they can never be completely ignored, however we scrub ourselves with postcolonialism. Even if they are not the only way in which we understand, they are whispered insistently. They form a large part of the framework. "The transportation system is a chaos, not a system at all. All I can do is to move close to its edge, and see from there that there is nothing to be understood—it is irrational. And the people moving about the buses—aren't they just going to mislead me, to use me as an opportunity for money or to laugh at the stupid foreigner or to put me on the wrong bus without much caring? Above all, it is not a bus station, not a transportation system at all." Those are the insistent clichés.

According to Said, when we travel we're moving among people, places, and situations that are not—not our people, not our places, and not our situations. As a result we're able to feel pleased at our orderliness and rationality and superiority and to place the strange in safe, limited categories.

Yet while all travelers move within those clichés and controlled encounters, to be a traveler means to experience the breakdown of those stereotypes, too. The man who wailed "many are called . . . ," for example. He was, first, negligible—sitting in the dirt, with a black hand reaching out. He was a "beggar"—wanting my money, a distraction, an impediment. An item from the news—impoverished Africa. And even when I'd listened to his call and found it interesting and admired its many levels, I was still operating within my own frameworks—religious allusion, multilayered meanings, irony, poetry. If I studied Ghanaian culture I could come to understand more about the many kinds of people who ask for money, about their histories, about their places in society, in tribal groupings, in the popular imagination. Or if I sat with him for some weeks or months, I could come to know his own stories, his origins, his sense of why he sat and called, his friends or surviving family members, his ills and complaints.

With a great deal of time and an unusual receptivity, I might end up like Susan Brind Morrow, author of *The Names of Things*. She travels in Egypt and East Africa, and her observations on skin color are characteristic of her subtlety: "Sudan, *elbelad asswadeeen*, 'the land of the blacks,' was a market term, I suspected, a term of the Arab slave trade. It was a bad joke, for the territory itself was an argument against the notion of race. It spoke of nothing but the astonishing diversity, fluidity, and adaptability of human life. . . . [T]he Sudanese [were] a hundred tribal groups, each with its own language and physical character. The Sudanese did not commonly use black to describe a person's skin but yellow or red (*Mahas, Danagla*), green (*Kirdofani*), or blue (*Dinka, Shilluk*)."[25] Her usual ways of understanding are fragmented, as by a prism, and the world is richer and more confusing.

But, even so, if I ever stopped, if I ever felt that I'd finally "gotten it right" and could begin to be knowledgeable about Ghanaians, it would only be proof—wouldn't it?—that I'd gotten it wrong. Without absorbing a culture from birth, it will always be "other," and so there always has to be the disruption of my understandings. And that's just what took place with the man in Accra. I needed someone to reach me a hand, to set me straight on the buses, and he did reach a hand, but not to set me straight. Who was he, what did he want? He disturbed me, haunted me, and still does. I feel that the disturbance is what's so valuable, more than a dubious learning. If the postcolonial critique is to alert us to the disturbances, I'm with it. If it's to provide us with a program for a cure, I have to leave it to others. I am interested in us as we stumble—and keep going. I am less interested at this time in what sets us straight.

Morrow's book is full of disturbances. She lived in Egypt for years, but she never became an expert; she never seems finished with her understandings. She "loved nothing more than to sit with a group of strangers, speaking a strange language, in the middle of nowhere." It is a part of her that coexisted with another that wanted "only to stay home."[26] We're not at home as we travel. We move about with understandings that crack and decay, doing less and less work for us, and we need to tolerate the intolerable line between missing those understandings that come from home and appreciating their breakdown—perhaps, even thriving from it.

There's a further aspect of postcolonial travel. While the Western traveler is, beyond doubt, privileged and powerful, the speaker of the culture that dominates the planet, and while he reminds me of the Roman emissary of Empire, collecting tribute from subjected realms, he has also placed himself in a vulnerable position and travels, to some extent, as one submissive and dependent. Nothing establishes our identity as our own place does, with the acknowledgment of others and all the reinforcements of belonging. I walk into the New North Building at Georgetown University as a tenured professor. A student may be an Onassis, as one once was, but she still scribbles down my observations on William James and estimates her own intellectual accomplishment according to my comments on her essay. Her parents pay thousands a year for her to sit in my class and discuss how religious ideas function in human cultures. But when I fly to Morocco, I am nobody. I am always a Westerner, identified by my clothing and my skin, but I'm a Westerner out of place. I'm homeless.

I was in the Tangier train station, waiting to go to Fez. It's a small station and was crowded. A young Canadian came up to me and said, "Can I stand near you, please?" He'd just been robbed at knifepoint and needed to feel a bit safer, standing near someone like home. "Can I stand near you, please?" He'd also been shaken down that morning in the station, accused of drug possession by a policeman who demanded money. He and I traveled together for the next week, each needing to stand near the other. But since then, that phrase, that question, "Can I stand near you, please?" has echoed in my ear. It needn't be too close, just "near," and it needn't be too comfortable, standing is fine. But we needed it. We always need it. Standing near our parents, standing near our partner or spouse, standing near friends. But when we travel, we stand near fewer of those people or none. We are exposed. For the rest of the trip, to Fez and down to Marrakesh and back, whenever I had a particularly acrimonious conflict with a would-be guide, I feared a knife. Maybe that is just a fantasy of the lethal non-West, or maybe it was a legitimate fear: the situation is confused. And, of course, I was never totally homeless; there was the hotel and, I suppose, the consulate. Besides, everyone knows I'm a Westerner, wearing the aura and power of the West. But I'm also a child, bewildered and lost, and as easily hurt. "Can I stand near you, please?"

The postcolonial critics seem to have a social and political aim, whereas mine is personal and individual, though those are not clearly distinct areas. I see travelers (and tourists) drawn to excess, for example, and while some of that attraction might be stereotypical, limiting the "Orient" to qualities solely for the benefit of the Western traveler as he or she is drawn by "the strangely threatening excesses of Oriental mysteries," we can also shift our focus to the nonethical consideration of why the traveler is drawn to excess anyway and why it might nonetheless be of value.[27] Maybe those are simply two different ways of looking at travel. There can be a tendency among postcolonial critics to want to have the "master narrative," especially since ethical and political concerns can be so urgent. People are being hurt. There can be the insistence that travelers become aware and rid themselves of images and motivations. I am not so sure. Being confused and being disempowered can have ethical benefits. And there can be personal benefits quite aside from social and political considerations—those this entire book has been presenting. Neither the ethical nor the political trumps all.

We might notice that those whose concern with travel is primarily ethical are urging something Arnoldian: travel ought to improve us; it ought to enable us to encounter the person of the non-West so that we learn more about who they are and replace our stereotypes. We combat philistinism by seeing "what's there."

There's something admirable about such travel. We all ought to grow. We should increase our meanings and make them more adequate to our experiences. We ought to become more just and more understanding, and the postcolonial critique can make us so.

On the other hand, we might consider Whitman's endorsement of "dirty" travel in the last chapter. In contrast with Matthew Arnold's erudite and self-improving travel, Whitman insists that "everything comes out of the dirt—everything." Children play in the dirt or adults do when they're being childish. We might think that it's the "real travelers"—Fussell's travelers—who best travel in the dirt. No itinerary, no air-conditioning, no reservations, no fine restaurants. These travelers for "dirt" jump ship and disappear into the crowd. But it can be any traveler, even the tourist. Going odd places and seeing odd stuff—it's not much more complicated than that. Wandering out of the yard and crawling through the bushes into land that's someone else's, and perhaps finding ourselves politically or ethically over our heads. Finding a pond or a culvert, and then, beyond it what feels like the end of the world. The railroad tracks, rumors of accidents, and another city altogether through the far woods. And legends where the tracks point, either way. Was it Tolkien who wrote that there is really only one road and it starts here and then goes . . . everywhere?

But there's another kind of "dirty" travel, not the adventure away from home but, in a manner of speaking, the anti-adventure away from home. We'll see more of this in the chapter on strangers (and the erotic), but for now I want to point out that we can dirty not only our knees but our hands—by consenting to be too affluent, too superficial, to be the gringo, the one with a camera but no expertise, no reason for being present except to look and snap a photo. "Dirty" travel is travel with the might of the West but without a voice, travel with the invulnerability of the colonialist but a very vulnerable colonialist, nonetheless, who is more often silenced, caught off guard, fearful, dependent.

To travel as a tourist is to go about on the surface of a soap bubble. It is a gorgeous surface, to be sure, iridescent, floating, ethereal—like Fellini's cruise ship—but it is also on the point of bursting. How long can it last? The pretense of power and elegance and affluence need only touch the slightest edge (perhaps the slightest acid) and it will rupture. That's why it must stay off shore and why the tourist has to get back on board by nightfall. The agonizing if subconscious awareness of the dirt, the sure destiny of the bubble: there can be no traveling in a tourist bubble without it. And tourists have chosen this means of transport. They've decided to be blown out of the child's pipe and to float and descend, inevitably, to the dirt. Slowly they fall, perhaps because they, too, know that "everything comes out of the dirt—everything."

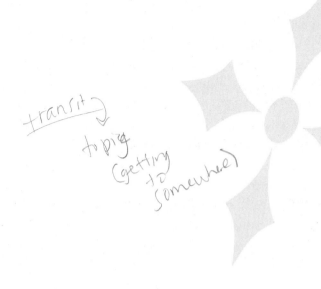

transit → *to bring (getting to somewhere)*

FOUR The Ride of Passage

"THE ROAD IS BEFORE US!" WALT WHITMAN PROCLAIMS IN "SONG
of the Open Road," asking us to drop everything in an endless
journey: "The long brown path before me leading wherever I
choose."[1] Whitman's poem—in fact, all of his work—establishes
the model for an American attitude toward travel. It is an attitude
that is not oriented around an end to be gained, but is a never-
ending movement, expansive, restless, and difficult. We can see
the attitude in Henry Miller, in Paul Bowles, in Mark Twain, and
in many contemporary travelers and writers—Alphonso Lingis,
Diane Johnson, Mary Morris, Susan Brind Morrow, and Jack
Gilbert, among many others. They all leave home, often for very
extended periods, and go to places which are not mildly but radically different: Morocco, the Philippines, the Middle East, India,
Nicaragua. When they go someplace familiar like Greece they
search for and discover what is most foreign about it (as Miller

relishes being cheated by guides or encountering a man who had been imprisoned for murder). They are all drawn to confusions that make the pulse race and are sometimes dangerous.

But what do we think? For while we might feel the lure of the highway, the ship, rails, or the airliner, we don't usually agree with Whitman and relish the going, only the being there. Going, we think, is only the price that we have to pay to get there, and what we wish for is to make that passage as painless, as fast, and as convenient as we can. Airlines advertise enormous seats so that we'll think we never leave the cushy easy chair in our living rooms. They try to convince us that we're in restaurants by serving us fine wines and meals prepared by outstanding chefs; they try to make us feel we're in a movie theater by showing first-run films. It's dinner-theater in the sky, not a ten-hour flight to Prague. Luxury automobiles seem to be mobile living rooms, with an atmosphere, sound system, padding, leg room, and communication devices that we can control to maintain the comforts of home. Trains, ships—we could go on and on. We seem to do all we possibly can to make passage pleasurable. Is there an advertisement for passage that does not mention comfort, safety, or convenience? They are our paramount concerns—when it comes to going. But what is it that we are trying so hard to avoid? What is it that so disturbs us about passage? What is it that we may actually be seeking, behind this screen of comfort—seeking because it cannot be hidden in spite of the meals, movies, and large seats? It is there, and to travel means to encounter it. In fact, if these aspects were not there, it would not be travel. I would suggest danger, trance, and failure are what we seek, and all three make travel especially religious.

It's Dangerous Out There

Mark Twain departs from New York in June 1867, and immediately confronts both a "full-blown tempest" and, as he puts it ominously, the "Outside."[2] He is the first great American traveler, pursuing and mocking the "Grand Tour," in the first of his many journeys. Throughout his passage across the Atlantic, he keeps our attention focused on dangers. Every storm is mentioned, with emphasis not merely on discomfort but on mortal risk: "the sea was still very rough [so] one could not promenade without risking his neck."[3] Witnessing the dangers of the seas was important to Twain and his fellow passengers: "Some thought the vessel could not live through the night, and it seemed less dreadful to stand out in the midst of the wild tempest and see the peril that threatened than to be shut up in the sepulchral cabins, under dim lamps, and imagine the horrors that were abroad on the ocean."[4] When the Azores are reached ten days later, there is a palpable sense of relief, even from the usually composed Twain. We might think that Twain is merely describing what must be described when he harps on the dangers, but that is not true; he chooses what he will notice and mention. Mortal danger is part of his journey; without the mortal danger it would not be the same journey. In fact, it would not be a journey at all.

Mortal danger—and it must be mortal danger—is surely an element of our own passages. Am I the only one who thinks about crashing every time I sit on a plane? I can sit reading while the plane fills and passengers settle down, arranging themselves for the next several hours. Anxiety rises a bit every time I hear the engines whine, and I have been known to imagine what the consequences might be if those turbine rotors disintegrated, as surely they must after millions of rotations. "Through the walls of the cabin?" I wonder, searching my memory for newspaper stories I might have read. The flight attendants go through their safety instructions, and I really do make a note of the nearest exit, as they suggest, my eye lifting from the page of my novel. For an instant I actually wonder if I will wait for the people behind me to file past in an orderly evacuation or whether I'll shove them aside in a panicked rush. It's only an instant's thought, but it is still there after dozens of flights. And as the plane roars down the runway, I put my book down and take my reading glasses off—I honestly do. In case of a crash I want no smashed lenses blinding me. I want to be able to see as I panic. In fact, can I confess? I uncross my legs so they're not broken in the crash, making that dash for the exit so much trickier. Is this only obsessive compulsive disorder or the unavoidable encounter with mortal fear? Am I really the only one with such tics, such fantasies, such fears?

I wonder if the anxiety that we feel about missing our planes or trains might be a displaced anxiety about death. So many of us rush to airports, stand very nervously in the line to check in, and dart forward when the airplane is boarding—when in fact there is very little chance of actually missing that plane. What, will the baggage compartment be full? Will someone else have taken our seat? Or was that a convenient place for anxiety to locate? Are we really anxious about missing the flight—or anxious about catching it? We all know traffic fatality statistics; know that we're more likely to die in a car crash within five miles of our homes than to die in a plane crash. But is that really a statement about the relative safety of planes or a fixation on the link between even the most ordinary form of travel and death? Even in our own cars, close to home. . . . The great age of train travel has passed, as has the period in which the coast of the United States was lined with rescue stations watching for sinking ships, but the media still report every derailment, every sinking of a freighter in a storm. And we still pay fascinated attention, as though in atavistic trance. A myriad of things takes place on ships, planes, cars, trains—books are read, babies are born, lovers meet, hands are washed, theories are conceived of, curses exchanged—but of the hundreds of thousands of events, it is the end of all events, the final plunge that fascinates us, so that to travel comes to mean to encounter and skirt death.

An activity through which we encounter death—isn't that familiar? The room with the dead man hanging on the wall in front. Chants for the dead. Sermons about death. Images of people long dead. Shrines with offerings to dead relatives. Reciting holy books as one readies oneself for death. When a person dies, religions step in, preparing the body, the person, the community for that passage. And while we are alive, we cannot avoid the usually taboo subject of death while we're in the church, temple, mosque, or synagogue. Religions drag out the uncomfortable topic and place it squarely in the front of the room. Religion is death-centered, perhaps death-obsessed, and so is travel. Christianity is not unique in this way, but it certainly is extreme. Its most central symbol is a man being put to death—the event of a God dying—and theologically that paradox gives rise to very fruitful reflection on the nature of being human and the nature of the Christian God. Through their religion, Christians are able to encounter death; through death, Christians are able to encounter their religion.

In 1623, for instance, John Donne, the poet who had become one of the most important religious figures of his day, a renowned preacher and dean of St. Paul's, nearly died. This journey became the occasion for one of his greatest works, *Devotions upon Emergent Occasions*. Donne travels through his illness, pausing at each phase—"The first grudging of the sickness" . . . "The patient takes to his bed" . . . "The physician is afraid" . . . "They apply pigeons, to draw the vapours from the head" . . . "From the bells of the church adjoining, I am daily remembered of my burial in the funerals of others" . . . "At last the physicians, after a long and stormy voyage, see land." And at each halt in the pilgrimage to death and to life, Donne mediates on his condition, expostulates in questions and remarks to God, and finally prays. Nowhere is there more wisdom in Donne than in this passage through sickness and death. But religion specializes in death.

When Donne reached the end of his life, he preached his own funeral sermon, "Death's Duell," then posed for his death portrait, keeping it with him in his room in his final decline. As he died, he posed his own body, "[disposing] his hands and body into such a posture, as required not the least alteration by those that came to shroud him."[5]

We could multiply illustrations from most cultures, religions, and historical periods. Donne is a vivid example, but he makes the point well: it is not only travel that is a journey to death. Religion is, as well. Travel, then, echoes or augments that crucial religious function.

Trance, Stupor, Lethargy

Death is not all that we encounter in passage. I drove to Vermont from Washington, D.C., one summer, a trip that took fourteen hours. During one pause in Massachusetts I realized how deeply I was in a trance—and how I enter some sort of trance every time I am in passage. Truck drivers are permitted only eleven consecutive hours of driving because even they are subject to the trance of the road, because it is so possessing, so robbing of the most fundamental recognition of surrounding, of judgment, of self. I should have stopped driving myself, I suppose, but in an odd way I enjoyed the trance and, perhaps, felt I could handle it. I was under its spell.

I'm tempted to call it a stupor, being not in our full faculties. The line between dream and wakefulness is not distinct, our judgment is impaired, we lose track of where we are, when we are, even who we are. Perhaps that is why literature and legend are so full of travelers who encounter spirits, witches, or demons who bewitch them far from shore or in the depth of the forest. Odysseus's second landing after leaving Troy is the land of the lotus eaters, where those who eat the lotus lose thought of home. Circe, too, makes them forget their origin and destination, and their being is changed entirely, becoming swine. Coleridge's Ancient Mariner comes under the spell of "Life-in-Death" and various spirits during his journey and, like many travelers, must tell his tale. But it isn't only that we can be snared by the dangers of trance; we also have the benefits of trance. The decks of ships, railway compartments, sitting behind the wheel of a car, and flying above the clouds are places for dreams. Literally they are the places of daydreams. I thought of the basic ideas that have covered all of my academic research twenty-five years ago during a two-hour ride on Amtrak. Once, on a ferry across the Channel to Hoek van Holland, I met a young woman, and we were both possessed by romantic visions—until we landed. As we squirm in our seats and the interminable hours refuse to pass, we dream illicit dreams and sometimes feel them taking shape. Diane

Johnson, one of our best querulous travelers, proclaims her "most sacred rule for airplane travel: never talk to the person next to you," and I nearly always follow her advice, but perhaps one reason why I so often hear the person behind me pouring out their life story is that they are in a trance, in a mood to see their life as a story, and to hope that their story will be heard and even understood. Well, we can dream, can't we?[6]

Torpor, stupor, listlessness, lethargy—are states of consciousness where all the definite frameworks of the mind lose their distinctness and their ability to orient us. It's as though the hard edges of the mind are gone and we wander without walls or floor. Or as though what Coleridge called the "esemplastic" power of the mind—its ability to shape the world around it—has disappeared. Diane Johnson declares that "for the traveler, time is suspended in an airplane as in a space capsule; one neither ages nor remembers. Life will start again on arrival."[7] We especially lack the frameworks of time and place when in the stupor of travel, and our minds feel filled with cotton, as though, lacking the solidity of those two fundamental categories of experience, nothing in our minds has a definite shape or a sense of importance at all.

Mark Twain delights in telling stories of disequilibrium, a variety of stupor. There is the very physical disequilibrium which results in seasickness. "They were [all] seasick," he says. "And I was glad of it. We all like to see people seasick when we are not, ourselves."[8] He tells story after story of the distinguished passengers, those who certainly had a very powerful sense of equilibrium on shore—the doctors, professors, judges, ministers, military men, and ladies—lurching for the rail as their inner ears declared them lost and then emptying their stomachs. Do airlines still provide airsickness bags? I think perhaps they do, but they don't announce it anymore. There was always something too blatant about those brown bags, as there was when the crew covered the deck with huge cardboard cups when I once took a ferry from Brindisi to Patras. Our vehicles of passage attempt to conceal the disruptions of passage. Those cups and bags stated too clearly that passage may be physically wrenching.

Temporal dislocation catches Twain's fine eye, as well. He tells the amusing story of Mr. Blucher, who believes that he's been swindled because his watch won't keep the correct time: "By George, [the watch] is good on shore, but somehow she don't keep up her lick here on the water—gets seasick, may be." Twain needs to send poor Blucher to the captain, who "explained to him the mystery of 'ship-time,'" that is, what happens to time when a ship sails east.[9]

It is not just that time is different in Egypt than it is in New York. That fact is a marvel of the powerful otherness that travel encounters (and the attempt to explain it to our children can show us just how paradoxical a notion it is). But the stupor is induced because we lose our sense of something as fundamental as time when we travel: time is not changed, it's lost. When are we as we're in passage? Time is simply liquid. In fact, we bear the scar of that temporal disequilibrium after we arrive. We all talk about the time changes when we travel. "Jet lag" is not only a widespread modern malady, it's widespread modern lore, one of the fascinating "realities" that we never tire of talking about or fully acclimate to. Could it be something we seek?

Mark Twain has a moral aim in seeking his own disequilibrium and inducing it in his readers back home. He feels that they have lost their moral compass; that they are complacent, proceeding on the wrong bearings. His fellow-passengers were to be a "select" group, representing the finest stratum of American society and accomplishment, yet, as in his novels, their superiority is mocked: when he considered their honorifics, he "fell under that titular avalanche a torn and blighted thing."[10] The moral blindness of Gilded Age America requires a travel-induced dizziness. Place all the worthies on a ship and then see what they are really worth.

Spatial disorientation is an aspect of passage as well. Occasionally we hear complaints about the plane, train, or car because we lose touch with the space we're moving through. In "Walking," Henry David Thoreau urges his readers to seek the wild, even to get lost in a bog, but in order to regain contact with our surroundings, to get in touch with place.[11] Yet passage is a passing, not a staying, not even a touring. The dizzying sight out of the side window of a car is exactly the right image for passage and place: the solidities of towns and homes, gardens, forests, museums, stores, inhabitants, and garages are blurred, warped, distended and thereby destroyed. We are no where. Place is liquid, too.

Experiences that are liquid have an important place in religion, too. In his seminal study *The Varieties of Religious Experience*, William James writes of the similarity of religious figures to psychopaths. The founders of religious movements, he says, are possessed by an "acute fever" that produces such "abnormal psychical visitations" as trances, hearing voices, and seeing visions.[12] Religion is closely connected to madness, especially as seen from the perspective of the nonreligious world. James's best example is George Fox. The founder of what we now consider to be the most sober religion, Quakerism, is described by James, so memorably, as a "psychopath or *detraque* of the deepest dye."[13] He seems to be a deeply, deeply purple psychopath. He quotes from Fox's own 1690 *Journal*. Fox is walking with friends when he passes the town of Litchfield and "is commanded by the Lord" to take off his shoes and walk up and down the streets of that startled town, yelling, "Wo to the bloody city of Litchfield!" He shouted in the market, too, and saw blood running down the streets and standing in pools. Visions are the stuff that religion is made of, and they are all a kind of disequilibrium. When Emerson was crossing the Cambridge Common on a perfectly, well, common winter evening with "snow puddles" underfoot and nothing special in his head, his experience became very uncommon, as he suddenly felt a "perfect exhilaration" and became "a transparent eye-ball; I am nothing; I see all; the currents of the Universal Being circulate through me; I am part or parcel of God."[14] Emerson, like many religious figures, came in for a lot of mockery. Emerson's essay *Nature*, which includes the "transparent eye-ball" account, was called "moonshine" and "dreamy" because he seems so out of it.[15] But religious figures are often out of it. What they see and hear is often bizarre. After all . . . gods? Spirits? An afterlife? The supernatural?

And I wonder if it's accidental that both Emerson and Fox are walking when they have the visions I describe above. Travel, trance, and religion are simply very closely related. As Nietzsche might say, don't trust your vision or trance unless it comes while traveling.

Shamans are religious figures whose function is inseparable from both trance and travel. Take the Mixe Indians from Oaxaca, Mexico, whose shamans are trained and assisted by spirits called *niwambi*. The shaman finds the *niwambi* either through a dream or a drug-induced hallucinogenic experience. The shaman is then initiated by ingesting hallucinogenic mushrooms, abstaining from talking, sex, and most foods, and then journeying up a mountain to pray. During the initiation, the shaman may temporarily lose his or her sight and be severely affected physically—all of it a process that the shaman repeats periodically. Once initiated, the shaman cures the ill by undergoing dream journeys, too, either to mountaintops, to the mountain homes of spirits, or to various lower worlds. There, the shaman is able to discover the prospects of the ill person, seeing how the person's life candle is burning down, for example, and perhaps replacing it in order to give them more life.[16]

The anthropologist Timothy J. Knab tells a remarkable story of a shaman of the Mexican Huichol tribe, a man called Jesus, Mad Jesus, or Chucho Loco. The psychologists who advise Knab call Jesus a psychopath, as William James might, but the anthropologist views him more broadly as "an artisan, a shaman, a seer, a self-styled prophet, a mad messiah, a murderous mystic."[17] And in most of Knab's numerous encounters with Jesus, he is simply in another world, as though he were constantly in passage out of this one. At their first meeting, he tells Knab his life story, but it is a fantastic and fascinating bending and bending of Huichol and Christian mythology, starting with the Hewi, revered ancestors who gave birth to various Indian tribes, to the Mexicans, the

Chinese, the Americans, and others. A virgin called Guadalupe dressed in blue came to the Hewi, climbed onto a roof, and danced to the violin of a boy named San Jose. The next morning she put a white flower on her skirt and soon gave birth to Santo Cristo. But some of the Hewi, the Judios, chased Santo Cristo, and after many miracles including an earthquake, he died on the cross he asked to be built and paid for. Afterwards for an entire night everyone ate peyote and smoked tobacco and drank tequila, until in the morning the shamans helped Santo Cristo rise out of his grave, now as Teayau, the Sun. Then (later, one supposes, but it is unclear) at the very ceremony of the rising of Santo Cristo, Mad Jesus himself was born, leaping and yelling from his mother's womb so that the shamans came running and named him Jesus.

Each of Knab's encounters with Jesus was thoroughly bizarre, as though he were living in that fabulous story continuously, fearing an evil spirit and battling her even as he sat with Knab: "He was becoming agitated, looking for an escape like a trapped animal. His eyes were darting all over the room and his words poured out so fast that they almost cascaded into a pool of Huichol gibberish. His knotted hair flew about as he went on looking around in every direction shaking his head. Chucho was disturbed, incoherent, ranting in a paranoid way."[18] And all that's going on is that Knab and Chucho are sitting on a church patio where artisans are constructing wax and yarn paintings. This religious figure is always in motion.

The Trivial, Mistaken, and Failed

Passage has a third characteristic, in addition to trance and the encounter with death. As we "pass" from "here" to "there," we engage in activities, too, activities that also seem to be part of the ride of passage. We see them rather clearly in Twain in his ruthless scrutiny and mockery of his fellow passengers (and often of himself). They adopt nautical language (everyone speaks casually of "eight bells"), write in journals, form a discussion club, dance, and play musical instruments.[19] Every single activity on board ship is skewered by Twain. What he reveals is the failure involved in all the activities. The movement of the ship makes dancing "full of desperate chances and hairbreadth escapes."[20] Journal writing is always begun with enthusiasm and ambition and abandoned before very long—"If you wish to inflict a heartless and malignant punishment upon a young person, pledge him to keep a journal for a year," Twain advises.[21] The passengers hold a mock trial that results in "an absurd decision and a ridiculous sentence."[22] Twain takes an especially perverse pleasure in the musicians who play frequently but always the same piece: "It was a very pretty tune— how well I remember it—I wonder when I shall ever get rid of it."[23] And in revealing the failure involved in all the travelers' activities, Twain does not exclude himself—it is a tendency that moderates his misanthropy. But we have to wonder why—why focus on failure? If it is true that our view of our fellow passengers is a means of viewing both ourselves and the strangers we will see when we arrive, then the situation is rather rich. Once Twain leaves home and moves "Outside," no activity succeeds. And each of the activities is a crucial cultural activity: writing, reading, making music, dancing, discussing, debating. Of course, it is true that Twain would skewer each of these activities back in New York, too. But once we begin to travel, there is a "systematic monotony" of failure.[24] To travel is to encounter some significant degree of failure in most of one's activities, and to witness the mocking of one's activities through the strangeness of customs. And isn't this something that most of us have encountered in travel? Once we have left home and left all of the activities that we have mastered and routinized, once we have begun our passage, don't we encounter an entire texture of failures? Just on the airplane we find ourselves eating in highly confined spaces, likely to shift suddenly and spill liquids in ways they haven't been since we were children. Our digestion is disrupted—we endlessly complain of airline food—and so is our sleep, trying to snatch just a couple of hours' sleep but failing to get any rest. And the activities of the passage— instead of Twain's discussion groups, choral societies, debating clubs, and journal writing, today they are reading, watching a movie, and talking with the stranger next to us. And could we generally call any of these activities successful? Isn't each of them worthy of Twain's mockery? Passage means engaging in activities that are failures.

Religiously it is not so strange to go "Outside" and from there experience the failure of all of our usual activities or look back at the failure even of virtue. In her 2004 novel *Gilead*, Marilyn Robinson tells the story of a midwestern minister, son of a minister who was himself the son of a minister. The men are to varying degrees "inside" or "out," but the most terrible and terribly impressing is the grandfather, who is most severe in his demands and condemnations. An abolitionist, he joined John Brown in his violent efforts to destroy the proslavery faction in Kansas, preaching "The Lord Our God Is a Purifying Fire," and meaning it in a most literal way.[25] When he returns home after the war he is missing an eye, shot out in the holy violence of "Bleeding Kansas." The novel's narrator, his grandson, reports the old man's presence, through and past his death, for the old man himself is a purifying fire. The grandson tells the story of seeing the old man being teased by children who sneak up on the side of his missing eye and tug at his coat, as though he were a simpleton. As John Ames, the grandson, considers how to drive the taunting children away, the old man wheels and casts his good eye on him, on the compassionate one. The boy's virtue is condemned—his virtue! Reason and compassion and good intentions are as insufficient as cruelty and taunts, he realizes. "They were trivial by his lights," John Ames says, "and that made them a little bit trivial by our lights."[26] From the "Outside" of travel, all that takes place "back home" is trivial, all is mistaken, all has failed. It is a religious vision.

We feel that the six-hour plane trip is merely a means; I would like to suggest that it is an end, part of what we want, that in an odd way we seek this encounter with danger, stupor, and failed activities. I cannot prove that this is true; I cannot cite studies or use conclusive logic. All I can do is appeal to the reader's own experience. I have to appeal to you. To agree a reader will have to dispel the notion that throughout our lives we seek only what is

94-97 fear

pleasurable in the most overt and simple sense. Surely we seek much more complex and equivocal "pleasures"—if we did not, films like *Jurassic Park* or the entire horror or slasher genres would not exist. We would not pay good money to scare ourselves out of our wits as a car hurtles seemingly out of control in an "amusement park." We wouldn't jump out of airplanes for recreation, leap off of cliffs suspended below a few yards of a hang glider's fabric, breathe from a tank of air beneath the ocean, race down frozen slopes on sticks of plastic. Can I go so far as to suggest that swimming at the beach means leaving a relatively safe (if inhospitably broiling) stretch of sand for the margins of an ocean that is unfathomably deep and dangerous? Hiking in the forest is also a momentary survival in an environment that has been hostile for as far back as human memory stretches. There is nothing unknown about humans seeking encounters with what seems threatening to our comfort, pleasure, and safety. What might be slightly more strange is our refusal to acknowledge that odd—but important—behavior.

fear of transit

Changing States: Rites of Passage in Religion and Travel

Why do we seek the confusions of passage, the prolonged encounter with danger, discomfort, disequilibrium, stupor, and failed activities? Religious theory offers two possibilities. The more traditional way would be to look at the ride of passage (yes, I know it is a corny pun) as actually a rite of passage. Standard theory states that moving from one state or status to another—from childhood to adulthood, being outside the social group to a member of it, being alive to being dead—requires a ritual passage. In that ritual, one's previous state must be erased and a kind of gestation period must take place (the liminal or threshold period) before one is "reborn" in the new state. So, to take a contemporary example, a college graduation ceremony moves a person from one level of schooling or one level of maturation to another, first by eliminating all signs of the prior schooling and maturation (dressing everyone in a uniform gown), subjecting them to a gestation process (the educative ordeal of speeches by their elders), and then releasing them into their new world and as their new selves (they leave the auditorium, rejoin their families, begin life in the "real world"). The rite of passage is the transformation of identity; one will be a different person as a college graduate than one was as a college student, and one will be seen differently, see oneself differently, be expected to act differently—to earn a living, find one's own home, have a career, perhaps launch a family. It is a profoundly difficult process, being a different person. It does not happen automatically, but requires the efficacy of the rite of passage.

There are numerous similarities between the ride and the rite of passage. We leave something when we travel. It is crucial, isn't it, that home is left? Henry Miller's vast distaste and disdain for America make necessary a strong break. When he is in passage from France to Greece, he meets a Turk, a Syrian, and some Lebanese who antagonize him by having absorbed "the American spirit at its worst. Progress was their obsession. More machines, more efficiency, more capital, more comforts."[27] Nothing is as likely to rouse deep antipathy in Miller as finding the aspects of home abroad. Paul Bowles seems often on a crusade against the Americanization of the people he meets in Morocco, Sri Lanka, Latin America, and India. He calls it "the Twentieth Century gangrene": "My own belief is that the people of the alien cultures are being ravaged not so much by the by-products of our civilization, as by the irrational longing on the part of members of their own educated minorities to cease being themselves and become Westerners."[28] When Miller and Bowles travel—which they do, of course, for years, even decades (and, in fact, it often seems as though their travel is nothing but an extended passage)—what they want is, as Bowles says, for a place "to be as different as possible from the places I already know," especially from home.[29]

As we enter the liminal state in passage, it is crucial not only that we not be where we've been, but that we not be who we've been. This is the trancelike aspect of passage, its blurring of our frames of reference, and of our sense of self. Like Odysseus's men, we are caught by a spell and become other. And it's an especially indistinct other that we become—sleepy, in a stupor, ensnared in an "in-between" existence. It's no wonder that our activities fail, that they must fail: just like the judges and generals on Twain's *Quaker City,* we lose our equilibrium, our sense of what we do well, and vomit out our competence. It was the self we left behind that was the professional, with poise and self-assurance. On the plane, train, or boat, we read trash, prattle on, in a "holiday spirit" in which the old seriousness—the old competence—is lost. When we're in passage, we become fools.

But in this ride of passage, what's the place of danger? Rites of passage always involve symbolic deaths. Before one can become a new self, the old self must . . . disappear. The old self has to die. It isn't only that we lost our competence, grow sleepy and disoriented. The threat that is involved in leaving is much larger than that. Any transformation of self involves the rupturing of who we once were, and that ripping of the self is a very violent act, indeed. William James argues that we have multiple selves and that they are social and material: we have as many selves as we have others who acknowledge us; and our selves are defined by our belongings.[30] A few years ago I wrecked my car, and while it may seem trivial to say that a part of me died as that VW was hauled away, I believe that it is true. When we leave, when we disembark, when we—as my son used to say—"blast off" on an airplane, and leave behind all those others and all those things, we leave those selves behind, too. Those selves die—temporarily. We seek the danger, the discomfort, the disequilibrium, and the failures because we seek a passage, and not just a vacation. Certainly we don't go "Outside," as Twain put it, in order to remain just who we were "inside."

Changing States: Disruption in Religion and Travel

A more interesting and contemporary religious theory that can account for the peculiarities of the ride of passage is that which deals with ruptures. According to this interpretation, we seek a break with home, a bumpy ride, bad food, pathetic conversations, nausea, terror, and blurs out the window not because of the outcome, not because they take us to a new and better state after the passage. A rite of passage is a means to an end, but a rupture is not evaluated according to its conclusion. It is what has value. The passage doesn't conclude with arrival at Charles de Gaulle or Ben Gurion. There is no arrival and no conclusion. The passage continues in France, India, Israel, Morocco, the Czech Republic, Indonesia, or Senegal. Of course, the travel does come to an end; one returns home. But as the postmodernists enjoy pointing out, that isn't an end. One's life continues, and life at home is influenced—made—by the passage and travel. Our homes are disrupted—by the clutter of souvenirs, by the odd stories, by the importation of microbes, and by the self that refuses to be domesticated.

The difference lies in a shift in imagery. We've been looking at passage as a continuity, a movement that passes from place to place. It's the mountain pass that allows access from one valley to the next; the forward pass that carries the ball (and the team) farther up the field. But a passage is also a break in a surface: we discover a hidden passage where there appeared to be a sheer rock face or stumble across a secret passage in an old house where there seemed to be solid wall. There are other broken passings: someone passes out—or passes away. There are the blurrings out the window, liquid time and place, being no where. As Whitman says of the "Open Road," "I believe that much unseen is also here": to stumble across the "unseen"—the strange, the exotic, the disturbing—is not just a smooth passage but a fall.[31] A passage can also be abrupt and disturbing.

Paul Bowles: "Suicide or Europe"

Passage and disruption are combined especially well in the writings of Paul Bowles, that most aggressive traveler. *The Sheltering Sky* transfixes readers with its presentation of a bleak landscape and the gradual swallowing of its characters into death and a cultural strangeness that does not give them back. In uncompromising fashion, Bowles shows us danger, trance, and failure and their disruptions of our ability to act, our sense of identity, and our very vitality. In Bowles those ruptures are valued not as a means to a ritual transformation or a greater good, but for their own sakes.

Paul Bowles selects the wonderful title *Without Stopping,* for his autobiography. It's a title that indicates that he never arrives and never returns, that he engages in a continuous passage. He seems to echo his maternal grandfather, who "never slept twice in the same town" during his own years of travel.[32] Bowles scarcely seems to pause, though those pauses can be months, even years long. In fact, he is still in passage as I write, living in Tangier.[33] That continuous passage, a characteristic he largely shares with Henry Miller, allows us to see the three characteristics of passage—danger, trance, and failure—in all of his travel: incessant movement through incessant dangers, being in a dreamlike trance and lost to the activities of home are the themes of much of Bowles's writing. They make Bowles's travel religiously significant, as well.

In early 1929, Paul Bowles returned to his room at the University of Virginia late one afternoon and knew that he "was about to do something explosive and irrevocable." He tossed a quarter in the air, realizing as he did it that tails meant suicide and heads meant he would leave for Europe (77). It's a more dramatic version of the disruption of travel than we saw in Mark Twain, and it makes that disruption more blatant. On the more immediate level, travel is the alternative to the death of the self: Bowles spent his childhood terrified of his father. When he was four years old, he was told by his father, "Your mother is a very sick woman, and it's all because of you, young man. Remember that" (10). Bowles remembered, and so did his father. Their hostility is continuous in Bowles's autobiography. The terror made it reasonable for him to believe his grandmother when she said, "your father wanted to kill you" (38). Departure, then, meant life.

On the other hand, however, flipping that coin—"suicide or Europe"—meant death in either case. Travel is the synonym for death—death of the life at home and death of the home self. In Bowles's case, it was the death of the victimized self, and since it was a death, his departure was not joyful or merely liberating. As he took the ferry to Hoboken and the ship *Rijndam*, he half hoped to be stopped by his parents (80). Departure was a rupturing of the predominant self he had known and been, and that is never easy. "I was not the I I thought I was," he states, as he recounts the flip of that coin (77). And in a sense Bowles does kill himself, fulfilling his father's desire. Bowles dies when he departs and when he travels, seeking the most intensely strange environs and experiences in the desire, as he writes "of getting as far away as possible from New York," where his father lived (124).

Writing of his first passage by boat from France to North Africa, he declares that "I had always been vaguely certain that sometime during my life I should come into a magic place which in disclosing its secrets would give me wisdom and ecstasy—perhaps even death" (125). Getting "as far as possible from New York" meant distinctly difficult realms, places that were "beautiful and terrible," as he wrote of his first landing in Algeria (125). He seems to have enjoyed coming quite close to death. Traveling with the composer Aaron Copeland during that first trip, he is challenged by an Algerian soldier and forced to walk with a gun trained on him, an event that makes Copeland express relief that they'll be leaving. Not Bowles. "Morocco's much wilder," he declares with seeming satisfaction (126). After some months in Tangier—"a madhouse, a madhouse," according to Copeland (127)—the two move on to Fez, and Bowles finds it "ten times stranger. . . . I felt that at last I had left the world behind, and the resulting excitement was well-nigh unbearable" (130).

Danger is an essential aspect of that unbearable excitement. Traveling to Ouarzazate, on the southern side of the High Atlas Mountains, Bowles and Copeland ride on top of the truck: "The trail over the Atlas was so hair-raising that the most sensible place to sit seemed the top of the truck, where at least we could see down over each precipice as we swayed over its edge" (135). We might be reminded of Twain and his fellow-passengers, coming up on deck to watch a storm, "prisoners," Twain declares, "to a fierce fascination."[34] On the way to Ouarzazate, because of a muddy road "above the cloud line," the truck carrying Bowles "skidded to within inches of the abyss" (135). Not many months afterwards, he is traveling in Mexico with friends and his future wife, Jane Auer, and he is "delighted with the hairpin curves, the sheer drops, and the unfamiliar, savage landscape." In contrast, Jane "crouched, frightened and sick, on the floor of the back of the bus," as many of us might (198). I ask, did Bowles really think that he had escaped suicide that day in 1929?

In many ways, *Without Stopping* is a chronicle of Bowles's illnesses, from typhoid fever contracted on his first trip to Morocco (152) (the disease, by the way, that kills Port In *The Sheltering Sky*) to sunstroke soon after he recovers (155) to multiple intestinal disorders from drinking bad water or eating tainted food (161). "The following day I felt like death," he writes of Mexico, but it could have been dozens of occasions in dozens of places (180). His account of collecting indigenous music in Morocco has the constant backdrop of illness, usually fevers. He reminds us, perhaps, of how prominent sickness is in our own accounts of traveling. I have had friends whose letters from India consisted primarily of commentaries on their bowel movements, commentaries more detailed, in addition, than those of temple sites. I have been regaled with descriptions of dengue fever—there is the proverbial "First you think you're going to die, then you hope you do die, then you think you have died." I once sat on a bunk in a government rest house in Sanchi, a village in India that contains some ancient Buddhist stupas, and listened for an hour or more as a traveler inventoried his traveling apothecary, one that might have exceeded the stores of a small drugstore in a rural American town. Again, is all of this illness and the preoccupation with illness merely the risk of travel? My friends boasted of their diseases. I've done it myself. I was once in an earthquake in Katmandu—it's a story I love to tell. I woke in the night, and the room was shaking (as I always put it) "like a small tree in a strong breeze." I knew I ought to get out of the building—it was just the sort of cement-block structure that the newspapers say collapses in an earthquake—but I was just too sick. Too sick to escape from an earthquake?! Yes, that's how sick I was! Paul Bowles might be hard put to admit it, but he traveled (in part) in order to be sick, in order to be that far from New York. I do, also, and so do you.

Danger, risk, and illness aren't just a means to an end for Bowles. We could view them that way: they take him away from a life in fear of his father and from subservience. They break with that old life and make autonomy possible. But on the other hand, where does Bowles get to? Does he ever stop? There is a pathology to this continuous passage; if he were my child, I'd want him to settle down, to take fewer risks. I find myself sympathizing with Jane Auer, cowering in the back seat. He seems to want the rupture to be as strong as he can manage, to be on the very edge of the tumbling abyss, infected with the more threatening bacillus. Keats wrote that he was "half in love with easeful death": Bowles is also half in love, but with a death that is not easeful, but wild and unbearably exciting.

The second characteristic of passage is its trance, I argue. We can see this in Bowles in his linking of travel with dreaming. When he arrives in France in his first passage, he writes: "I sat for a long time [in the hotel room] looking out at the empty port, trying to persuade myself of the reality of the situation. I touched the curtains and said to myself: 'They are France. This is France. I am in France'" (82). The sense of irreality is more powerful in North Africa, where he encounters the "magic place" he had always sought, the place of "wisdom and ecstasy—perhaps even death" (125). Tangier, most explicitly, is "a dream city." Bowles especially is struck by its dreamscapes, "covered streets like corridors with doors opening into rooms on each side, hidden terraces high above the sea, streets consisting only of steps, dark impasses, small squares built on sloping terrain so that they looked like ballet sets designed in false perspective, with alleys off in several directions" (128).

But it isn't just the mysterious and intriguing that make Morocco dreamlike. There is also the man who became a goat in Marrakesh. He is traveling with John Widdicomb, "an excellent traveling companion [because] he was well educated, highly adaptable

. . . and," best of all, I suspect, "blessed with a sharp sense of the ridiculous" (173). In the Djemaa el Fna, the great square marveled at by all who see it, Bowles saw a deformed man transform himself into a goat. The transformation "made it possible for him to move like a goat, to sound like one, and, in an indescribable and faintly horrible fashion, even to have eyes and a mouth that looked like those of a goat" (173). Apparently, the dream of travel has nightmares, too.

I argued earlier that the line between dream and wakefulness is not distinct while we are in transit: our judgment is impaired, we lose track of where we are, when we are, even who we are. Passage is a blur. A man became a goat? Not in Ohio. Not even in New York. But in the Djemaa el Fna we are apt to see miraculous transformations, or when we're in Fez to say, as Bowles does, that the place was "full of monsters" when a more sober and awake assessment might be that there were many people deformed by disease (176). Our usual frames of reference are gone—time and space, those essential landmarks that seem to situate us in reality itself, are fluid and so strange.

Those landmarks are artificial, we discover, where the places are strange, and we ourselves become strange, not only to the locals but, more importantly, to ourselves. Philosophers have long had a fascination with dreams—"how do we know we're not dreaming?" is a staple of philosophical speculation in nearly every philosophy classroom today, and not just in Pascal's *Pensées*. More especially the postmodern thinkers want to disengage us from the anchors of the real, from our sense that the things we deal with are things. They love to point out that those things are names—signs—and with no anchor in reality at all. We live "betwixt and between," using names of names of names, and don't stand on solid ground at all. The trance of passage is this "middle ground." The onanistic games of philosophers, as it turns out, are not so solitary and fit for the classroom alone. Paul Bowles sought those trances and so do we. Why do we travel? In part it's in hope that we'll see a man change into a goat in the Djemaa el Fna. What's more, we always do. It may not be a goat and maybe not in Marrakesh. It may be a statue of a dead man for Mark Twain or an epiphany of the blood of ancient Greece for Henry Miller. On the roof of the YMCA in Lahore, I was once shocked to notice that the city was populated by hawks—kites, my British companion called them—and not by the pigeons that we're more accustomed to in American or European cities. I sat transfixed one afternoon and watched hawks soaring, fighting, even copulating in the midst of the city of 9 million. Was I in a dream? Where was my ground, or my landmarks? Like Miller, Twain, and Bowles, I had passed out. I'd lost my consciousness. And I was both alarmed—terrified—and very pleased. *example*

Again, though, I can hear the objection: Paul Bowles may seek those dislocations. He might relish driving along a sheer cliff or witnessing a disturbing transformation in a square near the end of the earth, but we don't! But don't we? Why do we take all those photos, for example? Why is our own inseparable traveling companion not the "highly adaptable" John Widdicomb, but the highly reliable Nikon or Cannon? Why do we carry it everywhere, point it at objects and people, and capture them? The usual explanation—the one drawn out of the Victorian vision of educative travel—is that we want mementos of the great cultural sites, "bits" of them to take home with us. Religiously, these photos and cards are relics, images of the sacred that are much like holy cards with pictures of the saints. We are "ennobled" by these images; they are of our "best self," the self that can appreciate and even commune with the likes of Michelangelo, Christopher Wren, Gerard Ter Borch, Velasquez. We bring tangible evidence of our cultivation home with us; we bring home riches.

But is that all that's going on? While he is in France, Bowles composes a piece of music that he hears in a dream, transcribing it directly onto paper, note for note, as soon as he wakes. He's fascinated and pleased by this phenomenon, for he'd always wished (he writes) to be able to drag some bit of the dream world right into the waking world. Couldn't that be why we take those photographs, too? Don't we want to hold onto some part of the amazing things that we see and experience? We aren't only among

Titians, but in France. In France! The traffic is different, odd. The language is confusing. The customs are strange, enticing. The entire world is just "off"—and that's a very considerable "off" when it isn't just France but Bulgaria, not to mention Indonesia. If we were transported suddenly to Mars, wouldn't we wish to snap a few photos before we were whisked back, just to show our friends how it really is? Just to hold onto a piece of that impossible place? And wouldn't we most surely take a photo of a dream if only we could? Well, we do, and just as our dreams bore everyone but our analysts, our travel photos fascinate only ourselves.

The final aspect of passage is the failure of our activities—Twain's pointless shipboard debating societies, and orchestras that can play only one tune. In Paul Bowles's endless passage, there might seem to be no failures. He writes most of his novels and stories abroad and is, after all, one of the finest writers of the century. *Without Stopping* is not only a chronicle of his illnesses; it's also a catalogue of an impressive number of his remarkable writings and musical compositions.

Yet Bowles's writings belong to the "other world," the world of dreams, drugs, and the unconscious. They are not "failures" in the same sense that Twain's are, by being worthy of scorn. They are, rather, part of the more general trance of passage. As a teenager, he contributed to a surrealist magazine, *transition,* published in Paris: "I sat at the typewriter practicing the invention of poetry, 'without conscious intervention.' At length I could type an entire page literally without any knowledge of what I put there" (70). As he presents his method of composition in *Without Stopping*—which is to say, as he presents writing in the context of his life of continuous passage—a similar absence of "points of reference" is essential. He spends years composing music that is largely in support of others' poetry, choreography, plays, and films and that is a world that he needs to leave, a world from which he must depart. The break comes when he has been back in America and one night dreams of Tangier. There was no content, he says, but "a changing succession of streets," and when he awoke and realized that it was a real city, the Tangier of 1931, his "heart accelerated." In entering the world of dreams (and adrenaline)—and leaving the world of consciousness—he enters the world of fiction (274).

He had already resurrected the surrealist technique "of abandoning conscious control and writing whatever words came from the pen." In writing *The Sheltering Sky* when he returned to Morocco, he seems to have used a related method. Once he conceived of the title and basic plan (on a bus riding up Fifth Avenue in New York, that is, in passage, interestingly enough), he "resolved to give it no more thought until [he] started the actual writing" (275). The unconscious, alone, would do the planning—that and Morocco itself. Bowles's account of the actual writing gives strong creative credit both to accidental incidents during each day's writing and to a derivative of cannabis called *majoun*. Details from the day would be incorporated into his writing, "regardless of whether the resulting juxtaposition was apposite or not. I never knew what I was going to write on the following day because I had not yet lived through the day" (278). The state induced by the *majoun*, a state, of course, quite close to trance, enables Bowles to imagine the death of Port, *The Sheltering Sky*'s protagonist: "Very consciously I had always avoided writing about death because I saw it as a difficult subject to treat with anything approaching the proper style; it seemed reasonable, therefore, to hand the job over to the subconscious" (279).

Bowles's actual method of composing is one that the literary historians can better discuss. Like any autobiographer, Bowles himself is uninterested in the factual; rather, his autobiography is an autobiogony, a creation of the self. And what he creates is a self who writes in a manner essentially connected to passage, to without stopping. He must write without reference points, without the conscious, either by allowing random events to hold the pen or cannabis to open the doors of the unconscious. Only the unconscious can write about death, he says; in fact, in passage, even a passage lasting decades, any activity must be a death, a rupturing of the usual, the accomplished, a rupturing of home. The unconscious can write about death because the unconscious is death.

In a endnote to this chapter, I noted that Paul Bowles has now "passed on," that phrase which seeks to keep him almost within reach. One of the more important tasks of religion has been to manage the relations of the living with the dead, to maintain communication, emotionally and otherwise, with the dead, and keep us informed. Death is not an utter rupture, after all. One of the images frequently used for death is the journey, of course. The dead have simply gone across the waters, into the West, over the mountains, or into the sky. A religious ritual is used to begin the voyage of the departed, and then prayers to keep in contact. Danger, trance, and failure might describe the barrier between the living and the dead, and religion is the means of those three not creating an absolute severance.

It's tempting to think that the religious aspects of travel suggest another possibility. We can follow the dead across the waters and the hills and become like the dead ourselves. The three aspects of passage that we have focused on—danger, trance, and failure—describe death reasonably well. Separated from life, they are severed from safety, from full awareness, and from the accomplishments of the living. We fear for them, and for that reason we want to keep in touch, to feel that they're just a little way away. If travel means that we take on the danger, trance, and failure of the dead and that we do so in extreme form, then we can take their journey. We can die, as Bowles did, and experience, even enjoy, that ultimate journey. The religious importance of travel might, then, even exceed that of the more usual forms that had to content themselves with remaining among the living, staying home (in the house of worship), and sending messages. The secular religious form of travel can imitate the dead. It can take the journey of the dead, assuming the danger, trance, and failure of the dead, and pass away. It gives an additional meaning to those words of Whitman's that I have been using throughout this book, that travel is a journey to dirt.

FIVE Holy Strangers

I ONCE POINTED TO SOMEONE WALKING PAST MY HOUSE AND asked a three-year-old friend of my daughter's who it was. "The stranger," she said with an ominous tone. Our culture is fascinated and obsessed with "strangers." We warn our children about strangers, insisting at a very early age that they distrust them. Sexual predator, kidnapper, thief—one might think we lived on the frontier, our security and safety constantly in peril. The Neighborhood Watch is vigilant, fortunately, and we're glad that there are retired folks on the block, sitting by the curtains, just keeping an eye on things while we're at work. At night there is a Citizen Patrol, wearing bright orange vests and carrying cell phones: Moms and Dads walking the circuit. Twenty-five years ago I was visiting my sister in Hollywood, and a police cruiser pulled to the curb as I walked to a shoe repair shop: "I didn't recognize you from the neighborhood," he said. I resented it then;

these days I'm glad that the police are alert. And since September 11, Homeland Security is watching for the deadly strangers with ceaseless acuity.

Unfortunately, strangers are hard to spot, especially since they look a lot like "us"—or are us. The crime statistics warn us, above all, against friends, neighbors, and family members. The supermarket tabloids are much more likely to shout a story about one family member who murders another, and maybe that's why the JonBenet Ramsey murder or Susan Smith's drowning of her children or even O. J. Simpson stories ran for so long. David Lynch's *Twin Peaks* touched a very raw nerve when Laura Palmer's murderer turned out to be her father—or, better yet, the evil spirit, Bob, inhabiting her father. For that matter, Oedipus and Hamlet have lethal strangers in the home. Patricide, fratricide, suicide—they are the crimes that are simply too heinous, the crimes of the stranger in the home or the stranger in the mirror.

What is a stranger? Strangers are from "there," not "here." They are unfamiliar—not of our family, our culture, our values, our understandings. Their customs are funny and their clothes are, too. They speak with an accent. Above all, they make us uncomfortable by reminding us that there *is* a "there," and that "here" is *only* here, not everywhere. They hold values that are in conflict with ours; in fact, they have values that seek to undermine ours. They are the vanguard of invasion, spies, the singular point of not here, not us.

A friend tells a story of approaching remote villages in India, nothing yet visible except trees, but everyone already knows he's there. It's as though there's a small but detectable alteration in the rhythm, he says, an alteration that can be heard, felt. A stranger is around. He knows he's been detected because as soon as he goes into some bushes to pee, some boys are already there, waiting and watching.

Strangers exist only where there are borders (though they might be the borders between our own towns or between our home and our neighbor's). We cross a border and encounter strangers immediately, a fact that seems as odd to me now as that it should rain on one side of the street and not on the other when I was a child. On one side, San Ysidro, California, and on the other, Tijuana, Mexico. On one side, ranch homes, safe water, English, and people who know what I mean when I speak about . . . well, anything: the Republican National Convention that was going on in San Diego (I saw James Carville outside a hotel and said, "Keeping 'em honest?" "Tryin'," he said), the trolley ("Does this one leave next?" "No, the one that will arrive over there"), lunch ("Large fries?" "No"). On the other side, a waiter rushing to get me a taco that may or may not have beef and a glass of water that he may have understood I wanted to be from a bottle; a four- or five-year-old girl on Avenida Revolucion, smiling up at me, but smiling because she's friendly or to slow me down to look at her mother's handicrafts spread on the sidewalk? A hotel manager scowling as I check into the Hotel Nelson, but is it because I hesitated at the exchange rate or because of his conversation (in Spanish) with the man next to him? A couple of hundred yards, and all of the smooth fabric of understanding and ease is torn, and as a result I'm isolated, my health is at risk. I'm a stranger so I'm confused.

If there were no borders, there would be no strangers, nothing strange about culture or language. The entire world would be like a proverbial midwestern town, where everyone knows everyone else, and their parents and grandparents, and there are no serious deviations, no street crime, no atheists (except gentle ones), no one who objects to the Nativity crèche or the Fourth of July parade. But since there are borders, we're jolted not just into political or religious dispute, but into dislocation, unsure, anymore, whether the 1990–91 Persian Gulf War was just, or whether religion really is synonymous with decorous ceremonies and neat clothes. But even more pervasively, borders mean that we become strangers among strangers in the thousands of details that are the texture of every day, in eating and drinking and shitting and peeing, in eye contact and stepping from a sidewalk and staying alive. Even in as familiar a place as Britain, "Look Right" painted on the street corner reminds us that our instincts in crossing a street can kill us (and this does kill many).

Most generally, there are strangers only where there are ruptures. If there were seamless continuity, a continuous family, nation, or culture, an unbroken surface, there would be no strangers. But since our families, cultures, values, and understandings have borders—since they end, that is, since they break off and there are outsides to them—people can bring us the news of those breaks. Those are strangers—the ones who announce the rupture because of their clothes or accents or customs. People can even bring the breaks themselves. They can be the breaks. Strangers are emissaries of ruptures. That is why we seek them.

Religious Strangers: The "Downright Repulsive"

Novelist and short story writer Flannery O'Connor is preeminent among American writers in presenting religious strangers. Her significance is greater than that: she is not just a fiction writer who uses strangers; she simply understands the religious role of strangers more profoundly than any other American of the past century. It is impossible to belong, to be a member of the community in good standing, and still to be genuinely religious in O'Connor's fiction, for "the religious feeling has become, if not atrophied, at least vaporous and sentimental" among those who comfortably "belong."[1] The good Christian folk in churches with soaring steeples, the fine people who sing hymns in tune in O'Connor's stories and novels are in need of a good shock, which they usually receive—from a stranger. Yet it isn't only the superficially pious who require a rude awakening. As O'Connor wrote in one of her letters, "there are long periods in the lives of all of us, and of the saints, when the truth as revealed by faith is hideous, emotionally disturbing, downright repulsive."[2] And O'Connor's strangers provide a good smack not only to the religious, but to the secular, also. Her novels and stories are full of rationalists, atheists, and cynical nonbelievers who need—and get—a life-altering, religious shock. Those who reveal the repulsive religious message are necessarily quite repulsive themselves: they are strangers. If we would understand the religious fascination with strangers, we could do no better than to look at

O'Connor's novels and short stories, especially in the American context of this book.

The urge to put ourselves among strangers is a common religious urge, though it is as paradoxical religiously as it is in travel, for who in their right mind would want the rude and repulsive disturbances that O'Connor's religious strangers offer? Yet that is exactly the religious urge: it is the one from beyond the ordinary and beyond the mundane who is the religious figure, the one who moves us from the ordinary and mundane to the religious. In O'Connor's "Good Country People," the three women of the household are flawed in very ordinary ways. Mrs. Freeman is dense, blunt, stubborn, and nosy. She moves forward, implacably, never admitting she is wrong. Mrs. Hopewell, who employs Mrs. Freeman, is blindly and vacuously optimistic. "Nothing is perfect!" and "That is life!" are her favorite expressions, and yet she cannot accept her own daughter's deformity. Neither of those women receives the advantage of a religious encounter. Only the daughter does. Misnamed Joy, she is a typical O'Connor "sinner": she is a rationalist. A Ph.D. in philosophy, Joy is a woman who has seen that there is no truth and who is insistent on revealing that bleak fact to all, especially to her mother. She has renamed herself Hulga simply because the name sounds ugly, and she is proudest that she has not a shred of joy about her. Enter the religious stranger. He is a Bible salesman who fabricates a story of a heart condition, a father dead in an accident, and a frank awareness of death, and Joy hopes for a deep commonality. Joy entrusts herself to him, feeling affection without realizing it. She climbs into a barn loft, kisses him, and, most astonishingly for a woman who seems as resolutely skeptical as Nietzsche himself, allows him to remove her false leg. That is the profoundest religious encounter and typical of O'Connor: Hulga allows herself to be vulnerable. She says to herself that she does it because she is touched by his innocence, but it is her own innocence that she is experiencing, a unique occasion of utter trust—it is entirely misplaced, but it is trust, nonetheless. Of course, he steals the leg. He takes the prosthetic leg and runs off as he has already with a woman's glass eye. But he has been a good antidote for her nihilism, the only sort of religious response that O'Connor allows: a brief moment of redemption that brings no lasting good. His lies have revealed her hopefulness and trust, something that neither her mother's (nor Christianity's) platitudes could do, for only a stranger could bring the violence that alone could benefit her.

Little Strangers

On the ferry from Algeciras, Spain, to Tangier, Morocco, the Strait of Gibraltar is a ten-mile thickness of border, a passage I strongly wanted to take, though it meant a laborious journey: a flight from Britain to Malaga with a planeload of British vacationers extravagantly ready for their holiday, the confusion of finding the bus station in Malaga, a bus I was never completely sure was the correct one. Not to mention the uncertainty about the ferry itself: there seemed to be lots of companies selling ferry tickets. Was this the "right" one? I had a fear of the wrong destination or of paying too much because the ferry was especially for tourists. But though the ship looked exactly like the ones used by the Massachusetts Steamship Authority to carry cars from Woods Hole to Martha's Vineyard and Nantucket, I knew I'd left Europe because the ship was full of strangers.

Mostly they seemed to be "guest workers" in Germany, on their way back to Morocco for a visit, and the strangers who broke into my reverie were the children, five or six years old. "Was schreiben Sie?" they asked as four of five gathered around me and looked at my open journal. I replied in Dutch, which was close enough—and all I can really manage with relative ease—"dagboek," and then I tried it with a more Germanic pronunciation, "Dagenbuch." They were pleased, smiling and running over to tell others, who gathered around me, too, and asked more questions I couldn't understand.

Who were they, these slight, dark children speaking German? I usually feel somewhat comfortable in Germany—a fact I attribute to my family's consciousness of its German roots and my German name. It's a very discomforting comfort, feeling "at home" in the land I can't help but associate with Buchenwald as well as with Beethoven. And here were these Moroccans, looking so un-German, and, according to all the news reports, of very mixed welcome in Germany. Strangers in Germany; strangers, perhaps, back in Morocco. And loosening the gaps in my own patchwork of identity. German American? As in O'Connor, strangers bring about vulnerability.

But there's more to it than that. Why do I feel best and worst around children when I travel? Why do I seek them out—the smallest strangers I can find? What else do they pry open? It surely must be the distance from my own children. What a silly thing: I travel thousands of miles from my kids, just to feel best when I'm with others their age. I worry about the harm that may come to these little strangers (can't they fall from that railing?), use my little magic tricks to entertain them, fantasize about sending them a *real* soccer ball when I get home (to replace the only slightly round, wrapped-up cloth they are kicking). Why did I leave home in the first place if it's just to find these replacements? I'm ten miles from Europe, and already I have found strangers to make it as poignant as possible that my kids are *not* with me, that they miss me, too, and that they may be walking on railings without my hands nearby. Here, again, are strangers making us vulnerable.

Strangers and the Slammed Door

Novelists and travelers Paul Bowles and Henry Miller seek out strangers to open their wounds, too. Bowles is not really all that interested in intimate relationships. It's evident in his fiction, which generally is populated by estranged couples and parents and children who prey upon one another. Emotional intimacy simply is not present in his fictional—or personal—world. His autobiography, *Without Stopping,* presents his excitement on first arriving in Africa, an excitement composed, as he writes, of intimations of "wisdom and ecstasy—and death."[3] In that book there seems little distinction made between the landscape, the culture, and the people, all of which are "beautiful and terrible."[4] When he and the composer Aaron Copeland enter Algeria, a soldier points his gun at them, an event that frightens Copeland, as it would any of us, but it strangely attracts Bowles. Copeland calls the Spanish in the North African enclave Ceuta "raving mad," but Bowles isn't disturbed. He enthusiastically echoes the assessment when they cross into Morocco, saying "the impression of confusion and insanity was redoubled."[5] The farther Bowles traveled into North Africa, the greater the strangeness and the greater his delight.

The ancient Moroccan city of Fez elicits a similar reaction. It isn't the cultural history of Fez, the fact that it's the oldest of Morocco's imperial cities, or that it has dominated the religious, cultural, and political life of the country for a thousand years. What fascinates Bowles is that it is "full of monsters."[6] "The cafés of Fez-Djedid swarmed with beggars deformed since birth by phocomelia, with unfortunate victims of Koranic law who had had both hands amputated, with faceless lepers and syphilitics, with men whose bodies had been twisted by disease or accident into fantastic shapes and who pushed themselves along using their spines as runners."[7]

◆ ● ◆

He tells a brief anecdote that summarizes his view of strangers and the role of strangers in his traveling. We can use it for the role of strangers in all bewildered travel. He meets Gilbert Grosvenor (longtime editor of *National Geographic Magazine*) and his daughter while traveling by ship from America to Europe, and they trade stories of Beni-Isguen, "the 'holy city' of the M'Zab, where, as soon as a stranger arrives in the town, everyone who is in the streets rushes into the house, and all one hears as he walks along is the slamming and bolting of doors."[8]

Here is the role of the stranger: we need to slam and bolt our doors against the stranger—that is the degree of threat. The stranger is a risk to us personally; it's meeting the stranger face to face, on the public street that we must avoid. Is it the sight of the stranger, the outrage of what she wears or how she walks? Is it the fear of what will be said, the heinous or blasphemous words?

Or is it the rank odor, an offense that will penetrate into our organs? No matter which, the stranger must not be met.

And why is it that the Moroccans (in the story) do not flee to the mosque or to the civil guard? It is home that is their refuge. Maybe it is home that is threatened, too. Why leave the homes open to depredation as they flee to the police? The stranger's fingers touching the food, his eyes on the bed, and his shoes on the floor. The home must be protected with a bolted door, and then in their homes, the stranger will remain outside. That threshold must not be crossed, and with the power of the home and the family, it will not be.

Yet a bolted door is enough protection—we are not faced with the leveler of homes or cities. The stranger is not an armed invader or a plague. She can be halted, and she won't burst through the window or batter down the door. The stranger is certainly frightening, but she is not a power beyond the usual resources, for the stranger is human; the stranger is one of us. There are two sides to the stranger in Bowles's telling of the story: he travels among strangers, surrounded by those against whom he must slam and bolt his door, but he is also the stranger in his story. He arrives in town and the Moroccans slam their doors. Oh, to be the stranger, whose mere presence is sufficient to cause the townspeople to flee and hide. How powerful such a stranger must be. And yet he is not a criminal; he'll never be arrested or expelled. He's legal. He can walk through town. He's been given access. He must be at the extreme of what is permitted—any more fear from the inhabitants, should it move, for example, into terror, and he is not tolerated any longer. He is expelled or punished. On the other hand, how lonely it is for this stranger. He is closed out of every home. His turn of the doorknob won't gain him entrance. He is homeless. His desire for home is rejected. He's locked out. More, he won't even be seen. He arrives, a stranger. Those who belong, those with homes, flee.

It's my theory that the roles we find ourselves in are roles we put ourselves in and roles that we want. To some degree, the roles work for us. So we travel in order to become strangers and to be among strangers. But Bowles's personal example seems too extreme, again. Perhaps he wants to be the stranger who arrives and hears the doors slamming and bolting, but do we? I would say yes.

Strangers Making Blood Flow

The stranger who is a threat, the stranger we must avoid, the stranger in whose face we slam our door, the stranger against whom we protect our very home: that is the religious stranger. That is the stranger who is, in Flannery O'Connor's words, "hideous, emotionally disturbing, downright repulsive," for she or he threatens us with a transformation that is powerful enough to be called religious.[9]

Flannery O'Connor's first novel, *Wise Blood*, centers on just such a figure, Hazel Motes. He is an exaggeration and a distortion, as O'Connor says, for in that way he can reveal what he must reveal.[10] All of her religious figures are extremes—grotesques— and, thus, all of them are strangers acting very much like strangers in the holy city of Beni-Isguen. When we read Bowles's story, we think that the holy city protects its sanctity by slamming its doors on strangers, but in O'Connor what makes a city holy is the disruption caused by the stranger. It was not holy at all until the stranger arrived. The slamming of doors is the sounding of religious bells: a slam is the sound of the holy. *Wise Blood* begins as Hazel Motes is riding a train home from the army, and there he disturbs Mrs. Wally Bee Hitchcock, a nice lady who rolls out the usually comfortable clichés, that the evening is the prettiest time of day, that there's no place like home, that time flies, and that life is an inspiration. Hazel Motes is like a finger in her eye, insisting that nowhere is home, nothing is pretty, and no one is redeemed. He is the same for all those in the novel, haunting them and, paradoxically, attracting them. Above all, he affects them powerfully, for religious strangers are not a mild presence.

Wise Blood presents two who encounter the religious stranger, and together and separately they show the effect of the religious stranger, an effect that is echoed in the best confusions of travel.

There is Enoch Emery, the naïve believer, and Asa Hawks, the experienced one. Together with several minor characters they make up a rather good list of who is affected by a religious stranger: in a phrase, those who need a strong correction, regardless of their experience. The basic pattern is given in a description O'Connor provides in one of her letters where she describes humans as "wingless chickens."[11] We like to think of ourselves as capable of flight, of astonishing flight, in fact: eagles are what we think we are. But O'Connor's strong sense of sin ridicules such pretensions. Humans are chickens, and chickens are birds that don't fly well. How far off the ground can they get? Five feet? Six? Wingless chickens don't fly at all. So in spite of our pretensions, we cannot fly, though we need to, and since we must fly, since we must exceed the scratching and pecking, the only way for us to leave the ground (even if temporarily) is if we are hurled. We must be forced off of the ground. O'Connor's religious strangers do the throwing. Her image shows how close travel and religion are: both are often said to involve moving beyond—beyond the ordinary, beyond the merely human, beyond limitation. Transcendence is travel, and travel is transcendence . . . yet not exactly transcendence, not in the view of this book, nor of Flannery O'Connor. Instead, travel is disruption, as is religion. Travel and religion force us off the ground.

Enoch Emery is eager, trustful, and hopeful—he is like a tourist as he searches vaguely for something. He meets Hazel Motes when both are watching a man working a crowd to sell potato peelers. Enoch is the perfect rube, glad to be ridiculed, fumbling for money to buy one of the useless objects, like a man buying a souvenir. He is lonely, yearning, and waiting for something meaningful to take place. Hazel Motes is who this tourist meets, but, as with so many tourists, completely unintentionally. Enoch takes Motes (touristlike) to a museum to show him what Enoch believes is an absolute wonder, a mummy, a man who is shrunken just as O'Connor thinks all humans are. At the museum, Enoch comes to feel just what all tourists seek, too, "exalted," but it isn't the "wonder" that exalts but a rock that Motes throws, hitting the boy on the forehead, opening his "secret blood."[12] It isn't what the tourist thinks he will see in a museum. It's what's strange; it's what breaks the skin, what causes the "wise blood" to flow, that is, as O'Connor describes it, the part of us that leads us in the right direction.[13] Bewildered travel and religion agree on this point.

Wise Blood has a second character who meets the religious stranger, a second character who shows that the bewildered encounter with strangers in travel is a religious encounter. Asa Hawks seems to soar religiously as his name suggests, but, as we saw, for O'Connor humans are just wingless chickens, so anyone claiming to be a hawk is a fraud, as Asa Hawks certainly is. Where Enoch Emery might be a wide-eyed tourist, Hawks has been there and done that. He is weary, cynical, and manipulative, like a far too experienced traveler. In O'Connor's novel, he plays a blind prophet, calling for repentance and donations, but he is hardened, impervious, and utterly unreceptive. In a word, he is spiritually blind. And yet Hazel Motes affects him, too, staring into his eyes until Hawks blinks, recoils, and flees. There is both a "deeper darkness" within Motes and the ability to "reflect something," and after looking into those eyes, Hawks leaves town, "just a crook . . . [not] even a big crook."[14] The stranger is revelatory, and not of some transcendent truth but of the "darkness" in Hawks himself, the revelation of his own blind confusion.

O'Connor shows us that the strangers encountered in travel—by the tourist as well as the jaded traveler—are religious figures.

Strangers Dismantling the Heart

Jack Gilbert is a more delicate example of a life both among and as a stranger. He is a poet and a superb one, winning the Yale Younger Poet's award in 1962. He chose to live in Greece for many years. His sensitivity to foreignness is exquisite and painful. I read him on a daylong ferry from Santorini, near Crete, to Athens, a day spent among achingly beautiful young Scandinavians, men and women with huge backpacks and deep tans and scandals. Gilbert lived in exile from his youth and strength and love, grimly satisfied to be among stones and a relentless sun (he calls it "the sun nailed to the stony earth"), and among strangers.[15] He understands the ways in which strangers open wounds better than most.

❖ ● ❖

He was a poet, in the home of poets, Greece, but there is no homecoming for him. He's old, and his poetry is not, he claims, what it used to be.[16] He is wrong. Gilbert sang in Greece, alone, under "the sun / hammering this earth into pomegranates and grapes."[17] To be among strangers is to have no home, no mate, no pleasures of the hearth. To be thousands of miles away. To be locked out from what we most long for and simply to go on, without pleasure or profit. Among strangers who do not listen. And yet Jack Gilbert chose to live among strangers.

He has many poems about his dead wife, Michiko, about her dying in their house, about his mourning for her after she departs, and about being away from her. Memorably and astonishingly, he writes that he wants to go back to the intensity of his mourning, "To the magnitude of pain, of being that much alive."[18]

But he cannot go back to when he lived *with,* when he had a home and wasn't among strangers. It's a similar being away that he experiences—that he seeks—when he wakes one night at four thirty, taps out his shoes ("because of scorpions"), and turns on the radio "through the swirl of the Levant," searching for a football game, Cleveland against Los Angeles: "It makes me feel acutely here and everybody somewhere else."[19]

Youth, love, poetic fame, sport, life—all seem inside a bolted door, in an inaccessible home from which Jack Gilbert is excluded by biology and destiny, and the predicament comes painfully to us as we travel: surrounded by strangers who are hidden behind bolted doors. As in O'Connor, Gilbert encounters a "blankness" when he's among strangers. He seeks it by seeking them.

As I read back through my travel journals, there are dozens of pages written about home and dozens about the Greeks or Ghanaians or Moroccans or Czechs who seem so far and so unapproached. I feel more comfortable in the Netherlands than anywhere but home—I spent a year in Haarlem when I was eighteen; I have good friends there; I've spent time in most cities of any size and many towns of no size at all; and as I walk I recognize the pattern of the path's brickwork, the shade of brown of those bricks, and the particular downward gaze of bicycle riders speeding toward and then past me that seem a primordial recognition. I understand Dutch as closely as any (I wander about in the language pretty much as I wander about in a Dutch city—more or less knowing where I am though not precisely). But I also sit in cafés and watch people talk and feel acutely that they're too far away—too far to overhear, too far to understand.

It's Maastricht, on the central square, the Vrijdhof, in a café called the Rombouts. It's late afternoon deep into September, and people are walking home. Several tables away are two women sitting together, talking. The university is close by—are the women discussing a lecture? There's a performance of *The Marriage of Figaro* tonight: are they arranging dinner before or after? Are they complaining about a man or about a parent? Of course, I can sit in a café in Washington, too, and feel as distant, but I don't. In Tangier or Prague or Jerusalem I watch strangers and feel how much I'm *not* a part of their life.

But that's why we put ourselves among strangers. "Of course it was a disaster," Jack Gilbert writes.[20] What else? But it isn't only to feel the bolted door, at least not to him.

Estrangement isn't all we encounter in being among strangers. Perhaps that's largely true of Paul Bowles, but not of Jack Gilbert. What we discover among strangers is how much loss is required for intimacy, how much the wood of ourselves needs to be burned, as Gilbert puts it in one poem. I meet only myself unless there's a consumption that takes place, unless there's a breakdown of some of what's usual and taken for granted and true. I need to be disrupted—consumed—if I really am to meet another or myself. Jack Gilbert submits to the fire of loss, of distance, in order to discover what matters. Again, that is not a common need but a religious one.

The core of Gilbert's poetry—the loss that is necessary for intimacy—is a religious notion and not just one of poets. It's religious and very common, though not necessarily commonly acknowledged.

◆ ● ◆

One of my trips was to Ghana, where, in the old colonial capital of Cape Coast, my nephew and I met a young boxer named Ali. A waitress at our hotel had asked if we'd like to see a nightclub, and we'd surprised her by saying yes. Ali became our companion and perhaps her guarantee of safety. Of course, the nightclub was closed, but we wandered for hours, as Joanna, the waitress, grew sleepier, and Ali kept us gentle company with information about his life and questions about our own. He was, in fact, our guide, but was he doing it for pay? I've known few people anywhere as pleasant and companionable, so ingenuous that he allowed us to see a decency that would have embarrassed an American. I've had many foreigners talk about the importance of social harmony— it's a very tired cliché of two cultures meeting. "How can I get away?" I wonder. But Ali spoke about the peacefulness of the various tribal groups in Cape Coast with a sincerity that made me feel jaded and coarse and very pleased to be with him.

We spent four days with Ali, sitting with his twenty-odd "brothers" at a road junction in town that was their social center, eating chicken and rice with our fingers at a chop bar, walking along the garbage-heaped beach. His "sister" cooked us a meal, and we bought him breakfasts at Dan's Paradise Hotel. He washed our shirts by hand, bending over a tub in the rain. Eric gave him his Georgetown baseball cap; Ali gave Eric a ring. When we drove off, back to Accra, he stood at the junction with his friends and waved, looking as sad as anyone might at a family departure.

I gave Ali money when we departed, but was he a friend or a guide, for hire? When he wrote me letters, as he did, weeks and months after our return, with something of the nineteenth century about his phrasing and penmanship, was he maintaining the friendship or hoping for money? We'd all be very naïve to think that money had no part in it. But I'd also be too hardened and harsh to think it was only money.

I went to Ghana in August 1998 knowing something of friends and of money. I know not to sell a friend my old car, and when I ask the French au pair across the street to watch the kids for an evening, I keep in mind that she's only nineteen and needs the cash for the summer trip the au pairs always take to California. I'm not hiring her; I'm helping her out. Same with Sam, a friend's teenage son. When he works with my daughter on her soccer kick, he's not my employee, he's still Tina's son, and I'm giving him five bucks for helping out. I know the rules of friends and money, and I'm able to keep the lines straight so that Laurienne and Sam don't feel I'm less their friend because money moves from me to them.

But if someone asks me for directions on the street (and, for once, I don't get them lost), I don't expect to get paid. We have nice and clear customs about that. If they hand me a dollar, I'm astonished, and perhaps insulted. A prospective student once came to me, sent by someone I'd taught with a long time ago. I took him on a long tour of the campus, two hours out of a busy day. No money passed hands. When I went across Turkey, Iran, and Pakistan to India twenty-five years ago, I met up with an experienced traveler who served, in a way, as a guide through all that astonishment. His help was immensely valuable, but I never thought of paying him. Yet, when I said good-bye to Ali that morning, I knew he expected to be given some money, though he'd never given as much as an oblique hint, and though it undermined my native sense of "friend." I handed him not only 50,000 cedi but my comfort with the line between "friend" and "money." As Jack Gilbert writes, "We find out the heart only by dismantling what the heart knows."[21] Such dismantling takes place especially poignantly and well among strangers, as our hearts' wood offers itself for burning.

Strangers Incinerating the Heart

Sometimes we travel among strangers to experience something more powerful—the heart's incineration. Paul Bowles does. *The Sheltering Sky* is often considered one of the finest novels of the second half of the twentieth century, but precious little sheltering is performed by humans or by the sky. It's a wonderful title, really. It seems to promise nurturing at an organic level, but it's an ironic, mocking title. We have the cultural model of the sheltering stranger, the one who takes in the refugee or the traveler—Philemon and Baucis in Ovid's *Metamorphoses*. Strangers needn't be afraid: they will be taken in. And we needn't be anxious about our reception: even strangers offer shelter. Bowles's novel takes place as World War II has ended. It is a time of refugees and of especially harsh estrangement. Japan proved to be vicious to its neighbors; Germany was murderous to many of its own citizens, as well. It was a time in which Philemon and Baucis were butchered by the millions. But Bowles's title seems to suggest that at least the sky is beneficent.

It's not. At one point in the novel, Bowles describes the sound of locusts, "a high, unceasing scream like the sound of heat itself."[22] Not much shelter if nature screams. Nature, culture, and humans: all are hostile and strange, instigating and exasperating every possibility of a rupture, and each of them bloody.

The novel's two married Americans, Kit and Port, are emotionally and sexually estranged. They are on one of Port's "impossible trips" with a friend neither especially likes, Tunner (14). They push farther and farther into the continent until Port is dead of typhoid and Kit is deranged—and yet, perhaps, liberated. She travels farther into the desert, where she is coerced into marriage with an Arab whom she in some sense loves. She flees, seems rescued by the French, but maddeningly flees back into the crowded city where, as the novel ends, she is not even visible.

It is a novel of two sorts of strangers, those from whom Port and Kit flee and those toward whom they move. What separates the two groups is not that one is appealing and the other not.

Instead, Port and Kit are attracted by the strangers who are most unusual and repellant and repelled by those most familiar. While few if any would envy what eventually befalls Kit and Port, the novel does present the strangest encounters as nonetheless attractive. "Pleasurable agitation" is what Port calls his emotional state as he moves more and more deeply into the Sahara, "leaving behind all familiar things," and the same is true of the attractive strangeness (109). It seems that the door that is slammed and bolted is not at all an absolute barrier. The door is both transparent and porous; the stranger is shut away and accessible; his or her strangeness is alarmingly, enticingly near.

Port and Kit flee two British strangers nearly as soon as the Americans meet the Lyles. Just to read about them is to feel the fingernail on the blackboard—they are too loud, too boorish, condescending to the Arabs, bickering between themselves. On a daylong car trip with them, Port resolves "to remain wholly on the periphery of this family . . . [and] the best way of assuring that, he thought, would be to have no visible personality whatever" (65).

If Bowles weren't so fine a writer, the Lyles would be entirely stereotypical: the countrymen we all meet abroad, despise, and seek to avoid, with an acuteness that makes it seem that maybe we're really trying to avoid ourselves. The accent we're utterly accustomed to is now so nasal and so harsh; the background-filling patter that we've mastered back home is now stupid and banal; the garish clothes, political clichés, petty materialism—all of it our own and all of it now so ugly. It's like looking at our faces too closely in the mirror and discovering how hideous the pores and little hairs really are. The Lyles are just that sort of mirror, and Port and Kit do all they can to get away from them, but can't. We turn a corner in remotest Ladakh, and there we are, in all our boring and loathsome familiarity. As Bowles writes of Kit, "The blatantly normal always infuriated her" (61). Such normalcy can't just be disrupted. It has to be obliterated.

As Port is riding with the Lyles, Kit travels on the train, and she stumbles into the other sort of strangers, the antithesis of the "blatantly normal." It was the fourth-class railway car, "crowded to bursting with men in dun-colored burnouses, squatting, sleeping, reclining, standing, and moving about through a welter of amorphous bundles" (80). Her encounters with strangers crescendos, starting with a bearded man who glares at her sternly, then a man eating red locusts, crunching them noisily. Next is a man carrying a severed sheep's head, "its eyes like agate marbles staring from their sockets." Finally she turns and looks "directly into the most hideous human face she had ever seen," diseased and deformed. In all, it is a "dream of terror," the climax of what we bolt the door against (82).

Kit flees the train carriage and returns to Tunner, relieved to feel "the nearness and warmth of a being that did not frighten her," but he turns out to be a stranger of the first sort (85). It is Tunner that Kit flees at the end of the book, preferring the dreamlike terrors of the Arab quarter. What can we conclude other than that Bowles is seeking an escape from the familiar—even from the familiar *us*—and wants to be plunged among strangers who are as hideous as possible?

It goes even further, for *The Sheltering Sky* is a descent into the company of the stranger who is often sexually embraced. There is Marhina, the woman on the edge of the first town they enter. Port cannot place her: "There was bewilderment, fear, and a passive expectancy in her face as she stared quietly at him. . . . It seemed to Port that she was much more like a young nun than a cafe dancer. At the same time he did not in the least trust her" (29–30). There is the blind dancer in the brothel in Ain Krorfa. Port can't be sure it is a brothel: "He was waiting for a licentious gesture, at least a hint of a leer. None was forthcoming" (140). When Port sees the dancer, he's further bewildered, for he cannot recognize the dancer's motions as dance at all: "It was as if she were saying: 'a dance is being done. I do not dance because I am not here. But it is my dance'" (142). Port becomes desperate to have her sexually, and when he fails, "he was persuaded, not that a bit of enjoyment had been denied him, but that he had lost love itself" (144).

The apex of Kit's encounter with the attractively (and repulsively) strange is a sexual one, as well. When Port dies, Kit flees the French fort, and seems liberated in a particularly dreamlike way: "She kicked off her sandals and stood naked in the shadows. She felt a strange intensity being born within her" (258). She presents herself (clothed) to a caravan, and within a day has been sexually assaulted, though in an otherworldly way, "a perfect balance between gentleness and violence that gave her particular delight" (285). That paradoxical combination—the "beautiful and terrible"—that has typified Bowles's view of strangers, characterizes her relationship with Belqassim, the caravan master who rapes, then imprisons, then marries her. Eventually she is both terrified by Belqassim and longs for his company. When she escapes from this intimate and savage stranger, it is only to reject a return to the West. There is no escape from strangers. Bowles's depiction of both strangers and sexuality is troubling, and I would strongly hope that none of us would experience it, and yet we cannot simply dismiss or condemn the incident (or the novel) and be done with it.

What is most fascinating is that Bowles presents Kit seeking this stranger, much as Bowles wrote that he, himself, sought "wisdom and ecstasy—and death" in Morocco. And in both cases (Kit's and Port's), the encounter with the stranger is in extreme conflict with what is not only usual and comforting and true, but what is necessary for life itself. And that encounter is sexual. We flee and are fled from because we are so utterly different and so mutually threatening; the door is slammed and bolted, but then we press so close to the door, in blinding desire, and the door becomes membrane-thin. Either Bowles is presenting us with a sharp warning, telling us, "Stay home, go no farther, slam and lock those doors!" by presenting us with the cases studies of two who wandered too far, who opened the doors and were destroyed by the stranger, *or* he is showing us the strength of the appeal of the utterly strange and destructive stranger. The stranger breaks, rips, opens wounds; the stranger introduces microbes to Port and madness and oppression to Kit, and yet we want the stranger.

We want the stranger so powerfully that it has to be put sexually. Again, please do not misunderstand me: what Bowles presents in his novel is deeply disturbing. In many ways, it is antithetical to life itself. We can strongly urge all those we know to avoid all such situations, and I do. We can and must condemn such ethically troubling events. And yet why does Bowles present the events? Why does the novel have such appeal? What might the *value* be of this view of sexuality and strangers?

Three facts about this novel: first, the "blatantly normal infuriated" Kit. Second, for Port to be interested in a thought, Bowles wrote, "it had to be inaccessible" (62). Third, as Port and Kit bicycled to a pass outside Boussif, some boys watched them in a "paralysis of surprise" (97). What Bowles seems to seek in strangers is access to such a degree of surprise that his accustomed world (the blatantly normal one) is paralyzed, made inaccessible, even obliterated. What Bowles seems to want is to *be* on the other side of the door with the stranger, his old self left locked outside, perhaps dead. Strangers, as it turns out, *do* kill us—at least they kill the normal, accessible, unsurprising us.

The idea that Port's view is actually religious is a paradoxical one. Not only is it the stranger who "breaks, rips, opens wounds . . . introduces microbes . . . and madness and oppression," it is the sacred. The sacred annihilates. It is inaccessible. It brings about "a paralysis of surprise." And so are the religious others who are and bring the sacred: prophets, messiahs, religious founders, and shamans, for example. Flannery O'Connor's Hazel Motes is a religious figure of that kind. We also see one in her 1955 novel, *The Violent Bear It Away*. In that work, a rationally minded schoolteacher can only come to feel love for his own son when he encounters the murder of the boy at the hands of a prophet. For O'Connor in that novel, love must be a "terrifying love" to affect us, and only the sacred can bring it.[23]

What can such an extreme view have to do with us—with spending a couple of weeks in Provence or Tuscany, Cairo or Jerusalem, Beijing or Calcutta? I assume that few readers seek, as Kit and Port do, the utterly strange and destructive stranger who breaks, rips, opens, and wounds, the stranger who introduces microbes . . . and madness and oppression. To be perfectly honest, I hope—for their own sake—that such travelers stay home. But I do think that many of us avoid the "blatantly normal," seeking, instead, those who are strange, even repulsively strange, straining as many of our boundaries as we dare. Jack Gilbert finds it necessary to "dismantle" the heart through the loneliness of travel. In that way he can discern what matters and move even closer to others and to himself. For Bowles, what is familiar and ordinary—our home selves—needs to be undermined more forcefully, not especially to get anywhere or anybody or anything, but to lose somebody or someplace—himself and home.

Isn't that true for some of us, too? In order to agree, we have to give up the notion that we all live close to the average, the moderate, and the reasonable. I believe we're all more excessive and more strange than that notion allows. The best indication is the one Bowles himself points out—sex. There are times when there is simply nothing average, moderate, or reasonable about sex. It can be sheer arousal, blind desire, a knifelike intensity of feeling, the near-obliteration of consciousness. Sex is sometimes simply excess in action. And it (often) takes place with others. The peak of our loss of the moderate, average, and reasonable, the peak of our loss of the home-self just might take place with those strangers with whom we live or whom we love or whom we want. With that other, we often lose ourselves and become lost in a way we deeply crave. I said that strangers, for Bowles, "kill us—at least they kill the normal, accessible, unsurprising us." Can't we say the same for the "little death" we seek in sex? And if that is true, mightn't it be true in travel, too?

The Pain of Strangers

Alphonso Lingis is the contemporary heir to Mark Twain, Henry Miller, and Paul Bowles: a subversive of established values who travels to find the "dirt" rather than to enlarge himself through "commerce with the ancients." He is a philosophy professor from Pennsylvania, the translator of the most important work (*Totality and Infinity*) by, arguably, the most important ethicist of the second half of the century, Emmanuel Levinas. Yet our stereotypes are getting in the way if that information leads us to think Lingis can be found in Oxford's Bodleian Library or the reading room of the British Museum. No, he's at transvestite sex shows in Bangkok; the Havana office of a plastic surgeon who treats torture victims; a prison in Thailand (jailed for buying drugs); the lobby of a cheap hotel in Bangladesh (as he's being thrown out); or a jungle in Nicaragua (pursued by the Contras). He's as offensive to contemporary sensibilities as Twain, Miller, or Bowles were in their times, and as appealing.

His passion is strangers, who need to be alien in a particular sense. He looks for "persons my nation and my culture have made my enemies . . . people my nation and my culture have conquered and silenced."[24] That's why his strangers are Sandinistas during the Reagan administration's support of the Contras, or a renegade Philippine soldier loyal to Colonel Honasan who led a revolt against America's democratic darling, Corazon Aquino. His strangers are sex workers and transvestites and the healers one sees and ignores on the streets of Indian cities. A toilet cleaner in India invites Lingis home, and, amazingly, he goes. A male prostitute joins him in his Thai jail cell, and Lingis is with him for days. Lingis is a political traveler, and his writing can be exceedingly preachy. He hectors and reprimands his readers for the political and economic abuses of the First World. It's easy to be put off by Lingis's lessons; I put the book down for a year when I was part way through the first chapter. But that's a bit like putting down Twain because of his burlesque or Miller because of the zipless sex or Bowles because of the desert tedium. Lingis's ideological preaching coexists with a deeply personal ethical compassion. He feels the harm that strangers have suffered. He hears the effects of silencing. *Abuses* may in part be a book of politically correct harangues, but it's also a transcription of Lingis's many responses to the pain of strangers.

To read Lingis is to be reminded of how many people I ignore when I travel. There are, in fact, extremely few that I speak with at all, and those few are likely to have accosted me. I tolerate them for a while until I can escape. I sit in cafés, alone, and watch or wander the streets, alone, looking. It is as though the external appearance, the clothes, the gestures, the sounds are all sufficient—are more than sufficient. I can go no closer, and I have all I need. I can feel accused by a traveler like Alphonso Lingis—as I once was by a beggar in Tangier.

I was sitting at a sidewalk table in the ville *nouveau*, the French colonial section of the city, outside the French consulate, wondering (in my journal) about my error in spelling "consulate" as "consolate." Morocco was very aggressive—especially men asking if I wanted a guide and never relenting, creating an intense friction that only paused when I sat at a café table and came under the protection of the waiter. I needed a "consolate." And as I wrote about it and watched the people pass, an old man in rags stopped right in front of me, glaring, belligerent. "Fuck you, guy! You write all my prick!" he shouted. I'd thought I could hide, sit inconspicuously in cafés and write down my thoughts. I thought I could be the invisible stranger, investigating from a distance. But I was spotted and denounced. Cursed. Condemned. Exposed as a voyeur. For me, Morocco was about never being able to hide. My door was never bolted.

And that is religious, too. In O'Connor's *The Violent Bear It Away,* as in most of her works, those in need of the sacred try to hide from it. The schoolteacher, Rayber, wants to turn Tarwater, his nephew, into an echo of himself, grinding everything of value into numbers. If Tarwater were as empty as his uncle, then Rayber needn't be affected by the boy. Tarwater, himself, tried to hide from his own encounter with "terrifying love" by misunderstanding his mission as a prophet, to tragic end, when he drowns Rayber's son. If the religious is as violent and disruptive as O'Connor depicts it, inevitably the wingless chickens would try to sit quietly in cafés, silently on trains, passively beside the strangers, not meeting their eyes. But it is nearly impossible to be invisible either as a stranger or to one. The sacred spots us and denounces us, as the man did me in Tangier: "Fuck you, guy! You write all my prick!" Can we not see his words as sacred words? They rattled me then and they rattle me now, shaking my comfort and ease, rupturing my "me."

Alphonso Lingis denounces me, too. It isn't because he becomes personally involved, as Henry Miller did (as we'll see), whereas I can't. In fact, Lingis claims that all we have is the "surfaces" of strangers. We can't speak for them without silencing them, can't hear them without hearing our own ways of hearing them. The notion that we can "get close," that we can share and deeply understand strangers is rejected by Lingis because we're bound by our own cultural understandings. They're "transvestites" or "prostitutes" or "toilet cleaners," and we just can't drop the associations and hear them. So both Lingis and I remain on the surface, but he carries it further—much further—by literally moving to the surface. He listens to what strangers say through their bodies. He meets strangers by touching them.

He is often astonishingly poetic in telling about the value of touching, as in his essay (or letter) about Peru, "Tawantinsuyu." He feels that he is a man locked inside his own cultural "codes" but that simply seeing someone's "cheek, forearm, stomach, rump, flank, wrinkles, hair, moles, scars" is a way of getting past those codes by seeing the harm they can suffer, even the harm of his own look: "The glance at the skin grazes it already. . . . The face is not a barrier, shield, or mask, . . . The face exposes the body to the world. . . . The harsh sunlight, the grit of the wind, the damp, the lithic silence push against it."[25] Bodies suffer, and Lingis can approach strangers through their suffering. "But one has to touch them" in order to feel the suffering and to feel one's own inability to heal.

Unfortunately, "tact and tenderness themselves prohibit the contact."[26] The Peruvians politely move away, and Lingis is respectful, not crossing barriers. The result is a banquet of accidental contacts, "a child who touches your leg, a somnolent old man in a truck whose body touches yours when the truck reels on a curve. An old woman who stumbles, and your arm goes by itself to hold her. The old woman whose gnarled hand grazed yours when she handed you a cup of maté de coca in the rarified air that left your heart pounding against your ribs."[27]

❖ ● ❖

Lingis's book has several sexual encounters, too, often with sex workers. Sometimes he writes of them as a way of learning about strangers, as he did about the old women handing him a cup of mate. They are poetic touchings, just more intense. As he is writing about the transvestite sex club in Bangkok, he notes that he would like to *feel* what it is like to be one of the performers. Then "one would have a feel for the weight and the buoyancy, the swish and the streaming, the smell and the incandescence of the costumes, masks, castes, classes, cultures, nations, economies, continents."[28]

Lust, on the other hand, is not learning. "Lust does not know what it is"; "voluptuous pleasure engulfs and obliterates purposes and directions and any sense of where it itself is going."[29] Lust is confusion and a means of getting lost, while orgasm is loss of consciousness. Lingis seeks contact with strangers' bodies to experience a loss of his bearings. He is thrown into a turmoil that forgets who that other man or woman is or should be and forgets, too, who he is and what his prior understandings of that stranger are.

There is something of the postmodern romantic in Lingis's craving for foreign bodies (*Foreign Bodies* is the title, by the way, of one of his books). How else can we really leave home—leave *all* of our preconceptions, our profession, our socioeconomic class, our family upbringing, our education—except by so thoroughly losing our consciousness as we do sexually? It isn't that we can arrive at a romantic epiphany by having an ecstatic sexual vision. Rather, we accomplish something valuable by losing our minds. For Lingis, strangers are our most appealing sexual partners if what we want is to get lost.

A staple of travel writing—and of travel experience—is the romantic and sexual liaison. Alphonso Lingis is more frank and blunt than most, especially in writing about illicit sex, but I think he presents the significance of sex in travel quite accurately. Once again, we might think that travelers fall in love with foreigners and thereby widen their world. My town has several Peace Corps volunteers married to Africans or Latin Americans. My friend Lew is married to an Italian journalist. The world is shrinking, we like to say. As children we believed there was one person "right" for us and that we would find them and marry. But are we really seeking (or creating) a domesticated planet when we become involved with a stranger? Sometimes, yes. But aren't we also bringing a stranger into our bed? Isn't the very center of the familiar, our own bed, at risk of becoming a foreign place? Lingis would want to point out that there is an injustice done when we presume we are anything other than strange—other—to one another. There is a curious kind of hubris in presuming that we are two halves of one egg or that in love—or sex—two "become one." Don't we often mean, instead, that you become me? Doesn't the romantic or orgasmic "fusion" vastly oversimplify "you" and impoverish "you," as well? Instead we might be "sleeping with the enemy" (as in Bowles) or awakening to the surprising otherness of one as intimate as a lover.

For Lingis, nothing better presents the strangeness that cannot be overcome than the body that is touched and remains—always—another body, not my own. The body that halts my touch, even if it accepts it. And instead of the dissolving of that stranger into me, Lingis discovers the dissolving of himself into lust. It isn't just coincidental that Freud theorized the vast strange region of the unconscious as a result of his observations of sexuality. I think I understand myself—I teach and I write and I play soccer with the kids and have a glass of wine with friends—but at the touch of another a barrier shatters, and my own body becomes alarming and surpassing.

Lingis puts it better:

Lust does not know what it is. The mouth lets go of the chain of its sentences, rambles, giggles, the tongue spreads its wet out over the lips. The hands that caress move in random detours with no idea of what they are looking for, grasping and probing without wanting an end. The body tenses up, hardens, heaves and grapples, pistons and rods of a machine that has no idea of what it is trying to produce. Then it collapses, leaks, melts. There is left the coursing of the trapped blood, the flush of heat, the spirit vaporizing in exhalations.[30]

It isn't, I think, that we pacify our world through foreign affairs. That might be the hope of the new Victorians. Rather, intrigue, espionage, clashing cultures, and the acrid fertility of conflict are what may come of sex with strangers.

Few are as willing as Lingis to write of their sexual encounters with strangers as they travel. Far fewer to write of sex with prostitutes, though it's hardly just the local population that frequents the sex workers of Tijuana or Bangkok, Prague or Moscow. What we usually think is that men abroad have escaped the bonds and bounds of home. Like truckers far from home, their libido is free to roam. I'm sure that is part of it, but I also wonder if it isn't reversing the causality. Is it that men are free of restraints and so they have sex with foreign prostitutes or that they have sex in order to be free of home restraints? We can condemn it. The harm for sex workers and for those who engage them can certainly be enormous, but in addition to our ethical response, we need to understand the function. That's part of what Lingis and Bowles are saying. As Lingis writes of the Antarctic: "in domestic perception our eyes and ears pattern the flux of sensation—finding an elementary rhythm in the dripping of a faucet, in the waves of a lake—and our minds extrapolate those patterns to domesticate the universe. My eyes have been nowise gestalting this frozen intricacy into patterns; they have been de-domesticated."[31]

❖ ● ❖

Both men seek—crave—"de-domestication," and they both find that sex (and for them it is often sex outside of the usual social codes) reaches that end. We might recommend that "de-domestication" take place in ways less troubling, and it does, but I ask that we all inventory our imaginations as well as our actions as we travel, the mild and dim ones as well as those more powerful and more overt and notice the role of the sexual. Momentary fantasies and hopes, even fears can benefit us by "de-domesticating." These are the suggestions of one person, as I say in the introduction, and that fact may be nowhere more evident to some readers than here. My suggestions are partial. Can they be otherwise? I could try to gather in more views, and perhaps I need to, but if travel is a "rich thicket," as William James says reality is, then I crawl through and report on my own cuts and scrapes. I hope to see other reports.

The first deeply foreign city I visited was Lahore, Pakistan. I'd traveled across Turkey and Iran in winter. The bus we were on had broken down in frozen eastern Turkey, and as the driver hitchhiked on to get a new water pump, we waited in a teahouse full of men who seemed both contemptuous of and fascinated by our presence. Billows of freezing vapor at the door. Lucky Strike posters enticed smokers with women naked to the waist. We walked far out into the snow, and I saw the shadows in the snow a deep violet I'd simply never seen before. Days later there was another bus from Teheran to Zahedan, in southeast Iran, then a minivan jammed with nineteen burly Baluchistani tribesman, forcing us into corners of the seat. At night the van would stop for chai, and rebels would wander in from the night and squat around the fire, rifles at hand. One night my traveling companion, named Jack, woke to find the entire van's company laughing, stoned, as the young driver's helper lowered a huge stone onto my chest as I slept. "No, no," he said, and the stone was returned.

Several days later, we were in Lahore, the great city of the West Punjab. Women totally veiled, the city full of hawks—kites— soaring, fighting, even fucking, as common as pigeons in Europe or America. I knew I'd left the known world. But I hadn't gone quite far enough until one night when a man took us into the Old City. I still remember it as though it had been a dream—huge ancient walls, narrow, winding streets. Walls of burlap behind which families bedded down. Bare electric wires above me, within easy reach. Crumbling brick. Nothing of appeal, nothing of beauty: worn, decayed, collapsing. I felt that I was descending into Fellini's *Satyricon*, a labyrinthine hell of the utterly not-home from which I could never ascend. And then a stranger said he'd take us to the sex district, which seemed to insinuate that he could bring us much closer to the ruin of Old Lahore; he could strip us and take us to it, stripped; he could bare its crotch and we could be as utterly enmeshed with its raw lewdness as ever humans could. Oozing membranes rubbing membranes stretched and engorged. It was a terrifying thought—but also (I won't deny it) appealing. We fled, and those old worn walls and dark, lost streets—still—seem to me to be the pit into which I could at any moment fall. The bottom of that pit is "de-domestication," the complete loss of home. But who doesn't wish for it, even by fearing it; even, perhaps (as Nietzsche might say), by despising it.

Strangers and Strong Love

That is one face of the stranger, a face that both Bowles and Lingis present, though from different angles. Yet there are other relationships to the stranger besides those Bowles and Lingis present, as we all know from our own travels. We've probably all experienced the slammed and bolted door that Lingis and Bowles describe—and I think, for example, of the shopkeepers I encountered in Prague in 1995. I could feel that their instinct was to welcome the foreigner who wandered in through their door, but the sheer inundation of Germans, French, Americans, Brits overwhelmed and frightened them. It seemed another sad occupation of their beautiful city. It seemed, too, that their doors had only just been slammed, that soon after the "Velvet Revolution" there was a warm reunion with the strangers from the West, but there had simply come to be too many as the tiny streets came to be packed like midtown Manhattan.

But that is not all we've experienced with strangers, though we've certainly encountered it a great deal. It's also common to fall in love with strangers, and to fall in love because they're strangers. To feel an appealing spell of a foreignness. Henry Miller presents us with a voice so bewitching and an ear so eager to be beguiled that doors are thrown opened. We don't revert to the Victorian model of educating savages or a Romantic one of learning nature's secrets from them. Their strangeness is still strange. Henry Miller draws upon the attitude presented by Walt Whitman when he asked, in "Song of the Open Road," "Do you know what it is as you pass to be loved by strangers?" Reading Bowles and Lingis, we would think that there is no love from or for strangers possible—without deep injury or uncrossable distance, that is. Miller loves strangers without greatly diminishing their strangeness—in fact, by accentuating it. It's a kind of encounter that many travelers have had.

Miller left France for Greece in the summer of 1939, propelled, in part, by stories told to him by an American art student named Betty Ryan. "Her experiences were strange," he writes. In listening to tales of her travels, Miller says, "I found myself wandering about in a strange land."[32] Miller gravitated to strangers and to those who could make him feel strange, that is, those who could induce disruption in him.

"I had a strong desire to talk to Arabs and Turks and Syrians and such like . . . in preference to the Americans, the French, the English," and on the boat to Greece he takes up with a Greek (4). What he chiefly loves in that man is "passion, . . . contradictoriness, confusion, chaos" (6). When he is grossly overcharged by his first guide in Athens, Miller actually loves it, admiring that the man is "wily and cunning" (10). His great travel book *The Colossus of Maroussi*, is really an account of his intense delight in meeting strangers, chief among them the colossus of his title, a man named George Katsimbalis: "Nobody can explain anything which is unique. One can describe, worship, and adore. And that is all I can do with Katsimbalis' talk" (32).

There is nothing measured or restrained about Henry Miller. He is defiantly unreliable as a reporter of events or a describer of places. Since he is so hyperbolic, he may be an illustration of Lingis's claim that when we speak for the stranger, the stranger is not heard. We certainly hear Miller, without restraint and fullthroated, when he writes. But it is also possible that he gives us another way of seeing strangers: he is delighted in their strength and power and seems to want to devour and be devoured by it, a Nietzschean embrace of friends and equals. And crucial to his intoxicating love of a stranger like Katsimbalis is his deep pleasure in being lost in a large personality.

The stranger is no longer a stranger if the threat to "home" disappears, if the stranger becomes wholly a "familiar." If there is to be a stranger, there must always be discomfort, anxiety, a sense of borders violated. Some have the notion that Henry Miller simply subsumes all otherness into his own large and loose personality or that he comes to adore a man like Katsimbalis simply as an act of narcissism—the two seem so alike. One of the most memorable observations that Miller makes of Katsimbalis is this: "He seemed to be talking about himself all the time. . . . He talked about himself because he himself was the most interesting person he knew. I liked that quality very much—I have a little of it myself" (28). "A little of it"! Miller strikes many as so fatuously self-absorbed that he could only find a mirror image interesting. But that analysis of Miller neglects the tension and risk that he feels in Katsimbalis or any of the other strangers who attracts him. If narcissism is staring into one's placid reflection, Miller is no narcissist. What he loves about strangers—and Katsimbalis especially—is losing his bearings.

In discussing his travels in Greece, Miller takes up a wall metaphor something like Bowles's. It's France that has walls, he says: "The Frenchman puts walls about his talk, as he does about his garden: he puts limits about everything in order to feel at home" (32). What Miller loved about France—where he spent many years, of course—was that he was allowed inside the walls and felt a familylike nourishment. But there comes a time, he says, "when you are well again and strong. . . . You long to break out and test your powers. . . . You long to make friends, to create enemies, to look beyond walls and cultivated patches of earth" (33).

Miller has to leave home, even an adopted home, and subject himself to the risks of strangers. He is confident, of course—he is "well again and strong"—but the enemies he makes are hostile and harmful, and the friends don't just stroke him: they *encounter* him. He reminds me of Emerson's advice, that a man should compare favorably with a river, an oak, or a mountain—that there should be a *solid* encounter. Miller uses the same image when he writes of a man he met at the Turkish fortress in Nauplia (called Nafplio today). The man had committed murder, had served twenty years in prison, and says he would do it again in the same circumstances. "He had no remorse, no guilt. He was a marvelous old fellow, stout as an oak, gay, hearty, insouciant" (50). We can't dominate an oak. We encounter it, admire it. As Miller wrote of Katsimbalis, "It was definitely a meeting" (27).

Miller's encounters with Katsimbalis are solid, and yet they also enfold him. It isn't a dialogue—he isn't speaking of the long conversations with the stranger sitting next to us on the plane. Katsimbalis offers monologues, and ones that are so masterful that Miller describes one as "the Ninth Symphony of his travails and transgressions" (58). To listen to his monologue is to be overcome with admiration, and to become hypnotized, to enter into a dream, and to continue under its spell long afterwards. In fact, it's an "imprisonment" and a kind of "drowning" (71). Miller enters the stranger's room and allows it to enter him, and he's never the same. Isn't this what intimacy means? Doesn't it mean coming so close that we abandon our own safety, losing our certainties to experience someone so closely that a great deal is new and able to become new? Miller doesn't seek self-abandonment, like Bowles. He risks transformation.

He spends a lot of time describing Katsimbalis's difficulty at beginning a monologue. It is, after all, a masterpiece (and is any masterpiece easily begun?) as well as otherworldly (and ecstatic vision doesn't come without preparation). He stutters and fumbles, he casts about for a topic, "trying to get the damned spinet working." He finally got started, Miller says, "when he had come to a knot-hole . . . and [took] a tremendous step backward . . . [and] tumble[d] into the deep well in which all his stories had their source" (72). Of course, I love it that Katsimbalis himself began in a hole, that is, in a rupture. Intimate encounters with strangers who are to remain strangers must involve disruption on both sides. It isn't the smooth patter of the suave foreigner, welcoming you to lovely Venice. A miscue is crucial if there is to be an opening in the border that allows the stranger across. In Miller's view, it's a disruption of the usual talk. Even better, it's a "knot-hole": the tight roughness of the wood that hinders smooth flow and that's actually a hole, the hole of the branch. If we're sliding our hand along the grain or if we're sawing the wood, we're stopped, we're thrown off, and we need to draw back. Only if our progress is halted will we go off in the unaccustomed direction that will produce art or vision or the fresh start that a stranger requires.

Katsimbalis's talk is omnivorous—"When he described a place he ate into it like a goat attacking a carpet"—but it's not an eating that destroys. Rather, it vitalizes. Into the dream spell of his talk goes everything, "poison and ambrosia," "travail and transgressions," but especially loss and ill-health, and within the "flawless anarchy" of his talk, it was all "alive and flourishing like a smoking dung-heap" (30). As Whitman said, "Everything comes out of the dirt—everything." What comes out of the dirt is life. Katsimbalis has the ability to incorporate an entire world, and an exceedingly untidy one, at that—to meet that Greek stranger was to meet a world, and a world that lacked a tidy order, a world that was a "smoking dung-heap."

Surely this is what my friends have encountered when they have lived with or married strangers met in the Peace Corps or at academic conferences abroad. I once had a student who married a man she met during a two-week stay in Peru. He spoke no English and she little Spanish. He worked in the hotel in which she stayed. The marriage didn't last. What did she think she had found? It was impulsive, perhaps. Maybe it was a ruse to get him a green card. I can't be sure. But to one degree or another, many foreign involvements are the same—a very close encounter with the heap of customs and practices that is ultimately impenetrable—one that seems like a smoking dung-heap. There just must be the sense (isn't there?) that one might uncover something in that stranger's world that will simply be unrecognizable or unpalatable or repulsive or a brilliant surprise. What has he absorbed from his grandfather as a child in Benin or from the communal childrearing on the kibbutz that will be as foreign in your life together as sheep brains on the dinner table?

A wonderful aspect of Katsimbalis's talk is that he became lost in it, too. Miller says that he loved to redesign cities. It's very hard to know what to make of this: "He would take a map of London say, or Constantinople, and after the most painstaking study would draw up a new plan of the city, to suit himself" (58). All of this he would relate to Henry Miller and his friends in his rambling conversation, but, Miller, says, he would frequently become lost in his reconstructions, especially since much of the redesign would take place in his sleep. I won't attempt to try to make sense of this—how could he know he was lost if he had made the city himself? What was the reference point for "lost"? What's important, at any rate, is that being lost, even in one's own inventions and in one's own talk, is so crucial to Miller. He says, too, that it isn't only his listeners who are hypnotized by Katsimbalis's talk, but Katsimbalis himself. He, too, is a prisoner. It's a notion that destroys the myth of the omnipotent stranger, even the omnipotent Demiurge. It places both strangers, both sides of the border in the same world, a world without absolute reference points and without infallible guides. The stranger who bewitches us is not beyond bewitchment. She in whom we feel lost can be lost, as well. There is no master, no slave; no native, no tourist.

◆ ● ◆

In *Breaking the Waves,* the Danish film from 1996, a woman is interrogated by her village elders on a small, isolated, and extremely traditional Scottish island. She wishes to marry a Dane, a man who works on a North Sea oil rig, but the elders are fiercely determined to protect their way of life. The film shows that he will bring travail to her life beyond anything she can imagine or guess. Her life will be ravaged and she will die, but she will also discover a bewildering love. "What have strangers ever brought us?" the elders ask her, derisively, dismissively. They anticipate no possible response. "Music," she says. Maybe it's enough. Maybe it's much more than enough. But, as Jack Gilbert might remind us (and Odysseus, too), we hear no music without dismantling what the ear used to know. The difference between strangers as they are seen by Paul Bowles, Alphonso Lingis, and Henry Miller is the degree of pleasure and pain given by their music and its dismantling of our homes. But pleasure or pain, life or death, talking to strangers (says Naomi Nye) is the most important thing we do in our lives.[33]

SIX Guides for the Perplexed

I WAS IN MATANZAS, CUBA, IN AN URBAN NEIGHBORHOOD OF cement row-houses nearly flush against the narrow street. We had been through this part of the city several times, racing in Lied's wired-together East German Lada, but I knew I would never be able to find my way in—or out—on my own. There were so many turns down streets solidly lined with identical one-story buildings, and my eyes could not pick out the distinctions that residents would recognize instantly. There were resorts a dozen miles outside the city—"sun, sand, blue-green water and everything that goes with it," the *Lonely Planet* guidebook proclaimed—but Matanzas itself was, as the guide also pronounced, barely worth a visit. We got out of the car: Joe Murphy, an American expert in Santeria, the Afro-Cuban religion (and a professor at my university); Maria Galban, a respected elder in the religion; Elton, an

English teacher who was translating for us; and Lied, our driver and guide and the glue of this group.

Two hours later, we were in a room filled with chanting *santeras* and the complex rhythms of the bata drums. A man was writhing as a spirit, an *orisha*, took possession of him, as though divinity were much too large for a human. It was a scene that William Butler Yeats might have described in "Leda and the Swan," as the god Zeus overpowers Leda, mother of Helen. Yeats's vision is not our schoolbook Greek romance. No, when divinity and a human meet, the woman is "so caught up, / So mastered by the brute blood of the air." The man in the small room in Matanzas was in the process of being mastered.

The spirit danced with the community for forty-five minutes or so, playing tricks (giving children some of the money that had been collected and throwing other coins out into the street), greeting various *santeros*, whispering messages, and even mocking the two North Americans who stood and observed, shoving his cigar into the mouth of one before dancing off.

When Joseph Murphy writes of a *bembe* such as this one in his influential study *Santeria: African Spirits in America,* he describes it as "the heart of the religion . . . a harmony of the human and the divine in dance and joy."[1] How did we get to this "heart" when we were in Cuba? How does one travel to the "inside"? Of course, the only way to get "there" is with guides: Maria, above all, and also Lied, and Elton, and Murphy.

Our usual view is that guides can get us inside, that they're the way to avoid being mere visitors and tourists. As our ship or plane arrives, we engage a guide and then we can get not only to what is genuine but we can get past the dangers, past the discomforts, past the confusions. My view is that, in fact, it's the guides that lead us to the confusions, dangers, and discomforts. If we manage to get to anything like the "heart" (an overrated organ, it's been said), it's not "large and light" but "doorless, crudely lighted" and "darkly, unimaginably tenanted," as poet James Merrill noted.[2] What, then, is a guide that he or she can bring us to such an "inside"? I believe that we can't simply go to what is strange, we can only be brought. It takes another (in some form) to lead us to the tenants who we cannot yet imagine. These others are our guides. What are their qualities?

The guides that are to lead us past the dangers come in many forms, and we can learn about the guides who lead us into dangers by looking at those more idyllic types. Guides are, first, people, locals who walk ahead of us. They speak our language, know what our desires are, and are skilled in getting us to just what is most beautiful and most genuine, while helping us avoid the traps of what is banal or second-rate or risky: the pickpockets, the dangerous sections of town, the cons. The good guide leads, clarifies, enables—or so we think.

Our guides are also books, guidebooks. The eighteenth century proliferated books about travels in the Grand Tour that then became a means of propagating the same trip for others. The young men who had traveled for several years after Oxford or Cambridge then produced a volume recounting their journey and passing on their adventures, advice, and wisdom learned to others. As mass tourism began in the third or fourth decade of the nineteenth century, Karl Baedeker and John Murray III wrote the first books specifically designed to guide. Baedeker eventually produced guides to thirty-one countries and regions. Do we ever set off to travel without a guidebook? People urge their guidebooks on you almost as though they were religious tracts, guides of another sort. I use the *Lonely Planet* guides, and I have a friend who only uses the *Rough Guide*. *Let's Go, Fodors, Frommer's, Moon Handbooks,* and, of course, still *Baedeker's.* But other books are guides, too. Like many, I try to read the local literature or literature situated in that place. Kafka's home on Golden Lane in the shadow of Prague Castle is as small and frail as we expect, the streets as convoluted, and even in the summer or fall, there is a gloom that we wouldn't see without *The Trial.* Buying a postcard, I still feel the looming yet indistinct threat of that authority just up the hill. Ivan Klima, Milan Kundera, and Jaroslav Hašek's *The Good Soldier Svejk* just contribute more angles to this literary guiding. "All this history, all this Central European literature," we say as we walk the narrow streets. And I notice the three-inch cube cobblestones, ideal for being dug out and hurled at tanks in 1968.

Other aspects of culture can be guides, too: music, art, photography. I'm sure there are many who listen to Italian opera as they travel in Umbria or to Edith Piaf (or anything with accordion) in France or to *Buena Vista Social Club* in Cuba. I have been thinking recently about what it takes to be a "good listener." What does it take to really listen to another person? It isn't really that we remember all the details—the names of the friends, the story of her mother's refusal to let her cook? It's not facts that show we've listened; it's that we feel her presence. That we have absorbed a strong sense of what it's like to be her. That we feel how she feels toward her mother or toward her friends, that the imagery we get runs parallel to her imagery. The cultural guides allow us to feel the culture's presence more broadly. Being in Casa de Tradiciones, a music club in Santiago de Cuba, musicians playing guitars, bass, trumpet, bongos, claves, maracas, and the cow bell, and a large crowd dancing rhythms my body just can't perform, and yet all of it entering every pore. I don't know what that club enables me to say about Cuba, but I can feel Cuba physically. They aren't matters of fact (to know Kafka's name or the titles of the Cuban songs isn't enough), but are ways of experiencing Prague or Cuba through more senses, through richer imagery, through much wider emotions.

These are our guides, then: people, books, elements of culture. In no case can we encounter a strange place without being conveyed to it, opened to it through some sort of guide. But, again, does the guide simply provide us with cultural nourishment— providing us with "the best that has been thought or known in the world," with the ease of access to sweetness and light, as Matthew Arnold would have said? Or do we need to be opened, ruptured more violently since what we meet is not "large and light" (in Merrill's phrase) but "doorless, crudely lighted," and "darkly, unimaginably tenanted"?

Hybrid Guides

One of the earliest accounts of Santeria in Cuba is Irene Wright's. She lived there on and off for ten years, writing her account of life in the island in 1910. Cuba is a place she both despises and craves. That "logic and rational sequence are not the rule" seems the root problem, and Wright abandons the island three times "in disgust," but each times she returns, like an alcoholic, she says.[3]

Santeria is one object of her contempt, and it would be easy to see nothing but the racism and condescension that are surely there. She attends a *bembe*. The music's "maddening rhythm" is "unquestioningly African," the images of the *orishas* are in bad taste, their altars decorated with "cheap hangings and tawdry trinkets." Devotees who are seized by a spirit are actors. Behind the religion and its rituals, Wright sees "immoralities," "nefarious mysteries and the trickery of witchcraft."[4]

If denunciation were Wright's sole reaction, that would be one thing. But she is also attracted and intoxicated. It is the turn of the century and she is attending a *bembe,* for God's sake. Not many Caucasian North American women were. She actually observes quite well (well enough that specialists can tell the *orisha* that comes down is Oshun, though Wright herself does not know it), and her account is still used. Murphy sees harmony as the heart of Santeria, but it's possible to see greater difficulty and deeper conflict as spirits and humans interact, something less logical and rational, something more maddening. Murphy's own book highlights three disturbances: the blood sacrifice—for the *orishas* must be fed blood, fresh from the chicken, dove, duck, goat, pig, or dog; the monetary sacrifice (memorably Murphy says one initiation expense is considerable but nonetheless he takes the "plunge," a term I love for it indicates how risky the initiation is; if we plunge, we must know there may be rocks); and the disturbingly ambiguous relationship between humans and *orishas.* After reading Murphy's account of an *asiento,* the ritual where an *orisha* is "seated" in a devotee's head, a student pointed out to me that the spirit is both husband and father to the *santera,* an incestuous relationship that severely troubled my student. We might take the spirit's roles as "additive": both father and husband (and king and teacher and healer). But religious theory often points out that gods are not gods unless they break human concepts, unless they "interrupt" and interrupt absolutely. Perhaps Wright was disgusted in a way that was derogatory and dismissive; perhaps she was disgusted in a way that was perceptive. Perhaps she intuited that the spirit that is the tenant in the heart of Santeria is unimaginable.

But how does she enter this "doorless" heart? With a guide. "When we attended its dance, we were accompanied by a member, a mulatto, the leader of an orchestra well known in Havana."[5] Wright begins from a surface, a musical one that she shares with the orchestra leader who can help Irene Wright depart from that musical surface because he is of it too. He is also mulatto, white as well as black ("not all [of Santeria's] members are negroes. Our guide was, as I have said, a mulatto").[6] The guide meets you on your turf, where the sea meets the land, as you step off the ship, or at the hotel, the home abroad, and he offers the trust of being nearly one of "us." Nearly, but not. The guide must be a hybrid: both of the surface and not and thus capable of facilitating the breaking of that surface. And as it turns out, this orchestra leader is a *santero* of some importance, for "he compelled by a glance" a young woman to prostrate herself before him in a manner that strikes Wright as sexually suggestive. But Wright, herself, has plunged into a "heart" of "fanaticism and ignorance . . . hard to equal anywhere": she has been able to get to that world.[7] And she never would have managed without the guide. Unless she'd trusted this orchestra leader, she never would have experienced the *bembe.* Unless he'd also been a *santero,* she'd never have made it into the room. Irene Wright's surface cannot be ruptured without this guide.

Andrei Codrescu is another hybrid guide. A Romanian American who departed the deeply communist Eastern-bloc country in the 1960s and then reported on the collapse of the Ceausescu regime in the late 1980s, he is well-suited to travel to Cuba in what may be its late communist years, and just before the pope's visit in 1998, and to be a guide through his book *Ay, Cuba!* He is best known for his many commentaries for National Public Radio, where he displays a taste for surrealism and anarchism, an apt quality for a guide who is to help us leave and not really arrive. In addition, his book reveals an extraverted personality and powerful idiosyncrasies that owe a good bit to near-Beats like Henry Miller. What is the ideal personality of a guide? Docile or assertive, an invisible blade or a solid wedge? In 1997, Codrescu visited Cuba, ostensibly for the Havana Film Festival and to see the nation just prior to the pope's visit, but, in fact, not to study anything but to place his idiosyncratic personality in the Cuban cauldron and report on the results. Not only is he a guide for those who read the book in Cuba, but he has many guides himself, for guiding is a very jointed line.

Santeria, for Codrescu, is one of the ingredients in the Cuban pot, and naturally he has a guide, identified only as Pablo. He meets Pablo outside his hotel, a very fine one, the Capri, and while his NPR companions ignore the brash Cuban, Codrescu characteristically enjoys his banter and takes him up on an offer to guide them to "the real Cuba." What appealed to Henry Miller in a guide was the prospect of being hustled, and Codrescu seems to share the taste. It would seem to be an important one for, if our surfaces are not to remain intact, then we have to be "taken." Pablo criticizes Fidel, he jokes cynically about theft, he discomforts Codrescu's companions: he's a "fast-talking hustler," and Codrescu is ambivalent but takes the plunge.

Like Wright's orchestra leader, Pablo is both of Codrescu's world and other. He's quick-witted, politically savvy, and personally engaging, like Codrescu, but when they arrive at his Santeria *padrino's* place, they discover he's a *santero,* too, shifting from his Capri banter to reverence about the *orishas.*

Codrescu participates in two rituals, a divination in which the *padrino* throws a string of cowrie shells to read the American's condition in a process Murphy calls *ire/osugbo.* Codrescu's account is amused, even smug, as he notes the generic diagnoses, and he describes a group of ten onlookers, rooting for the *baba-lawo* to win him over ("all the ten heads watching bobbed up and down with delight and pride in their *santero*").[8] But the transition comes when the *padrino* mentions alcohol and his father. If there is such a thing as sacred time, Codrescu has entered it. He's departed from his skepticism: "The room felt sparklingly alive and Miguel [the *padrino's*] words had found their target. . . . I didn't care who was in the room. I was ready to do whatever the man said."[9]

A cleansing ritual (a *despojo*) follows, and what is notable is that Codrescu is able to submit himself to its strangeness. His cockiness, his ability to engulf all in his capacious personality are gone, and he is off-balance. At the threshold, as it were, he makes final use of his skepticism: "I knew . . . from previous encounters with psychics, that I was an easy mark. Pass a hand over my eyes and I go under like a fish." But up on the roof, as a live rooster is passed over him and then beaten against his bare back, drawing blood, Codrescu submits in a way that seems quite genuine. He shouts out his name when told to, suffers the bloody beating, and ends up feeling "quite good—oddly lighthearted." The ritual has been to free his father's spirit, and, in fact, Codrescu is able to experience pity for the man who had "hung around no longer than six months when he was alive."[10]

Codrescu is in the mold not only of Henry Miller but of Mark Twain, men who pride themselves on not being gullible, who are on their guard against ever being taken for a fool. They live on a surface looking constantly at their feet for evidence the dirt is not worth trusting. Yet Codrescu submits to the *babalawo,* and he even affirms it benefited him. Again, the guide was instrumental, just as he was for Wright. By being an echo of Codrescu himself, Pablo lures him from his world and suspends him in Santeria.

Once when he visited my class, Murphy played a song about a North American who wanders into a Santeria ritual and begins to eat the offerings placed there for Shango. "Please don't eat the banana," the lyrics say, "the banana is for Shango." There is a history, Murphy explains, of outsiders wandering into a *bembe* and becoming prematurely involved in the ritual, eating Shango's banana because they slip into a trance, becoming Shango. It happens to Murphy himself, as he explains in chapter 9 of *Santeria: African Spirits in America*. Once the guide lures the traveler away from his world, anything can happen. One leaves and yet one does not arrive; they're in a "doorless" heart. Wright and Codrescu and even Murphy in that *bembe* do not become *santeros;* they do not arrive in the "large and light" heart. They are there and yet not there. In a word, they are bewildered.

In the jointed line of guides, Codrescu becomes a guide, as well. Murphy and I traveled to Cuba in 2001, and I carried *Ay, Cuba!* along with other books. I read it on the Air Canada flight from Baltimore, wondering if I should be so open about it. There is a strong sense of the forbidden about going to Cuba. When the Canadian immigration officer asked why I was in Toronto, and I told him I was on my way to Cuba, I was puzzled and concerned by his silence. I expected disapproval and discovered that I was carrying it all by myself; the Canadians didn't care. Did Codrescu feed that anxiety or help create it? For he has an acutely skeptical political sensibility, born out of his upbringing in Romania, perhaps, but spreading like water to all else. He knows that harmful political tides move everything, for his inner ear can sense a rolling that most of us never detect. As a guide he may be a caricature, exaggerated and boldly colored, but he also harmonizes with our own suspicious sense that political forces overwhelm and drown.

Codrescu begins *Ay, Cuba!* with the day in 1997 he was asked to go to Cuba for NPR, a day "when communism seemed to have prolapsed forever and the world looked in danger of becoming eternally boring."[11] There follow twenty-seven pages of political framework, American, Cuban, international, and personal. His reporting on the fall of the Ceausescus in Romania; the transformation of Cuba into a tourist haven since the fall of the Soviet Union; anti-Castro bombings in Havana; the day he learned of the Cuban Revolution from Comrade Papadopolou in Transylvania; his ambivalent attitude toward Cuba, Fidel, and Che as a Wayne State University radical in the 1960s; the story of Margaret Randall, an American revolutionary who moved to Cuba in the 1970s and "swallowed hook-line-and-sinker the mind-numbing sloganeering of the regime"; and on and on and on. To be guided by Codrescu is to begin as one of the "many Americans who came of age [in the 1960s and] still have a soft spot for Cuba."[12] True, true.

But is it true that Codrescu is a guide as Pablo and the orchestra leader were? Does he pull us from our surfaces and leave us suspended, neither here nor there? Does he take us to the heart of Cuba that is "doorless"? Perhaps. Although Codrescu engages us with politics—Fidel, Helms-Burton, CIA plots, Bay of Pigs, Che posters—he leads us toward sex. The subtitle of his book is "A Socio-Erotic Journal," perhaps in the mode of Henry Miller. While we can be comfortable enough with his politics, his erotic interests (and those of Cuba) are very discomforting. That is the "doorless" heart.

Codrescu is fascinated with *jineteras,* women who are involved in the sex trade. Cuba is a major destination in sexual tourism, and Codrescu is fascinated with it. Early in his book he tells the story of his friend "Jack," a fifty-two-year-old man who met a fifteen-year-old girl on a trip to Cuba and carries on a long-distance relationship that might well be statutory rape were there sufficient legal reciprocity between the United States and Cuba. This might be the reason that Jack is one of just six pseudonyms in the book. *Jineteras* trade sex for dinners and trips to clubs. They tend to be quite young, and the men who engage them a great deal older. It seems a straightforward barter: women with little to offer but their bodies gain food and some luxuries, and the men buy the company of a young woman and sex. It can certainly engage a man's fantasy, as it does Codrescu's, but it is also quite disturbing.

Sex is one of our surfaces always apt to rupture. Are we ever finished with sex? Delight, desire, surprise, urgency, vulnerability, guilt, intimacy, ecstasy—all are the disturbances of our sexual surfaces, and those surfaces are always trembling with them. The secular theologian Charles Winquist called this "incorrigibility," a wonderful term. There are certain aspects of our experience that are simply incorrigible, always unruly, never tamed or fully domesticated but apt to act out at any moment. God, he says, is the ultimate incorrigibility: God cannot ever be tamed through language but resists all articulation. The body, too, is incorrigible. Whatever we say about the body, it never matches our descriptions of it. It always resists, always demands. It is always other.

At home we have made an uneasy peace with the incorrigibility of sex, but as I wrote in chapter 1, travel means exposing our surfaces to other forces. It means leaving our piece of earth and moving to strange shores upon which we walk uneasily. If we love to travel, we love the experience of our surfaces being broken. Codrescu goes to Cuba to experience sexual disturbance, and if he guides us, that is the "doorless" heart he brings us to.

Murphy and I were in Santiago de Cuba, staying in a *paladare* guest room owned by a very hospitable *santera* who was also a professor of folklore. One evening she and her cousin Fidel took us to Casa de Tradiciones to hear music. It's an ordinary neighborhood, and the club is just a house. The music is rolling when we enter, a mixture of traditional and "romantic" music, as our *santera* put it. Bongos, claves, maracas, bass, guitar, all seemingly on different rhythms, all intertwining and producing an intricate and satisfying musical shape. The crowd is large, filling all of the smallish rooms, and everyone so friendly, nodding to us, smiling. Everyone is in motion.

As I squeeze through the crowd to get to the wooden plank that serves as a bar, I felt a hand on my leg. I turn, and it is a woman sitting against the wall and smiling directly at me. Is it a *jinetera?* I have to confess I found her overture alluring. She was in her early twenties with short dark hair, pretty eyes, and a dress that showed her legs. I thought of Codrescu at once, and felt a sharp mixture of desire, curiosity, and fear. I bought her a rum and then stood with her, trying and failing to communicate, for neither of us knew the other's language. We'd make sounds, we'd lean to get closer to the sounds as though that might help, we'd shrug. After a while she gestured to the back of the building and pulled my arm, and I became afraid, leaving her to go sit next to the band with Murphy, our *santera,* and her cousin.

Where was she leading me? Where was Codrescu? Was she inviting me back to taste the sexual rewards of buying her continued rums or was that a fevered imagination fanned by too much Codrescu? Where had he led me? Did she wish to be my guide? I simply had no idea who she was or what she wanted. I lacked the cultural and linguistic knowledge to know. I was in a space without gravity, without orientation, trying to guess what was going on. Codrescu's book provided me with a story to make sense of a friendly woman in a club, but he also loosed the diffuse power of sex, so I both followed his lead and was overwhelmed by it. He had, in fact, led me to a broken and shifting surface— and I chose to sit by the band and listen to the music, instead.

Guidebooks: In the Hands of German Professors

What does it mean to be led by a guidebook instead of Codrescu? The *Lonely Planet* guide to Cuba has a 350-word discussion of *jineteras,* including an excerpt from a German traveler's letter. The usual sociological and economic perspective is provided (it's "an alternative means of obtaining Western consumer goods"), and yet the guide presents it as nothing other than a clear-cut social problem in which "fat, ugly, old European men" benefit, and "pretty young Cuban women face three years of prison if caught."[13] There is no difficulty there.

The purpose of a guidebook is clarity, not confusion. The *Lonely Planet* guide opens with fifty-three pages of history, geography, climate, economy, culture, and religion, written in high school textbook style, which is to say, an account that presents itself as factual, dispassionate, and purely objective. The message of those pages is that we can enter the country with reliable facts. Contrast the whispered rumors of an ignorant companion or the self-serving comments of a local guide. A guidebook expresses the presumption that one can be objective, factual, dispassionate, and impersonal, none of which qualities are possessed by Codrescu or Pablo or any other human guide.

The young British men taking the Grand Tour in the seventeenth and eighteenth centuries had personal guides—typically, educated clergymen who could guide culturally and morally. The older man had education, maturity, and experience in the countries visited so he could reproduce his own travels in the younger man and nourish the values of importance to his culture. Such guidance was reinforcing, not disruptive.

With the end of the Napoleonic Wars and the improvements in transportation (for instance, the steam powering of ships and rails), mass tourism began. Those now traveling were not inclined to an accompanying clergyman. The *Baedeker* and *Murray* became the substitute.

Baedeker did not produce a guide to Cuba or any other part of Latin America, so let's look at his *Palestine and Syria: Handbook for Travellers*, published in 1894. It is, at least, a guide to a non-European country, and I think Baedeker would guide us to Cuba in a similar way. Our guides, the authors, are three German professors, Dr. Albert Socin, professor of Oriental languages in Leipzig; Dr. Immanuel Benziger of Tübingen; and Professor H. Kiepert of Berlin, "the well-known cartographer."[14] It has to make us laugh a bit, being guided by three German professors—as we'd laugh being guided by a British parson. What adjectives come to mind? Stuffy, pedantic, fastidious, authoritarian? This guidebook replaces all unreliable guides, for, as the preface says, the editor "knows by experience how little reliance can be placed on guidance and information sought from the natives."[15] In the place of Pablo and Codrescu is a group of sober, highly rational, scholarly German professors, seemingly a clear gain.

The *Baedeker* existed to enable travelers to encounter Arnold's "best that has been thought or known in the world," and to do so while avoiding the confusions and dangers along the way. What it promises is that we can leave the familiar without really landing in the unfamiliar; what it avoids is disruption. The first chapter reminds readers that a trip to Palestine and Syria is not for pleasure. It will be tiring, monotonous, inconvenient, and uncomfortable, the professors say. One by one, all dangers are presented and addressed. There will be fleas, lice, mosquitoes, and scorpions, but if the bed straw is taken up and shaken and then the ground sprinkled with water, the fleas can be controlled, as can the other vermin: "Scorpions abound in Syria, but they seldom sting unless irritated." There will be sun stroke, fever, diarrhea, and dysentery, the first avoided with correct headgear, and the others the "consequence . . . of camping on damp ground," the germ theory of disease not having fully taken hold, apparently. Camp on dry ground, avoid mists, and what killed Port in *The Sheltering Sky* won't kill you. Another danger is the weather, to be addressed with proper clothing. Curiously, "if it becomes necessary to camp in the open air, the eyes should be carefully covered, as the dew and the resulting cold are very prejudicial to the eyes." The *Baedeker* provides the names of "medical men . . . in the more important towns."[16]

Perhaps more important to the authors are the financial dangers. The professors point out that travel is not cheap. The prices that travelers can expect to be charged for every item, service, admission, and transport are detailed in multiple currencies. The cost of washing shirt collars (two to three francs a dozen); of hiring a man as a valet (thirty to sixty francs a month); of a night in a hotel, without wine (fifty francs). They hasten to add that Bavarian beer is one to two francs. By following the guide's advice, the traveler will avoid being taken advantage of, and the professors sternly warn against overpaying.

The *Baedeker* presents three competing guides: those provided by Thomas Cook (and other European tour companies); that of the native "dragoman"; and the guidance of the truly local individual, the "Pablo," or the "orchestra leader/*santero*." The *Baedeker* spends little time discussing the European tours. They make the trip "as comfortable as possible" but allow little individual choice for the traveler.[17]

The dragoman is a local man who arranges an entire trip, contracting for horses or camels, tents, food, equipment, guards, watchmen, and local guides. He is the master guide, equivalent of the *Baedeker* itself, looking after all aspects of the journey. What is so fascinating is the *Baedeker's* attempt to manage the dragoman, to minimize the degree to which the traveler submits him or herself to the guide. The *Baedeker* presents a model contract, one that attempts to cover every possible contingency and to eliminate the uncertainty.

The contract binds the dragoman. It's a crucial point. Instead of being subject to him, the traveler binds the master guide in the legal contract. The route is specified "with the utmost possible accuracy," for the dragoman will attempt shortcuts in his own interest.[18] Exact costs are specified, including tips, and "during the journey no demands for bakhshish should be entertained for a moment."[19] Precisely what kind of saddle or bridle is stated in the contract, and the travelers are indemnified against damage to animals or equipment, while the Europeans are also to be allowed to use the horses as much as they please, to take detours of their choice, and to take any steps necessary to guarantee the speed of the trip. What is to be served for breakfast, the services of a "good cook," and the dragoman's own courtesy are also binding elements of the contract.[20]

What is eliminated when the dragoman is "bound" is a negotiation between the traveler and a guide. That is what took place between Irene Wright and the orchestra leader. Suppose she had entered into a *Baedeker* contract with him. She might well have stipulated that there be no encounters with those violations of "logic and rational sequence" that she so despises. She might have insisted there be no "immoralities" or "nefarious mysteries." She never would have been subjected to the *santero*, conveyed into a ritual that was an "astounding confusion of heathenish and Catholic worship" and been able to leave home as she never would have otherwise.[21]

Yet unless we are slaves to the guidebook, we are always suspended between the German professors of our chosen guide (even if they are lefty and hip, as in the case of *Lonely Planet*) and the other guides—local, literary, musical, artistic. The *Baedeker* fears we'll be used by the unreliable and unscrupulous local guide, and indeed we are—fortunately—by all the guides. Each has its own purposes. Codrescu wants us to witness the decay of communism and recall our old admiration of Che. And there near our hotel is the neighborhood Committee for the Defense of the Revolution with an open door and a table and chairs, and I feel a little shiver recalling an ex-student whose family announced its intention to leave Cuba and was compelled to walk a gauntlet of neighbors who pummeled and slapped them. Codrescu also wants us to feel the incorrigible tug of sex. And I do. Ry Cooder's *Buena Vista Social Club* (and the Wim Wenders film of the same name) is a complex and insistently kinetic sound of old musicians in sunny, yellowed, worn porches and rooms, making a music that is older than Fidel. And I feel it as we walk along the colorful and peeling Malecon (seeing Ry in the old convertible in Wenders's film), and wondering what Ruben Gonzalez or Ibrahim Ferrer is sitting behind the chipped railings. And as Murphy and I walk through the narrow streets of Havana Vieja, he points out the beads, the *elekes* of Santeria, designating a devotee of Shango or Oshun, spirits who require and provide. Each guide demands my response, and the traveler is broken in unequal pieces. No *Baedeker* or *Lonely Planet* could pull them together again.

A guidebook is designed to prevent or minimize the leaving of your own surfaces. It is not a hybrid. It is regrettably, in a word, reliable. Fortunately, it often fails.

◆ ● ◆

We were in Maria Galban's home, a twelve-foot-square room with a tiny adjoining kitchen holding a tiny propane stove and, separated by a curtain, a toilet. An old Russian TV is in the room and no other luxuries unless you count her shrine, a very diverse collection of soup tureens and dolls and statues and beads. On her stove, Maria is cooking turkey and rice, sweet potatoes, and French fries. Joe and I bought the food and beer, too, and when it is done, Maria serves it to Lied and Elton and us. She says she has eaten earlier. On the open wooden steps going to the room above lounges her son, in his mid-twenties, smoking a cigar from the box Maria sold me, pausing now and then to study it, and looking utterly content. Maria begins to tell stories from Santeria, as though they were family lore. In a Spanish I do not understand and Joe and Elton translate, she talks about Shango's two wives, Oya and Oshun, how one (I do not understand which) cut off her ear to attract Shango.

I have been brought to a home in Matanzas where I am paradoxically both utterly far from home and at home. During the day, Mother's Day, as it happens, Maria has declared that she is Joe's mother, which is a gesture of hospitality and a statement of spiritual relation, for a *Madrina* is a spiritual guide in Santeria. Joe has had a *Madrina* in the past, and he tells me later that he feels drawn to becoming Maria's godson. It is a religion I do not belong to and, frankly, will never really understand. I cannot even say that I feel emotionally drawn to it. But I do feel Maria's warmth, and I feel happy in her home. Occasionally I glance out the door, into the night, and wonder how I managed to get here, so "deeply" in the heart of Cuba.

SEVEN Street People

I RETURNED TO THE NETHERLANDS TWENTY-EIGHT YEARS AFTER
first going there as an exchange student, seeing the same orange
roofs as the plane approached landing, driving past the same flat
fields, reading signs written in a language that was open where
all others but English are closed to me. It was a sense both of going
and of going back. There is no place I feel more at home than the
Netherlands due to that year's residence. The very color of the
bricks, the width of the bicycle paths, the contents of a living room
glimpsed through a window are simply embedded in my nerves,
as though our physical stuff were made of a place we have lived
and to return to that place is to reawaken the rightness of being
there. Yes, my body said, that is the odor of October, that is the
shape of the Friday fish market, that is the clatter of feet in a narrow stone street just behind St. Bavo's.

Joseph Brodsky wrote that he lives from his nerves, not from principles, meaning that we operate according to what we feel instead of from rational principles. Our nerve endings guide us through the world with all of their imprecision and wildness though we might wish we were on the iron rails of abstract principles. Places make those nerves.

We had been in the Netherlands for only a few days, staying with friends in Maastricht, when my daughter said that Holland seemed so "weird." It was true. What was so uncanny was that this place was not only so familiar but so strange at the same time, a feeling that I remembered from my original stay. People who looked so much like the people we lived among every day but with another language coming from their lips. Places that are so recognizably homes, and yet in ways that are almost too subtle to name, those homes just crucially "off." Every place was a place we knew—streets, stores, schools—and yet not. That the familiar could also be strange. That the places which place us— that root and establish us—that those places could displace us by being simultaneously familiar and strange. That is what I experienced in this most familiar of foreign places, as my children did, too.

Walking but Never Arriving

The greatest American travelers, the models for all who followed, were Walt Whitman and Henry David Thoreau. This chapter will discuss the places that we visit when we travel, although both Whitman and Thoreau despised places, preferring open spaces instead. Both men were prodigious walkers. Thoreau left his home each day for at least a four-hour walk and sometimes took to the countryside for days on end. Whitman lived in more urban environments—Brooklyn, Manhattan, Washington, D.C.— but wrote hymns to the open road. Travel involves leaving a place— home. It also involves arriving someplace. So if Thoreau and Whitman give us a model of travel in which we do not go places, we are left with a riddle: when is a place not a place? How can the places travelers visit not be places at all? The answer is, when they are particularly unstable places, never places where we can rest.

We never simply go to Paris or Cairo or Jerusalem. Instead we go to a series of hotels, restaurants, cafés, and "sights": museums, churches, mosques, and other houses of worship, none of which is "ours," each of which is worthy of distrust, where we find disease or fraud, or more power than we can withstand. Above all we walk the foreign streets, which typify all of the places of travel, for each is a place of transit, a place in motion.

The anthem for American traveling—the original *On the Road*—is Whitman's "Song of the Open Road," written in 1856.[1] The theme is similar to what we've seen in Henry Miller, Paul Bowles, Alphonso Lingis, Mary Oliver, and others: the need to leave rather than the need to arrive.

> Afoot and light-hearted, I take to the open road,
> Healthy, free, the world before me,
> The long brown path before me, leading wherever I choose.

It's hard to match that openness, facing forward to a road that has no impediments, no boundaries, no destinations.

Whitman wants an open road because he loathes home. We do not often think of Whitman being troubled. He is the poet of the blue-sky temperament, as William James puts it. And yet when Whitman describes the place from which travelers depart, it is a "dark confinement" in which we feel a "secret loathing and despair."

His father is reported to have been stern, violent, and manipulative, and as a child, Whitman says, he had a "yearning and swelling heart."[2] In "Song of the Open Road," Whitman describes us as living in disguise in our homes, for we are compelled to conceal and to obey. We dress and act conventionally; we are "polite and bland." And yet we are secretly tortured and slowly expiring, for we speak "not a syllable" of ourselves.

It is as though the boundaries that exist around places—the walls of the houses, the fences around the yards, the city limits—were iron bands around Whitman's very throat. Laws and authorities, customs and conventions, clothing and etiquette, all have the rigid boundaries that do not allow for the eccentric or the out-of-bounds—for those who are gay, like Whitman, for instance, but for all humans, in fact.

Whitman wants "great draughts of space." What a wonderful phrase: a great vivifying drink of space, space that will enable us to expand into the enormous song of the self. The open road, he says, allows the "efflux," the flow and movement of the self, a gaseous ever-spreading that is the antithesis of dark confinement. And so as Whitman travels on this "open road," he scarcely stops:

> However sweet these laid-up stores—however convenient
>   this dwelling, we cannot remain here;
> However shelter'd this port, and however calm these waters,
>   we must not anchor here;
> . . . .
> You but arrive at the city to which you were destin'd—you
>   hardly settle yourself to satisfaction, before you are call'd
>   by an irresistible call to depart.

What, then, is the "place" we go to when we travel? For arriving is inevitable to travel; visiting and seeing are vital to travel. We go to France or India or Morocco or Ghana. We are asked, "Where are you going?" We say, "I am going to the Yucatan." We arrive, and we begin to walk through Fez, looking and listening and speaking. We set our bags down in the small hotel and sit there, in Accra. Can we be travelers in the Whitman mold and go anywhere?

The first city I arrived at after dark was Salt Lake City. I was twenty years old, hitchhiking across the country with my friend Danny, and we'd caught a ride in a van from Nebraska right to Seattle, as lucky a ride as we could have gotten. Two large bearded guys with tattoos were in the front, the sort of guys who intimidated college kids from the East, so we sprawled in the carpeted back and dozed away the hundreds and hundreds of miles. Sometime in the night we came over the Golden Pass, and I looked below us at Salt Lake City, spread and lit like the Milky Way itself, constellations of lights but right there, just below us, as though an entire galaxy of discoveries were just a few minutes' drive away.

I never arrived in Salt Lake. The guys drove right past the city and on into the western night. But maybe, in fact, looking down from the Golden Pass was as close as we ever come to arriving. Maybe we never get to such places as "Salt Lake City" or "Delhi" or "Jerusalem" or "Tangier."

◆ ● ◆

Susan Brind Morrow goes to Cairo in 1989. What does that mean? What is a place, anyway? Well, perhaps the most important thing to notice in reading her account is that she never goes to "Cairo." In fact, we never go to Prague or Accra, either. Our experience cannot encompass a city. She comes into the city from the airport and never sees "Cairo": She sees, instead, donkey carts and women in Islamic dress, cripples, men in Western clothes, cars. She gets to the river at Giza and descends past a blue iron gate to a friend named Galal, who jumps off an old paddleboat and embraces her. Where is this "Cairo"?

To watch Morrow in Cairo is to watch her movements among places that are much smaller than a city, places that she can observe directly. She can be on a staircase to the river; she can be on a stretch of road. She fails to be in Cairo.

In fact, here she is, returning to Cairo after a visit with her husband outside of Egypt: "I come into Cairo disoriented, exhausted and feeling like I should leave immediately. I stay. And gradually over the days I begin to remember the city."[3] How does she remember? Does she come to be in Cairo? No.

She is neither situated in Cairo, nor does she go into the "open" as Whitman does. Instead she moves from place to place. That is the point. To be in Cairo is to move from place to place. She goes under the Azhar flyway to a café, Feeshaway's, and then, after a glass of mint tea, she goes back through the tourist bazaar, through craft streets to the oldest mosque in Cairo, the Ibn Tulun. Later she goes to the Windsor Hotel, where she meets a friend, David, who takes her to still other places, "back dirt alleys," "the concrete shells of unfinished apartment buildings," and the Saida Zeneb, a mosque.[4] Travel is to places, but it's a movement among multiple ones that are within our field of vision, our range of hearing, of touch, and of smell.

So is Whitman wrong? Is travel not to the "open road" but to the local place? Or is Morrow not in the tradition of Whitman and Thoreau? Look at what she says of her friend David. In his work as an urban planner and in his travels, he has wondered, "What holds people together when everything around them is falling apart?" This expert in places, planner of urban places has no answer to that question, for all of his experience of places has been of decay and multiplicity, not of firm walls, not of strong centers, not of limits and authorities and all the rest that terrified Whitman and caused him to flee to the open road. To travel to the thousands of places of Cairo is to travel to mere juxtaposition and conjunction, not to any single constraining "Cairo" that would be the "dark confinement" that causes Whitman loathing and despair. As Morrow puts it, Cairo is a "mess," not a place we need to escape because it is authoritarian. In being a mess, the multiple places of Cairo are an open road.

But what triggered Whitman's loathing and despair wasn't "Brooklyn" or "America," not some place-name: it was home that caused his despair. The local places of home are exactly what are wrong: Whitman mentioned specific loathed places, the parlors, the streets, the railway cars, the steamboats, the dining rooms, and the bedrooms. There—no, here—is where we suffer "dark confinement." Home is the problem place.

Poet James Merrill writes of a similar predicament. In fact, nearly all travelers write of the need to leave home, but Merrill writes of it especially well. Let me retell "The Friend of the Fourth Decade" as a story instead of presenting it as a poem.[5] He recounts a conversation with a friend who is weary of understanding all that he hears—"the tones, the overtones." He feels contempt for his language, his home, and himself. He wants to leave. In effect he stands in Whitman's doorway, facing the open road. The friend has an artful metaphor for the experience of leaving: he places postcards in water to soak off the stamps and to dissolve the words. The stamps float loose, and the photographs remain, but the inky words slowly swirl clean away, as do the relationships with those who sent the cards, his mother, great-uncle, and friend. Home can, in other words, be left. Sending postcards—traveling—is a way of dissolving words and home. Merrill's friend later writes him from somewhere in North Africa or the Middle East (perhaps it is Susan Brind Morrow's Cairo—wouldn't that be nice?) where he now feels indestructible. What has threatened him at home is utterly gone. Like Whitman, he is "strong and content" once he has left. But what has really changed? At the start of the poem he was in a café with Merrill, but then he writes to Merrill as he drinks sweet tea in that foreign city. He is exploited by merchants as he was by his own language and culture. Whitman's parlors, streets, railway cars, steamboats, dining rooms, and bedrooms exist on the road as well as in our town. But the difference, of course, is that they are not "ours"; we are not "home." Being in a place at home and a place away are not at all identical. We are never captured by the foreign café or even the foreign merchants.

At the end of the poem, Merrill has a dream of his friend, his entire civilization unwound from him, as Whitman would like a confining, loathsome home to be torn down, wall by wall. Merrill points to his friend's face: "See his eyes darken in bewilderment— No, in joy—." When we leave our home and are in a place that is not a place, inevitably there is bewilderment—and, of course (I would say), we love that confusion.

Whitman is wary of any place that might become a home. He tells us not to stop and stay while on the open road. "We must not stop here! However sweet . . . however shelter'd . . . however calm . . . however welcome." And Morrow doesn't stop, even though she loves Cairo, knows it well, has fast friends there, and knows the language intimately. Not only does she move from place to place (bazaar to café to mosque to hotel to alleys, unfinished buildings, and another mosque), but none of them is really her place. If one does become her place, then she is a resident and not a traveler at all. Then she would be home and—

according to Whitman—would need to leave home again. When we travel, we visit places, but all of them are "open" because none of them is home. Like Merrill's friend, in the places of travel, our eyes inevitably "darken in bewilderment" because we have lost our homes.

But there is more. Susan Brind Morrow may not be in "Cairo," as I claim. She may only be able to present us with smaller, local places, places where she can see and sit and speak and smell, but all of those places are affected by being "in Cairo." Being in Cairo makes them even less her own.

I was near a fire, squatting on my heels and eating curry with my fingers, while men with great whirls of cloth around their bodies and heads squatted and ate, too, all of us facing out into an utterly black darkness. I understood nothing of their language. There were noises out there, in the dark, and then men walked up, men carrying rifles, men wrapped in cloth, too, and with great beards. What was this "place"? Ground, fire, darkness, tribal men, curry? I was not home. That was for sure. I was bewildered. Yes. But I was also in "Baluchistan," and that had an effect on where I was. All I ever knew of Baluchistan came from the words of other travelers and from encyclopedias once I returned, that it was a place that colonial borders did not respect, like Kurdistan, a place that spanned parts of Iran, Afghanistan, and Pakistan. All I knew then was that it was the "place" where I was, and that it was not a "place" like "Iran," "Afghanistan," and "Pakistan" that were on maps and in school curricula. This small area of firelight and men in robes and fighters out of the dark spread very indefinitely into "Baluchistan."

The places that exceed our senses still work on our sense of place, and they do so both in a way that calms and one that disturbs. If I awaken from a nap in the afternoon, from one of those deep sleeps that leaves me wondering just who and where I am when my eyes open, it can be very orienting to think at last, "Oh, right, this is Washington." But when I was in a café above a sidewalk drinking a beer with Joe Murphy, he said, "Bud, we're in Cuba!" The sidewalk, the table, the beer, the people were all disfigured by "Cuba." We couldn't quite believe it. This? Cuba?! Henry Miller is in Athens, and after saying goodnight to friends, he walks around "in the dazzling starlight, repeating to myself as if it were an incantation: 'you are in another part of the world, in another latitude, you are in Greece, in Greece, do you understand?'"[6] As travelers, foreigners, we just can't comprehend Cuba or Greece. Cafés or streets or starlight or curries are distorted, overawed, even distended into myth by "Cuba," "Greece," "Baluchistan." Susan Brind Morrow frequently says that she is in "Um a Dunya, Mother of the World," the Arabic name for Cairo. Does that place calm or disturb the streets, stairways, rivers, boats, bazaars, hotels, alleys, and mosques?

Religious Space

Space is utterly neutral in science. Places are neutral, as are persons, for that matter. It makes no difference where an experiment is performed. In fact, the electrolysis of water, for instance, must be able to take place in any laboratory, not just in a lucky lab or in American labs or in labs staffed by Christians or Republicans or graduates of MIT. The space might be affected by the sort of gases present in the laboratory or by the atmospheric pressure—whether the lab is on the top of the Himalayas or at sea level—but not by the space itself.

The religious view of space is very different. For religion, some space is neutral but some is sacred, and that sacred space is utterly different. The sacrality of space is not produced by any scientific means—it is not the gases in the atmosphere or the barometric pressure, not the presence of radiation or of anything else in the space in a measurable sense. Sacred space is much more like the "lucky" lab or the "American" or "Christian" one. The space is experienced as sacred, and that has crucial consequences. The distance between inside and outside a mosque, church, synagogue, or temple is not measurable in feet or inches but in an absolute change. In one way of looking at it, inside is and outside is not. Sacred space is utterly real, and neutral space is comparatively unreal and without value. Who we are and what we may and must do are utterly different from inside to out. Inside, in fact, I know just who I am in the most powerful sense. In the parking lot, my identity may be certified by my driver's license, at the airport by my passport, in the drugstore by my prescription card or a credit card, but in the sacred space those identities are worthless. My identity is instead founded on the God who is (or the Gods who are), a motto of identity that transcends, negates, or alone validates all others. In the most extreme case, there are no degrees of such reality. One is or one is not, and sacred space alone is.

I was once in Holy Sepulcher Church in Jerusalem, the traditional site of the crucifixion, entombment, and resurrection according to some Christian traditions. It is a place of many places, the balcony to one side being where some Christians believe the crucifixion took place; a church within the church being the site of Jesus's tomb. There is no rigid order to the church: it is not symmetrical; the most sacred sites are not logically arranged. The building itself is just a kind of a canopy to the sacred places. I stood near the Armenian half of the tomb and watched an old woman, dressed entirely in black, her hand touching the wall of the chapel, the very place where Jesus lay dead, her eyes closed and in utter thrall. It was a mesmerizing sight of what must have been a profound religious experience for that woman. She was in contact with the utterly real, the divine, where Jesus himself rose from the dead. With an absolute lodestone, the woman knew where and who she was. It is the same in all traditionally sacred places.

And yet, there are analogous spaces for all of us. A sacred space for many is the home. Scientifically considered, it differs not at all from the home beside it, except in particulars such as floor plan, colors, decoration. And yet those homes are not interchangeable, as they ought to be in science. To say one space feels more "real" than the other is ludicrous, rationally. And yet, we all feel that our homes have more power to shelter, vivify, nourish. We trudge home after a trying day and close the door behind us, and we may feel as empowered as the Armenian woman in Holy Sepulcher Church. Other places may also provide us with a sense of reality, identity, orientation: the restaurant where we met the man or woman we love; the hospital room where we sat when our father died; the grandmother's house where all childhood vacations were spent; the field we accidentally set afire; the hillside behind the art institute where we hiked to be alone. According to religious theory, such places have religious—that is to say, overpowering—significance. Just as a traditionally sacred place—a Jerusalem, a Mecca, a Benares, an Ile Ife—have the power to found the world, so do these more modest places create the world for an individual.

And yet, when we travel we leave those places. We leave home; we leave our world. We enter chaos.

Homeless Places

If we look at the places where travelers go, none of them are places they fully belong, and yet all are places of temporary importance. We come and we go in those places. We and they are restless. We belong and are strangers. We are and we are not. There are four major places of travel: the hotel, the site (of religious, cultural, or historical interest), the street, and the traveler him- or herself.

HOTELS

I have a friend who recently bought a house and moved into it. The friend puzzled me because he chose to live in a town very far from where he works, a town in which he knows no one, a town without a character. Why would he choose that place above others to have as his central place, his home? Then I remembered just how often this friend had moved: in the six years I've known him he has lived in a dozen or more apartments. He seems nomadic, unrooted by place. If we are defined by our places—if someone is a Virginian or a New Yorker, if someone is Korean or Russian—then being nomadic alters our being. It makes our identity rootless.

One of the most plaintive lines from literature is by Faulkner in *As I Lay Dying*. Darl, the unloved son of the demanding mother, is moving through the countryside as the family takes the body of that vindictive mother, Addie, to its final resting place. As he lies emptying himself for sleep, he declares, "How often have I lain beneath rain on a strange roof, thinking of home."[7] Darl has no family, no love, and no home. He is without a place. He has only places.

When we travel that is precisely what we do to ourselves. We become Darl. We have a new home every night—a new bed, a new room, a new shelter. A new place to entrust ourselves as we lose consciousness and become most vulnerable. Can a hotel really be trustworthy? Can we really sleep all that well?

I was riding through the night across the Peloponnesus, toward Athens. In the driver's seat was a wealthy young Turk, Kamuran, and his friend beside him, returning from a ski trip to Switzerland. An old Italian on the ferry from Bari had gotten me this ride, a real find: it would take me all the way to Istanbul. There were two slight costs. Hours ahead when we would cross into Turkey, Kamuran would ask me to carry a package for him. Without knowing what was in the brown paper-bound bundle, I would put it into my backpack and carry it across the border. Was it a bundle of clothes? That's what it looked like. Was it gifts he just didn't want to pay duty on? Or was it drugs? I had no idea and not enough sense to ask.

He also asked me to loan him some cash for the drive across Greece, explaining that, due to the hostility between Turkey and Greece, he couldn't exchange his Turkish lira for drachmas. It was 1974, and that is how it was. Wouldn't I loan him a couple of hundred dollars? Again I didn't ask, but dug into the pouch under my shirt to count my money.

Those concealed cloth bags are a fixture of my travel, secret places to hold that most valuable object, money, for it is well known that the world is teeming with thieves skilled in picking pockets and utterly halting a trip. So there must be a hand-sewn cloth bag held close to the heart and containing traveler's checks. There is the innermost place of safety.

As the shadows of Greece flashed by, in the back seat of his leather-seated Rover, I counted my checks and was confused.

Here and there the numbered sequence was interrupted, a number or two skipped, then all proceeded fine, another skipped number or two, then nothing wrong again. I consulted my journal with its careful account of checks cashed, date and place, and as it became 2 a.m. then 3 a.m. then 4, I tried to reconstruct what had happened. It gradually took focus through the blur of sleeplessness and travel: I remembered my hotel room in Bari with a convenient peg for my clothes right by the door and, above it, an open window onto the hall. The image woke me, shook me, alarmed me. I all but saw the hand reach in, enter my room, my place, and take that money, that fuel for getting me to India and back. A clever thief stole only a few checks so I would be across the Ionian Sea by the time I realized he had done his work. From the backseat of Kamuran's car, I saw the trip break down and halt because of that break in the wall of my room, my place.

To travel is to need one place above all others: a temporary home, a hotel. It is the bed where we can sleep, the door we can close and lock. And yet, the hotel is not home. It is also a foreign place. It is where we are found by the foreign and most powerfully challenged and affected. It finds us where we sleep.

We haven't discussed Mark Twain's travels since chapter 4, when we watched the thirty-two-year-old author's passage across the Atlantic in the winter of 1867 aboard the *Quaker City*. His tour of Europe and the Holy Land involved all the principal places of travel—hotels, restaurants, cultural sites, and streets—though he has less to say of the first of those than the others. He simply stays in the hotel less than many travelers, being so active and so social, scouring a city with his pals to find what is worthy of scrutiny, humor, and scorn. Twain is a man of streets, not hotel rooms.

In a hotel, what he cares about is soap. He seldom finds it. He tells about his searches for soap, his tirades to the hotel management about soap, the low quality of the soap that is finally provided. He comments frequently on the personal hygiene of the French, Italians, Greeks, Turks, and others, not finding it to his satisfaction. One wonders about this attention to cleanliness that is like a similar attention in many travelers: those foreigners smell, we say. How can we stay clean and healthy? Will we be somehow contaminated by these foreign places? For to be home is to be unsullied and to be abroad is to risk microbes and filth.

But this is just what makes a hotel not a home: one meets more than the bell captain and the concierge and intriguing strangers in the hotel bar. We are staying in a bed that another person has slept in just hours earlier. And before him, another. And before her, others. Hundreds of people have slept in that bed. Thousands. Every year local TV news stations delight in revealing just how dirty those sheets are, too. They bring in special scopes that show the semen and blood still on the sheets and covers. Fluorescent light can reveal mysterious stains in the carpets and chairs. We don't need any assistance to smell the cigarette smoke or to see the insects. Bacteria teem.

As we travel, our beds are the beds of hundreds of strangers, of microbes and chemicals, of molds and fungi. A hotel room is not, in fact, a sanctuary but a place for us to meet those others, their traces, their effects. A hotel is a place of literal and figurative infection.

Alphonso Lingis, the philosophy professor I discussed earlier, meets people in his hotels, and, unlike Twain, he does not try to disinfect. In his querulous way, he meets a soldier hostile to Corazon Aquino, the American-supported champion of democracy in the Philippines, and brings him up to his room, despite the discouragement of the hotel security guard. There is nothing polite and nothing subservient about the soldier, who undresses and flexes his muscles and boasts of his invulnerability due to an amulet. He is stronger than Lingis, and physically intimidating, and bitterly complains of American influence in the country. "One day we will have to fight the Americans," he declares. "The American is very big, and I am very small. He makes a bigger target for my bullet than I make for his."[8]

At home we can see such a man on television or in the newspapers, and he is fully tamed by the media that present him. The news anchor makes it clear that such a soldier is hostile to our values. He would inevitably be followed in the news by footage of cheering crowds wearing the yellow of Aquino's political party. Only in the Philippines can one be confronted by the soldier, and if, like Lingis, we were to bring him to our hotel room, we would be putting ourselves at risk in a very powerful way.

In hotel rooms we encounter noisy neighbors or the buzz of traffic or the banging of drums. My room in Tangier was in the medina, and as I went to sleep each night, the city seemed to come to life, especially with a mysterious banging of drums. In the morning I went to the roof to see if I could spot the source—a festival or a clearing with evidence there had been a crowd, but there was nothing. And the next midnight there was more drumming and what might have been chanting, and a restless night of heat and mosquitoes, other visitors to my room.

To check into a hotel is to realize that we must be accepted, that these "homes" regard us with suspicion. In Dhaka, Bangladesh, Lingis enters a hotel tired after a long trip and in a bad mood. The clerk wants the slightly interrogating information that travelers must provide: name, nationality, religion, where Lingis has arrived from and where he is going. Lingis is not a "good" traveler, as Mark Twain isn't, and he lets his irritation show. For "destination," he scrawls "moon" in big letters, and the clerk calls the guards, who throw him out.

Twain and what he liked to call the "pilgrims" are trailed by a gunboat when they arrive in Livorno, on the coast of Tuscany, and they arouse suspicion again in Capri, where not only are they boarded and questioned, but a policeman remains on the *Quaker City* for their entire stay. Twain usually burlesques a political suspicion, writing that the police "have decided at last that we are a battalion of incendiary, bloodthirsty Garibaldians in disguise!"[9] Insurgency may have been a concern in Italy for these were unstable years, but of equal or greater concern was the fear of epidemics in a number of ports. Travelers not only encounter local diseases, they bring them, and the places of interaction are also places of contagion. As I wrote an early version of this chapter, the SARS epidemic was of anxious concern in much of the world, and it was travelers who carried it from place to place. As people of apparent Middle Eastern descent were particularly scrutinized post–September 11, so those of East Asian appearance were looked at warily in 2003. It is in the places of encounter, the places where the inhabitants shift, the places of exchange that contagion takes place. What is odd and remarkable is that we are attracted to those places. Like most others, I love staying in a hotel.

SITES

We check into a hotel, we study the guidebook, we eat a meal in the morning, and then we spend our entire day visiting the sights, places where residents seldom go, or, if they do, they visit as participants, not observers. Museums, monuments, fountains, ruins, places of worship, historical sites. These are the places of "commerce with the ancients," where we the build the "better self" that we usually associate with travel. We have read Victor Hugo or seen one of the films featuring Notre Dame Cathedral or studied it in Art History 101. Its West End facade is familiar to us, as are its flying buttresses, even if we'd paid little conscious attention to it, and we have associations of beauty or romance. These are places like "Cairo" or "Prague," places we have experienced culturally but not directly, places that serve to orient us, for better or worse. We are, we think, better, larger for having seen the actual Notre Dame.

Mark Twain and his companions visit exactly those sites. When he tells his readers about the cathedral, it's the history he recounts, and we might see him with his *Murray Guide* (which he does carry) in his hand as he walks around the cathedral and then as he writes the newspaper account that would later be gathered into *Innocents Abroad*. As he says, "We have striven hard to learn. We have had some success."[10] Telling us about Notre Dame means telling us how much it looks like the pictures he has seen. It means telling us about the Patriarch of Jerusalem recruiting for a crusade from the cathedral, about the St. Bartholomew's Day Massacre, the Reign of Terror in the French Revolution, and the rise of Napoleon. To see that cathedral is to take in history and culture, for Twain as for Matthew Arnold. It is to make us the size of all those places and all their history, added together. We would become a grand, imperial, and monumental self.

If we require orientation, as I claimed in the first chapter, places are especially effective in providing it. We need to know who we are, where we are, and where we are going. A monumental place emphatically situates us with all of its tonnage. I teach a course on autobiography, on the creation of a self that is accomplished by what we say of our life—our life story. Out of the countless details of a life, we select a finite number to present "us," our life. Which details we select are crucial. We often choose to begin from our birth, for instance, writing, "I was born on September 22," which makes a self that has a start. It may seem inevitable, for we all are born, we might say. What else can we do but start from the beginning? But there are alternatives. In my course, I ask my students to write a one-page autobiography, forcing them to make the hard choice of selecting what most crucially is them. While many begin "from the beginning," not all do. One student, for instance, wrote his entire autobiography about an afternoon when he was ten years old. Some boys stole a ball he was playing with, and his mother came and got it back. That was it. That was his autobiography. That was who he was: the boy whose mother rescued him from the bullies. He didn't begin on a date on the calendar. He was the rescued son.

But the most common element in our autobiographies is not the date of our birth for some omit that beginning of the self. A more common element is place. We mention where we were born, where we lived as a child, where we moved to at age seven, and then where we went to college, where we moved for our first job, where we were married, where our children were born. And on and on. If we assume that our autobiographies write a self, our selves are made of places. Such building is highly effective. We are made of New York or Chicago or Pottstown, Pennsylvania, or Laramie, Wyoming. We are further constructed of a suburb or a neighborhood, Red Bank or Evanston or Great Neck or Silver Spring. We add Michigan State or Columbia or Lewis and Clark or Colorado College. And our selves are larger and larger, more and more substantial, as though the self were a steadily expanding city, absorbing more and more territory, on its way to being a megalopolis at death.

I was lying on the physical therapist's table one day, listening to her vacation plans, perhaps for Latin America, perhaps for Morocco. And as I heard myself giving vacation advice, mentioning Tangier and Fez and Marrakesh, then the Yucatan and Cuba, finally adding Athens and Delphi and Corinth and Santorini, I could feel like Henry Miller's colossus, expansive, encompassing, large. The postcolonialists might denounce the imperialism of it, and I can, in fact, hear the pompous sage advice of someone like Paul Theroux: one should be made of a solid structure of the great cities, Paris, Rome, Jerusalem, Delhi, St. Petersburg, and all their finest sites, but also have the life-giving places of great vitality, Sienna and Benares, Angkor Wat and Machu Picchu. But don't neglect the places that give us color and texture, Provence and Kyoto and East Africa and Havana. As though we were wealthy collectors of art or imperialist powers. And yet we are made by places, and it isn't all imperialism. But what is distinctive of the travelers we have been looking at in this book is that they do not only add; they subtract.

Mark Twain, like many, does not let us rest satisfied with our enlarged self. He does not let a place simply be an edifice signifying how well situated we have become or how grand. Nietzsche famously wrote, "the more mistrust, the more philosophy," and Twain (like all the others in this study) wholeheartedly agrees. He wants to lift the edges of these important places and show us the dirt beneath, usually due to the ignoble motive that made them. He wants to amuse us by showing that the place is not really so grand. So he points out that those past events brushed past Notre Dame Cathedral like birds, and the present will, as well. He reduces the monumental events of history to mere fluff. I must confess that I sometimes enjoy discomforting my students in a similar way, by pointing out that we are unjustified in assuming that what we take for granted will always exist. It is not only communism that fell, as feudalism did or the Hanseatic League; democracy will, too, someday, as will capitalism. Nothing is forever, though it is a very distressing thought, and one that Twain makes often in the presence of monuments that pretend to eternity.

Even more to Twain's taste is the fact that the Duke of Burgundy paid for a section of the cathedral in order to gain absolution for assassinating the Duke of Orleans. He loves to point out the base motives that masquerade as piety. Twain is an investigative journalist, discovering fraud, self-interest, greed, and lust everyplace he can. P. T. Barnum was not the only one who knew that there was a sucker born every minute. Twain never saw a tourist site that wasn't eaten away with the secret rust of fraud, suckering the gullible.

Churches especially attract Twain's antipapist eye. They are easy targets for him. He mocks the priests who attend them, every one of them "fat and serene."[11] He relishes absurd claims about relics, declaring that he has seen about a keg of nails from the true cross just in Genoa alone, and sufficient bone from St. Denis in France to duplicate him. But the "wretchedest of all the religious impostures" is the liquefying blood of St. Januarius in Naples for it mysteriously transforms from solid to liquid in precisely the amount of time it takes to collect offerings from the congregation: in a small crowd it liquefies quickly and in a large one it patiently takes a longer time. His succinct attitude: "Splendid legend, splendid lie, drive on."[12]

Twain sweeps through Europe and the Middle East like the honest wind of common sense, refusing to be bamboozled. It is not only the religious fraud that he exposes—revealing "happy, cheerful, contented ignorance, superstition, degradation, poverty, indolence, and everlasting unaspiring worthlessness" (whew!)— but artistic fraud, too.[13] He is a bit like those who insist that children can drip paint as well as Jackson Pollock. Twain has been taught that Michelangelo, Rubens, da Vinci, Raphael, and the other masters are to be admired, but, frankly, he doesn't believe it. In Milan, he sees artists copying *The Last Supper,* and he is certain the copies are better than the decayed original. In the Vatican, he proposes that any painting set apart in its own gallery would be considered the better painting so he is skeptical of the ones so honored. Are they really better? Twain is the homespun man forever suspicious that he is being taken by the dandies, and he refuses to be fooled. "It may be thought that I am prejudiced," he says. "Perhaps I am. I would be ashamed of myself if I were not."[14] And yet Twain does not think for a moment that his is mere prejudice: he gives us honest common sense.

We think of a cultural site as a place that anchors a culture (and a self) for what could be more solid? It is made of marble, stone, granite. It does not shift or change. It does not respond to whims or weather. And yet it does not take much for us to be like Twain and see the human motives that underlie all of that stone—that require the stone, in fact. We all may wonder (as Twain does) at all that gold in the midst of considerable poverty. We may all suspect there may have been some ruthlessness that accounts for both the general's stature and his statue. We may be skeptical of proclamations of virtue or other greatness. The very insistence on permanence and importance may cause us to be skeptical. If it really does represent "the best that has been known and thought," then why all the marble coercion?

A traveler cannot help be an iconoclast, away from home where the icons are so much more fragile. It is so much easier to ridicule a pompous monument in Teheran than in Washington, D.C., or to scoff at the ornate uniforms on the soldiers guarding a tomb in Delhi when those at Arlington seem so right. But we may bring the habit home. The places that are to situate us may, instead, displace us.

Mark Twain displaces us through skepticism. Henry Miller displaces us by being so extravagantly receptive. Places overpower him. Instead of the educational model in which we enlarge ourselves by possessing so many grand places, Miller is possessed by places, though in such an idiosyncratic and maniacal way that there are at least equal parts Miller and place.

The best may be Mycenae, the palace and tomb of Agamemnon. This, too, is a place steeped in history and literature, and Miller reminds us just as every traveler would that it is legendary.

Being there is like being present in the *Iliad:* Agamemnon's decision to go to war against Troy to rescue Helen, the wife of his brother, Menelaus. Agamemnon's sacrifice of his daughter, Iphigenia, in order to gain a favorable wind to sail to Troy, and then, on his return, his own murder at the hands of his wife, Clytemnestra, herself then the victim of their son, Orestes. There are few places more thick with the blend of Western history and legend. The full list of literary and artistic works flowing from this gushing source of hubris, vengeance, intrigue, honor, and fate would take pages and pages. Other than the Oedipus story or that of Odysseus (to which it is connected and which echoes it in reverse), is there any to rival it? Mycenae ought to be the travel destination par excellence.

On the other hand, Henry Miller's presentation would be graded "F" by Matthew Arnold or any other teacher, myself (sadly) included. His account in *The Colossus of Maroussi* is utterly irresponsible, reading as though it were drug-induced or dreamed. Miller arrives factually enough at the train station a couple of kilometers down the road from Mycenae and at a real hour, 8 a.m., but "the magic of this world suddenly penetrated my bowels," he says, and we are off and running.[15] From then on, nothing else is factual. He immediately encounters a child wailing that he has lost three drachmas, like the farewell spirit of the materialistic world Miller is departing, and it is impossible to know if there was really a child there or not. Miller then enters the "world of terror and beauty." He sees the landscape covering the bloody bodies of heroes assassinated, describing it in R-rated detail, "a fresh-cut navel, dragging its glory down into the bowels of the earth where the bats and lizards feed upon it gloatingly."[16] The visionary blood and gore go on for page and page and page. He finally sees Mycenae itself, crouching, like a fighter—or a reptile or a dinosaur—and sucking all that is living into itself to be assassinated, as well, with copious and vivid details.

Clearly Miller feels sucked in and eaten. We might summarize such an experience as being "overwhelmed" or "stunned" by a place and its significance, but our descriptions are insufficient to how powerfully we can be disrupted by a place. There is nothing moderate or measured about Miller's presentation. He throws words and images as Jackson Pollock throws paint. Places eat us. They metabolize us into their bodies instead of the usual view: that we grow by consuming them.

Miller even mocks the usual expansion of the civilized self through travel. As he is about to enter Agamemnon's tomb, the beehive-shaped underground tomb several hundred yards from the ruins of the palace, he halts and spits out what he might have become, according to the usual concept of place: "I am gathering all of this potential civilized muck into a hard, tiny knot of understanding. . . . I shall be only a thing fabricated, at the best a beautiful cultured soul." But as he enters the tomb, he is shattered "into a billion splintered smithereens," as he is overcome by the place, happily.[17]

Could this really be part of travel—that we crave being consumed by a place and instead of growing larger we are chewed and bloodied, humbled and reduced? Don't we? True, if we follow the educational model, we ourselves want to consume, but don't we also look for strong places, places with teeth? Isn't that why Paul Bowles wanted each place to be as different as possible? Isn't that why Camus said that the motive of travel was fear? Isn't that why home isn't enough and we leap off across borders and oceans, where the world is "strange," by definition? The first sight of the Himalayas the morning after an earthquake when the air has finally cleared in Katmandu: jagged, brilliantly white, paralyzing. The bulb fields of Sassenheim, the numberless red petals vivid against the rain-wet green, as I repeat in my mind to the rhythm of the bicycle pedals, "vibrantly alive, vibrantly alive, vibrantly alive." The Old City of Jerusalem at night, looming above me with its vast stone walls and there, a twisting opening into a multitude of tiny streets, insisting I plunge.

In Sarnath, the place where the Buddha preached his first sermon after attaining enlightenment (that is, after knowing precisely where he was but knowing that there is no "where"), Alphonso Lingis speaks with a Hindu healer, a man skilled in knowledge of the "patterns and movements" in the planets and stars and in the most minute areas of our bodies. He could heal and advise because he could situate a person in the largest and smallest orders, he tells the American philosopher. In contrast with this pinpointing of place, a sort of global positioning system of Vedic medicine, Lingis speaks to him about "nomadic space," space without mapping, without location, and the healer is suddenly more interested in Lingis. As we read the passage, we can see him look at this traveler for the first time, for the healer, too, is more fascinated by wandering than by location. What both men love is streets.[18]

STREETS

When we travel we do not belong in the places we visit: that's what makes us visitors. The mosques, temples, cathedrals, synagogues belong to others. We are aware that we are trespassing. The houses of parliament, the opera houses, the palaces, the historical sites are not ours, either. We do not belong. We surely do not belong in those hotels, though they try to convince us that those rooms are our homes. There is only one place a traveler belongs: in the streets.

That is where Whitman wanted to bring us, on the road. There is a difference between Whitman and the English Romantics who also loved to walk. Wordsworth, Coleridge, and the others walked through the countryside, through fields and up hills. They wanted to get away from the towns and the roads with their carts carrying produce, their itinerant preachers, the families on their way. But Whitman wanted what he calls "the blab." He wanted the rude and ordinary sound of wheels on rough roads and people chattering. The English Romantics needed to get away from commerce and frivolity and ugliness and stink. Whitman wanted to move among it. Lingis, Twain, Bowles, Miller, Johnson, and Gilbert want it, too. For these travelers—as for many of us—the street is the place to be.

If we watch Mark Twain's progress across Europe and into the Near East, for example, he seems much happier in claustrophobic streets than anywhere else. When he arrives in Marseilles, his first stop in France, he plunges into the street immediately as though he were famished after the weeks at sea. A prior stop in a restaurant doesn't seem to satisfy his hunger: he needs to feed instead off the contact with the streets, trying to encounter as much as he possibly can.

As a place, a street epitomizes Whitman's desire to be "on the road." It is kinetic, and so are we when we are in the streets. Twain says it well, "I can not think of half the places we went to, or what we particularly saw; we had no disposition to examine carefully into anything at all—we only want to glance and go—to move, keep moving!"[19] To be in the streets is to be in motion, among others who are in motion. The streets and sidewalks (if they exist) define a rough direction of flow—and woe to the one who wants to stand still or to halt the movement—but there are many other directions, too, angled and cross, as well as descending and ascending.

Being in the streets means making contact, too—"we only want to glance and go." There are all of those others, after all, and all of the places we pass when we walk. It may be superficial contact—just a glance—but that is no reason to disparage it. Those are glances. There is contact. There are sure to be some to criticize it, but there is much to recommend it. For one is so open to the influences of the street. A traveler walks down a street without the protection of the bus or car and without the ordered presentation of the museum or a home. The contact on the street is visual ("to glance") but also involves most other senses, the smells of all that moves on the street, and the sounds (oh, god, yes) for nowhere is the decibel level higher or the mixture more radical.

On the streets of Zahedan, in the southeast corner of Iran, as Jack Perfect and I waited for our visas to be approved, we walked through the town day after day. We walked somewhat warily, for we had gotten this far by bus and we really didn't know what to expect. We were on foot. We were exposed. It was before the Islamic Revolution but still pretty much where the road ended as far as our experience went. We sat next to a street and ate dates, throwing the pits to join hundreds of others in the deep trench gutters by the road. We drank chai. We listened to the calls of strange birds and the passings of large trucks occasionally. It was January and pleasant. And one day we heard loud chanting and at a distance saw a procession of bare-chested men, striking their backs and drawing blood. We hoped to be left alone. But we weren't, for constantly during that week we passed almond-eyed children who smiled with delight and called "Hello, Mister!" to us.

We never entered a home, never learned the names of those children or their fathers, much less their mothers. "Hello, mister" was just a glance. The rough loud chanting of the men with whips was a glance, as well. So were the shifting gears of the truck and the nod of the man who sold us dates. The bare mountains up toward Afghanistan were a glance, and the gutters and the pits.

To be in the streets is also to be physical—to be a physical person in a physical place to a stronger degree than in other places. We are walking, not conveyed by a vehicle with a sheathing of metal, not standing before a painting or sitting in a pew or an auditorium. We are jostled, talked to, beseeched, cajoled. We are tired and hot, and the exhaust is thick so we cough, or we pass through currents smelling of curry or fresh bread. In fact, we are entirely in our own body-place. We are a place in a place. Our legs transport us, our eyes and noses guide us, frequently touched by hands, occasionally fearful of knives.

I mentioned earlier that Twain is obsessed with soap and maintaining cleanliness. He needs to because he is so often in the street. He is unusually aware of being physically assaulted, not in the criminal sense but by "dirt and vermin and ignorance," by "deceased cats, decayed rags, and decomposed vegetable tops, and remnants of old boots, all soaked with dishwater."[20] His denunciations of places for their ignorance, ugliness, and stench can strike us as small-minded and bigoted, but we can also see Twain as willing to be exposed. He is frank about all that hits him physically. He denounces it loudly—and then plunges back into the streets and all its physical powers.

The final aspect of the streets in France, Italy, Turkey, Syria, and Palestine that appeals to Twain (and to us) is summed up in Genoa. Twain, typically, loves the "corkscrew" streets that are only four to eight feet wide and lined with tall houses, so that he feels as though he is at the "bottom of some tremendous abyss."[21] And as he walks he is amazed to see beautiful, well-dressed women emerge from the "frowning, dreary-looking" houses beside the street. Streets are places lined with walls—unlike roads: the walls of buildings and homes. The other sides of those walls are hidden from us, especially from the strangers in town, we travelers. The doors are closed, and we have no keys. To be a resident is to be able to open the doors, doors of our own home or of those of friends, or of the businesses and institutions that we understand. Travelers never really belong behind those doors. Travelers belong only in the street. So we—like Twain—are surprised to see what emerges. The inside is never for us and never to be understood when it comes inside out.

TRAVELERS' BODIES

A traveler is a place as we travel to places, a place for our clothes to hang, a place some five or six feet off the street where our vision begins, a tactile surface, an opening for taste just below the vision and for scent between them, and for sound just aside. A traveler is a topography, hairy in some places, rough in others, totally hidden in quite a few. We have fauna and flora; we're a place for fungi and bacteria, viruses and mold, as well as follicle mites, eating the dried skin at literally everyone's hairs. Occasionally there are also ticks and lice, scabies mites, and more. Two hundred species of living entities live on and in our bodies, each square centimeter of skin inhabited by 50 million bacteria, with denser populations in the oily sides of our noses or under our arms and the richest populations just inside the openings, in the mouth or the anus, the populations of our places crowded around resources. Fewest bacteria live at the tear ducts and other places of frequent liquid flow, those topographic features of danger.

We are a place for our own exploration, searching for minor eruptions of the skin that we think may be unsightly, for small infections, boils, cuts, and lesions that we think may be unhealthy or dangerous (what is that tough patch on the side of my nose, invisible but felt by the fingertips, so like the skin cancer of years ago?), for the evidence of friction on the feet that will keep us from the streets and make us halt in the hotel. What of the deep openings, giving omens of deep illness: the throat and lungs; the nose and sinus; the anus and intestines; the urethra and vagina and sexual infections; ears and eyes: places we never want to find puddles of pus. We travel with a place that has around three thousand square inches of skin, more than we could ever fully walk, even the premiere place, the "real" us, our face. For all of our endless scrutiny, the face is a place as unknown as any of those nineteenth-century maps of Africa. The continent of the face with its gathering of all five senses, too much of a place for us to know, like a place with too many capitals, too rich and subtle and complex for us to be more than tourists, tourists to our own faces, never living there at all but limited to the surface, wishing for a soul.

As I was writing this book, I ruptured my Achilles tendon, brought to ground and then to surgical ward and then to bed. The traveler halted, much as I had been a month earlier when a friend and I tried to fly to Mexico and were marooned by Baltimore's "Storm of the Century," locked in a Marriott by thirty-one inches of snow and unable to move. Stopped. Bound. Hobbled. The night after my heel was cut open and the tendon resewn, I had a dream of lying in a bed that caught fire, the sheets burning into the mattress, which burned into the frame, then into the floor, then into the entire building, that dream the echo of a night where Percocet could not blur the heel's pain, and I realized just how deeply bound we are to the place of our bodies and inevitably to its pain. To be a place is to be in pain, and even if we forget it now, we have experienced it already (when we broke a limb or cut ourselves badly or were dropped on the tile as a baby or felt the painful squeezings of birth itself), and we cannot know the place—the being in a place—without feeling the pain. We are a place; we are in pain. But also, because of pain we know ourselves as a place and not just as disembodied eyes and mind. Pain sounds the full volume of our body-place. It is the sonar of the full substance, its mass and density, its loose fill and solid rock and open cracks. Pain is the sound that travels into the place but then never fully echoes back, because there is no other side, since the place we travel has reaches going back to childhood and infancy, so the sound of pain is changed in pitch as it moves through all those densities and temperatures and currents of the molten and moving. Pain is as intense as humans can feel. It is our absolute. And when that exploding charge travels beneath our floor, burning and ripping, and threatening the entire structure, we know at last that we are a place, large and long, and one that can be halted and maybe even destroyed.

The Achilles pain brought me on a trip through my body, through my body as a place. I was a traveler, guided by pain. It was as disruptive as any other journey I have taken. I hated it to be sure, but I also loved it like Istanbul or Lahore or Haarlem or Jerusalem or Accra or Athens or Venray or Sanchi or anywhere else.

One of the most memorable and humane passages in Alphonso Lingis is his account of touching, mentioned in chapter 5. He is traveling in Peru, visiting Machu Picchu, and is taken with the sight of people who will be ground up in economic development, narcotics traffic, and armed political struggles. There is an old woman who hands him a cup of maté de coca when he lands. There are others who are walking over the boulders or grinding corn or lying on the ground in the sun, fatigued. He sees them all so physically, and we know that these are people who will be in pain, whose hands hurt from working with rough implements, whose faces are creased. They work manually. They look eighty years old when they are only thirty. The contemporary carnage reminds him of the historic one, the millions of indigenous people killed by the Spanish conquest—8.5 million is the number he says were killed among these people. Lingis sees his own understandings of the people as offenses, too. How easy it is to "place" these people in terms of the systems and theories of economics, philosophy, and anthropology, how diminishing, even how violent. Any statement about "them" confines them to a code.

Lingis claims that touching is different. He travels in order to touch them, he says, for touching is mute, and without content. In touching we are just met by another body, which presses up against all of our confining systems and theories and mutes them. Another body is there—that is it. "A child who touches your leg, a somnolent old man in a truck whose body touches yours when the truck reels on a curve."[22] In touching we meet another place. It is not language or thought or even sight or smell. It is a bump—in the night, no doubt. Resonance. Place knocking place, revealing both of us to be places.

Pleasure does all that pain does in showing me to be a place. The echoes up and down that show my extent—how far a small sensual touch can travel so that a fingertip alone sends messages up to the coloring ears and thumps down the chest and causes the toes to curl. Pleasure opens the large domain of the self to reveal the vast extent, all of it alert and all lit, watching, listening. Everyone comes out in pleasure like on a sunny day, and we realize how large the population is. Like pain, pleasure dims the mind and allows the surface and volume to be heard, to speak.

Travel is being a place in a place. It is being visited as we visit. We are approached, entered, visited, left. Pain and pleasure are the echoes that someone is there. The smell of jasmine flowing thickly off a wall at night as we walk down a dark and narrow street in East Jerusalem. Every subsequent night we hope to find that sticky pool that woke deep regions of the head. The low notes of hunger moving our legs into the concentric streets of Amsterdam, urgent to satisfy the hollowing call, swelling into a panic as though the body will completely empty and drop if the food isn't found now. As Mary Oliver writes, "Listen, whatever it is you try to do with your life, nothing will ever dazzle you like the dreams of your body."[23] If we're dazzled by places as we travel—by the hotels, cultural sites, and streets—we're also dazzled as places. As a body, as a place our usual surfaces are broken by the gnawing, echoing, shouting, roaming, burning, shivering, melting that happen only in a place, not in a mind.

Pilgrims

My children and I were in Ocho Rios, on Jamaica. We had followed the advice of the *Lonely Planet* guide and checked into a "mid-range" hotel on a street described on another page (that we read too late) as unsafe. I could walk that street, accosted, entreated, but I couldn't let the kids. They would have to stay in the hotel room that gradually filled with cigarette smoke from the room beside ours. In the afternoon, we attempted to find Turtle Beach, driving back and forth in our scratched and dented rental, but unable to locate the beach. The map said it lay behind Main Street, but there was no access we could discover, unless we plunged through shops, but they were beyond our access, just as the street outside our hotel was. As a last resort, I turned into the Renaissance Jamaica Grande Resort, parked, and we walked through the lobby to the many pools and beach. We were the only ones without the red plastic bracelet that identified those who belonged.

It is not an extreme case of not-belonging, but it was enough. We had never been to a resort before, and it was gorgeous, like something out of a film. Everyone was foreign, mostly white. Everyone was in an attractive swimsuit. There were water toys heaped, a buffet-table, waiters standing attentively, and a couple in wedding dress being photographed by an artificial waterfall. We tried to look casual as we strolled toward the beach and then toward its far edge, where the public beach was just visible beyond a wall and chain link fence. We wanted to escape the resort, but as we finally crossed, we discovered we were equally out of place, now the only whites on the public beach, the only non-Jamaicans in a densely packed quarter mile of sand.

We walked to the far end, that much closer to the tall conveyer belt carrying bauxite for Reynolds Jamaica Mines, rented three chairs, and set to a hot and uncomfortable hour's swimming and reading, then left.

What kind of father would dis-locate his children like this? It was my first trip with just my children, who were now thirteen and sixteen, and I chose to take them to Jamaica, threading carefully between the Caribbean waters, with the delicate shades of blue and green, the coconuts trees, bananas, bougainvilleas, breadfruit, and Captain Clark, taking us out in his "glass-bottom boat" to snorkeling on the reef—all that on one side of the road, literally, and the jerk shacks, tin-roofed homes, herds of goats, "great Morass" swamp, ganja, and rumored political unrest on the other. We didn't stay with Jamaicans, and we didn't stay in resorts. We were, instead, on the roads, the narrow, twisting, ill-paved, barely two-laned roads with a fatality rate so high (ten times that of the United States) that it was one of only three places on earth that my Visa wouldn't cover the insurance deductible on the rental car (the others being Israel and Ireland—one assumes that many of the earth's countries are not even considered).

Why would a father drive his children on those roads? Why would a father take such risks? It is one thing to leave home and be in those places that are most vividly not-home, but it would seem to be another to transport home itself to a homeless place, to turn the family itself out into the street. Let me not exaggerate: this was not going to spend a year in Jamaica, much less in Mayagar. It was not putting the kids into local schools. It was not truly risky. But it was dislocating them in a way they'd never experienced before, in a way they are not likely to forget, and I am glad of it.

I am glad because they can, in fact, leave home. They can see their homes from a distance—see all of their places from a distance—and begin to discern what they require in a place. They can sleep, like Faulkner's Darl, under a strange roof, listening to rain, thinking of home, and yet not with the desperation of those who have never crossed a boundary. They can know, instead, what those who went on pilgrimage came to know.

During the European Middle Ages, pilgrimage was encouraged as a means of cementing a believer's identity. A common view of such pilgrimage is that pilgrimage countered the great disruptions of life—life's evils—be they physical, emotional, or spiritual. Life simply contained so many overpowering forces that governed and could destroy an individual's existence, both on earth and in an afterlife, that a solution was crucial. In fact, religious life had "a desperate, almost frenzied quality" in the later Middle Ages because present and eternal health, harmony, and happiness were so precarious.[24] Enter pilgrimage. Pilgrimage offered opportunities to reform the self according to healing models by journeying to sites which housed the relics of the saints or presented the scenes of Christ's life and death. But home had to be left. The pilgrim had to encounter the dangers and discomforts of the road. There had to be an ordeal before the benefits could result when the relics were finally in the pilgrim's view.

It was the same with my children. They had to leave before they could see what "place" means to them, before they could see if "home"—their room, their house, their town, their school, their fields, their country—really could cement their identity, and see, too, if it had cemented their identity too much. They had to wander on the roads, they had to be uncertain of food, had to be uncertain of the full safety of their beds, had to face the hazards of those drivers, and do so as pilgrims, seekers.

Don't we all?

Notes

Introduction

1. Gray, "Hospital Food."

ONE   *Love of Ruptures*

1. Bowles, *Their Heads Are Green,* 7
2. Bowles, *Sheltering Sky,* 199.
3. Emerson, *Journals and Miscellaneous Notebooks,* May 7, 1837, 5: 323.
4. Oliver, *Blue Pastures,* 4–6.
5. Barzun, *From Dawn to Decadence,* 24.
6. Eliot, *Notes Towards the Definition of Culture,* 30.
7. Oliver, "Whelks," in *New and Selected Poems,* 30.
8. Yeats, "Lapis Lazuli," in *Collected Poems,* 292.
9. Emerson, "Experience," in *Works of Ralph Waldo Emerson,* 3: 62.
10. O'Connor, "Revelation," in *Complete Stories,* 500.
11. Donne, *The Poems of John Donne,* 1: 328.
12. Bowles, *Without Stopping,* 77, 10, 38.
13. Lingis, "Matagalpa," in *Abuses,* 77–88.
14. Ibid., 88.
15. Miller, *Colossus of Maroussi.*

16. Bowles, "A Man Must Not Be Very Moslem," in *Their Heads Are Green,* 48–65.

17. Johnson, *Natural Opium.*

18. Ibid., 96.

19. Emerson, "Thoreau," in *Works of Ralph Waldo Emerson,* 10: 430.

20. Lingis, "Tawantinsuyu," in *Abuses,* esp. 55–61.

21. Gilbert, "Moment of Grace," in *Great Fires,* 49.

TWO   *Commerce with the Ancients*

1. Longfellow, *Life of Henry Wadsworth Longfellow,* 157.

2. Ibid.

3. Arvin, *Longfellow: His Life and Work,* 24.

4. Ralph Waldo Emerson, "Self Reliance," in *Works of Ralph Waldo Emerson,* 2: 80.

5. Emerson, *Journals,* 4: 68.

6. Ibid., 4: 78.   7. Ibid., 4: 74–75.

8. Emerson, *Nature,* 16.

9. Emerson, *Journals,* 68.

10. Emerson,"An Address," 125.

11. Ibid., 143.

12. Arnold's *Culture and Anarchy* (1869) may be the best location of this argument. *Complete Prose Works of Mathew Arnold,* vol. 5.

13. See "Rugby Chapel," in *Poetry and Criticism of Matthew Arnold,* 174.

14. Arnold, *Culture and Anarchy,* in *Complete Prose Works,* 5: 140.

15. Ibid.   16. Ibid., 140–42.   17. Ibid., 143.

18. Ibid., 141.   19. Ibid., 145.   20. Ibid., 94.

21. Ibid., 167–68.

22. Arnold, "The Function of Criticism in the Present Time," in *Complete Prose Works,* 3: 261.

23. Ibid., 268.

24. *Condé Nast Traveler,* January 2003, 29–40

25. Ibid., 104.

26. Arnold, "A Word on Democracy" in *Complete Prose Works,* 10: 2; contrast, by the way, William James, who advises Thomas Ward *not* to go to Germany in 1867 because it is too similar to the United States (*Selected Letters,* 29; see also 37–38).

27. Arnold, "A Word on Democracy," in *Complete Prose Works,* 11.

28. Ibid., 18.

29. "Summer Sessions Abroad," Georgetown University brochure, 1997.

30. Arnold quoting Montesquieu, in *Culture and Anarchy,* in *Complete Prose Works,* 5: 91.

31. Trilling, *Matthew Arnold,* 252.

32. Arnold, "Pagan & Medieval Religious Sentiment," in *Complete Prose Works,* 3: 222; Arnold, "The Study of Poetry," in *Poetry and Criticism of Matthew Arnold,* 306.

33. Arnold, "The Study of Poetry," in *Poetry and Criticism of Matthew Arnold,* 306.

34. Arnold, preface to *Poems* (1853), in *Complete Prose Works,* 1: 13.

35. Kauffmann, "Monumental Lives," 34, quoted in Bush, *Matthew Arnold,* 40n.
36. Sexson, *Ordinarily Sacred,* 16.
37. Traubel, *With Whitman in Camden,* 232, quoted in Trilling, *Matthew Arnold,* 398.

THREE   *The Pilgrim's Progress*

1. Conrad, *Heart of Darkness,* in *Complete Short Fiction,* 3: 13.
2. Said, "Identity, Authority, and Freedom," 18.
3. Fussell, *Abroad,* 39.
4. Durrell, "Reflections on Travel," in *Spirit of Place,* 426.
5. James Clifford sees the hybrid life of the tourist more clearly than most. See *Routes.*
6. Miller, *Colossus of Maroussi,* 26–27.
7. Ibid., 108, 36.
8. Bowles, *Sheltering Sky,* 66.
9. Ibid., 48.   10. Ibid., 68.   11. Ibid., 54.
12. "The sedentary life is the very sin against the Holy Spirit. Only thoughts reached by walking have value." Friedrich Nietzsche, *Twilight of the Idols,* "Maxims and Arrows" #34. There are many other similar passages in Nietzsche.
13. The ability to fear or hate, that openness to assault might indicate that even the Lyles are encountering Morocco. They, too, might earn Nietzsche's respect.
14. Conrad, *Complete Short Fiction,* 3: 58.
15. Hansen, *Stranger in the Forest,* 25.
16. Ibid., 31.   17. Ibid., 30–32.   18. Ibid., 179–95.
19. Ibid., 30.   20. Ibid., 30, 44.
21. Eliade, *Sacred and the Profane,* 25.
22. Said, *Orientalism,* 38.
23. Ibid., 40.   24. Ibid., 49.
25. Morrow, *Names of Things,* 65.
26. Ibid., 95.
27. Said, *Orientalism,* 56.

FOUR   *The Ride of Passage*

1. Whitman, "Song of the Open Road," in *Collected Writings,* 4: 149.
2. Twain, *Innocents Abroad,* 25.
3. Ibid., 27.   4. Ibid., 50.
5. Walton, "The Life of Dr. John Donne," xlviii.
6. Johnson, *Natural Opium,* 187.
7. Ibid., 195.
8. Twain, *Innocents Abroad,* 28.
9. Ibid., 38.   10. Ibid., 23.
11. Thoreau, "Walking," in *Writings of Henry David Thoreau,* 5: 205–48.
12. James, *Varieties of Religious Experience,* 15.
13. Ibid., 16.
14. Emerson, *Nature,* in *Works of Ralph Waldo Emerson,* 1: 15–16.

15. http://www.transcendentalists.com/nature_review_emerson.htm.

16. Lipp, *Mixe of Oaxaca*, 148–53.

17. Knab, *Mad Jesus*, 3.

18. Ibid., 30.   19. Ibid., 31.   20. Ibid., 35.

21. Ibid., 34.   22. Ibid., 35.   23. Ibid., 36.

24. Ibid., 31.

25. Robinson, *Gilead*, 99.

26. Ibid., 98–99.

27. Miller, *Colossus of Maroussi*, 6.

28. Bowles, *Their Heads Are Green*, 8.

29. Ibid., 7.

30. James, *Principles of Psychology*, 279–83.

31. Whitman, "Song of the Open Road," in *Collected Writings*, 4: 149.

32. Bowles, *Without Stopping*, 19. Subsequent citations to *Without Stopping* in this chapter will be given parenthetically in the main text.

33. And, in 1999, he "passed away."

34. Twain, *Innocents Abroad*, 50.

FIVE   *Holy Strangers*

1. O'Connor, *Mystery and Manners*, 161.

2. O'Connor, *Habit of Being*, 100.

3. Bowles, *Without Stopping*, 125.

4. Ibid.   5. Ibid., 126.   6. Ibid., 173.

7. Ibid., 176.   8. Ibid., 172

9. O'Connor, *Habit of Being*, 100.

10. O'Connor, *Mystery and Manners*, 162.

11. O'Connor, *Habit of Being*, 90.

12. O'Connor, *Wise Blood*, 99–100.

13. O'Connor quoted in Elie, *Life You Save*, 155.

14. O'Connor, *Wise Blood*, 162, 168.

15. Gilbert, "Beyond Beginnings," in *Great Fires*, 77.

16. Gilbert, "Finding Eurydice," in *Great Fires*, 15.

17. Gilbert, "On Stone," in *Great Fires*, 31.

18. Gilbert, "Measuring the Tyger," in *Great Fires*, 7.

19. Gilbert, "The Edge of the World," in *Great Fires*, 82.

20. Gilbert, "Going There" in *Great Fires*, 16.

21. Gilbert, "Tear It Down," in *Great Fires*, 9.

22. Bowles, *Sheltering Sky*, 70. Subsequent citations to *The Sheltering Sky* in this chapter will be given parenthetically in the main text.

23. O'Connor, *Violent Bear It Away*, 182

24. Lingis, *Abuses*, viii.

25. Ibid., 58   26. Ibid., 60.   27. Ibid., 60.

28. Ibid., 118.   29. Ibid., 118, 120.   30. Ibid., 118.

31. Ibid., 95.

32. Miller, *Colossus of Maroussi*, 3. Subsequent citations to *The Colossus of Maroussi* in this chapter will be given parenthetically in the main text.

33. Nye, *Never in a Hurry*, 12.

SIX   *Guides for the Perplexed*

1. Murphy, *Santeria*, 99.
2. Merrill, "Part of the Vigil," from *Collected Poems*, 246.
3. Wright, *Cuba*, vii, 2.
4. Ibid., 147–50.   5. Ibid., 147.   6. Ibid., 149.
7. Ibid., 150.
8. Codrescu, *Ay, Cuba!* 82.
9. Ibid., 83.   10. Ibid., 85.   11. Ibid., 1.
12. Ibid., 16.
13. Stanley, *Lonely Planet Cuba*, 71–2.
14. Baedeker, *Palestine and Syria*, iii.
15. Ibid., iii.   16. Ibid., xxiv–xxvii.   17. Ibid., x–xi.
18. Ibid., xx.   19. Ibid., xxi.   20. Ibid., xx–xxi.
21. Wright, *Cuba*, 150.

SEVEN   *Street People*

1. Whitman, "Song of the Open Road," in *Collected Writings*, 4: 149–59.
2. Allen, *Walt Whitman*, 21–22.
3. Morrow, *Names of Things*, 102.
4. Ibid., 107.
5. Merrill, *Collected Poems*, 228–32.
6. Miller, *Colossus of Maroussi*, 209.
7. Faulkner, *As I Lay Dying*, 76.
8. Lingis, *Abuses*, 74.
9. Twain, *Innocents Abroad*, 178.
10. Ibid., 168.   11. Ibid., 115.   12. Ibid., 151.
13. Ibid., 146.   14. Ibid., 227.
15. Miller, *Colossus of Maroussi*, 86.
16. Ibid., 88.   17. Ibid., 93.
18. Lingis, *Abuses*, 175–80.
19. Twain, *Innocents Abroad*, 64.
20. Ibid., 185.   21. Ibid., 117.
22. Lingis, *Abuses*, 60.
23. Oliver, *American Primitive*, 62.
24. Sumption, *Pilgrimage*, 15.

Bibliography

Allen, Gay Wilson. *Walt Whitman*. Detroit: Wayne State University Press, 1969.

Arnold, Matthew. *The Complete Prose Works of Mathew Arnold*. Edited by R. H. Super. 11 vols. Ann Arbor: University of Michigan Press, 1960–77.

———. *Poetry and Criticism of Matthew Arnold*. Edited by A. Dwight Culler. Boston: Houghton Mifflin, 1961.

Arvin, Newton. *Longfellow: His Life and Work*. Boston: Little Brown, 1962.

Baedeker, Karl, ed. *Palestine and Syria: Handbook for Travellers*. Leipsic: Karl Baedeker, 1894.

Barzun, Jacques. *From Dawn to Decadence: 500 Years of Western Cultural Life, 1500 to the Present*. New York: Harper Collins, 2000.

Bowles, Paul. *The Sheltering Sky*. New York: Vintage Books, 1990.

———. *Their Heads Are Green*. London: Peter Owen, 1963.

———. *Without Stopping*. New York: G. P. Putnam's Sons, 1972.

Breaking the Waves. Directed by Lars von Trier. Denmark, Netherlands, Sweden, France: 1996.

Brodsky, Joseph. *Watermark*. New York: Farrar, Straus and Giroux, 1993.

Bush, Douglas. *Matthew Arnold: A Survey of His Poetry and Prose*. New York: Macmillan, 1971.

Clifford, James. *Routes: Travel and Translation in the Late Twentieth Century*. Cambridge: Harvard University Press, 1997.

Codrescu, Andrei. *Ay, Cuba! A Socio-Erotic Journey.* New York: Picador, 1999.

Condé Nast Traveler, January 2003

Conrad, Joseph. *The Complete Short Fiction of Joseph Conrad.* Edited by Samuel Hynes. 4 vols. New Jersey: Ecco Press, 1991.

Donne, John. *Devotions upon Emergent Occasions Together with Death's Duel.* Ann Arbor: University of Michigan Press, 1959.

———. *The Poems of John Donne.* Edited by J. C. Grierson. 2 vols. London: Oxford University Press, 1912.

Durrell, Lawrence. *The Spirit of Place.* Edited by Alan G. Thomas. New York: Marlowe, 1969.

Eliade, Mircea. *The Sacred and the Profane.* Translated by Willard R. Trask. New York: Harcourt Brace, 1959.

Elie, Paul. *The Life You Save May Be Your Own: An American Pilgrimage.* New York: Farrar, Straus and Giroux, 2003.

Eliot, T. S. *Notes Towards the Definition of Culture.* New York: Harcourt, Brace, 1949.

Emerson, Ralph Waldo. "An Address." In *The Complete Works of Ralph Waldo Emerson,* vol. 1. Boston: Houghton Mifflin, 1903–21.

———. "Experience." In *The Complete Works of Ralph Waldo Emerson,* vol. 3. Boston: Houghton Mifflin, 1903–21.

———. *The Journals and Miscellaneous Notebooks of Ralph Waldo Emerson.* Edited by Alfred R. Ferguson. 16 vols. Cambridge: Harvard University Press, 1960–82.

———. *Nature.* In *The Complete Works of Ralph Waldo Emerson,* vol. 1. Boston: Houghton Mifflin, 1903–21.

———. "Self-Reliance." In *The Complete Works of Ralph Waldo Emerson,* vol. 2. Boston: Houghton Mifflin, 1903–21.

———. "Thoreau." In *The Complete Works of Ralph Waldo Emerson,* vol. 10. Boston: Houghton Mifflin, 1903–21.

Faulkner, William. *As I Lay Dying.* New York: Random House, 1964.

Fussell, Paul. *Abroad: British Literary Traveling between the Wars.* New York: Oxford University Press, 1980.

Gilbert, Jack. *The Great Fires: Poems 1982–1992.* New York: Knopf, 1997.

Gray, David. "Hospital Food." On *Life in Slow Motion.* Ato Records compact disk, B000AA305M.

Hansen, Eric. *Stranger in the Forest: On Foot across Borneo.* Boston: Houghton Mifflin, 1988.

James, William. *The Principles of Psychology.* 2 vols. Cambridge: Harvard University Press, 1981.

———. *Selected Letters.* Edited by Elizabeth Hardwick. New York: Farrar, Straus, Cudahy, 1961.

———. *The Varieties of Religious Experience.* Cambridge: Harvard University Press, 1985.

Johnson, Diane. *Natural Opium.* New York: Knopf, 1993.

Kauffmann, Stanley. "Monumental Lives." *New Republic,* June 22, 1968, 22–34.

Knab, Timothy J. *Mad Jesus: The Final Testament of a Huichol Messiah from Northwest Mexico.* Albuquerque: University of New Mexico Press, 2004.

Lingis, Alphonso. *Abuses.* Berkeley and Los Angeles: University of California Press, 1994.

————. *Foreign Bodies.* New York: Routledge, 1994.

Lipp, Frank J. *The Mixe of Oaxaca: Religion, Ritual, and Healing.* Austin: University of Texas Press, 1991.

Longfellow, Henry Wadsworth. *Life of Henry Wadsworth Longfellow, with Extracts from His Journals and Correspondence.* Edited by Samuel Longfellow. 3 vols. Boston: Houghton, Mifflin, 1891.

Merrill, James. *Collected Poems.* Edited by J. D. McClatchy and Stephen Yenser. New York: Knopf, 2002.

Miller, Henry. *The Colossus of Maroussi.* New York: New Directions, 1941.

Morrow, Susan Brind. *The Names of Things.* New York: Riverhead Books, 1997.

Murphy, Joseph M. *Santeria: African Spirits in America.* Boston: Beacon Press, 1993.

Nye, Naomi Shihab. *Never in a Hurry: Essays on People and Places.* Columbia: University of South Carolina Press, 1996.

O'Connor, Flannery. *The Complete Stories.* Farrar, Straus and Giroux, 1979.

————. *The Habit of Being: Letters of Flannery O'Connor.* Edited by Sally Fitzgerald. New York: Farrar, Straus and Giroux, 1979.

————. *Mystery and Manners: Occasional Prose.* Edited by Sally and Robert Fitzgerald. Farrar, Straus and Giroux, 1969.

————. *The Violent Bear It Away.* New York: Farrar, Straus and Giroux, 1960.

————. *Wise Blood.* New York: Farrar, Straus and Giroux, 1962.

Oliver, Mary. *American Primitive.* Boston: Back Bay Books, 1983.

————. *Blue Pastures.* New York: Harvest Books, 1995.

————. *New and Selected Poems.* Boston: Beacon Press, 1992.

Robinson, Marilyn. *Gilead.* New York: Farrar, Straus and Giroux, 2004.

Said, Edward. "Identity, Authority, and Freedom: The Potentate and the Traveler." *Transition* 54 (1991): 4–18.

————. *Orientalism.* New York: Random House, 1978.

Sexson, Linda. *Ordinarily Sacred.* Charlottesville: University Press of Virginia, 1992.

Stanley, David. *Lonely Planet Cuba.* Melbourne: Lonely Planet Publications, 2000.

Sumption, Jonathan. *Pilgrimage: An Image of Mediaeval Religion.* Totowa, N.J.: Rowman and Littlefield, 1975.

Thoreau, Henry David. *The Writings of Henry David Thoreau.* 10 vols. Boston: Houghton Mifflin, 1906.

Traubel, Horace. *With Whitman in Camden.* 7 vols. Boston: Small, Maynard, 1906.

Trilling, Lionel. *Matthew Arnold.* New York: Harcourt Brace Jovanovich, 1954.

Twain, Mark. *The Innocents Abroad.* New York: Library of America, 1984.

Walton, Izaak. "The Life of Dr. John Donne." In *Devotions upon Emergent Occasions Together with Death's Duel,* by John Donne. Ann Arbor: University of Michigan Press, 1959

Whitman, Walt. *Collected Writings of Walt Whitman.* Edited by Harold W. Blodgett and Sculley Bradley. 4 vols. New York: New York University Press, 1965.

Wright, Irene A. *Cuba.* New York: Macmillan, 1910.

Yeats, William Butler. *The Collected Poems of William Butler Yeats.* New York: Macmillan, 1972.

Index

guides (*continued*)
binding of, 157; cheated by, 137, 149; clergymen as, 155; conflicted, 121–22; culture as, 146; *Fodor's*, 145; *Frommer's*, 145; idyllic, 145; to inside, 144; *Let's Go*, 145; literature as, 145; *Lonely Planet*, 143, 145, 154, 157; *Moon Handbooks*, 145; *Murray's Guide*, 155, 175; paid and unpaid, 121; as people, 145; *Rough Guide*, 145; suspended between, 157–58; spiritual, 159
guidebooks, 45, 66, 73, 143, 145, 154–58, 175

Haarlem, The Netherlands, 120
Hansen, Eric, 67, 69
Havana, 129, 148, 149, 151, 158
healing, 43, 44, 45
Heart of Darkness (Conrad), 56, 68
Holy Land, 172
Holy Sepulcher Church, 169
home: broken, 20, 33, 60, 77, 106, 136; closed to strangers, 115; as a danger, 15, 134; exaggerated, 56; as homeless, 190; inaccessible, 119; insufficient, 181; left in pilgrimage, 191; left in travel, 25, 27, 95, 98, 128, 170; loathed, 162, 165, 166; Netherlands as, 120, 160; protected, 115, 138; as valuable, 6, 13, 62, 115, 138, 169, 169–70; sex and, 153; to Whitman, 162–63
homeless, 170
hotels, 26, 162, 170–75, 189; as contamination, 172–73; as foreign, 172; and suspicion, 174–75; as untrustworthy, 171–72
Huichol, 90–91
humility, as tourist, 64

Iceland, 28
Iliad, 180
illness. *See* disease
improvement, 78
incorrigibility, 153
India, 5, 31, 100, 108, 129
Innocents Abroad (Twain), 175

intimacy: through loss, 121; and strangers, 139
ire/osugbo, 149–50
Istanbul, 28

Jakarta, 15–16, 18, 48
Jamaica, 189–90
James, William, 89, 90, 96, 135, 162; *The Varieties of Religious Experience*, 89
jineteras, 152, 153–54
Jerusalem, 51, 57, 62, 120, 162, 164, 169, 170, 175, 181, 187, 188
Jesus, 74, 169. *See also* Mad Jesus
Job, book of, 22
Johnson, Diane, 8, 13–14, 28–29, 81, 87
journals, 35, 38, 89, 91–92, 112, 119, 130, 172
Journey to the Center of the Earth, 28

Kant, Immanuel, 25
Katmandu, 100
Katsimbalis, George, 28, 137–41
Kaufman, Stanley, 52
Keats, John, 101
Knob, Timothy, 90–91

Lahore, Pakistan, 103, 135–36
languages, 19. *See also* Dutch; German
laughter, 23
"Leda and the Swan" (Yeats), 144
Let's Go guides, 145
Levinas, Emmanuel, 129
liminal state, 95–96
Lingis, Alphonso, 8; *Abuses*, 129; and disruption, 26–27, 48, 129; and endless travel, 81; and hotels, 173–74; and "nomadic space," 181–82; and sex, 132–34; and strangers, 128–30, 142; and touch, 30, 131–32, 187–88
literature: as guide, 145–46; as religion, 39, 42; and trance, 86
Lonely Planet guides, 143, 145, 154, 157
Longfellow, Henry Wadsworth, 34–35

Salt Lake City, 163–64
San Francisco, 31
San Ysidro, California, 109
Sanchi, India, 100
Sandinistas, 26–27
santero/santera, 144
Santeria, 143, 147–48, 149–50, 158
Santeria: African Spirits in America (Murphy), 144, 151
Santiago de Cuba, 146, 153
Santorini, Greece, 59–60, 118
Sarnath, India, 181–82
Satyricon (Fellini), 136
Sea Cliff, New York, 13
self: autobiography and, 176–77; "best selves," 39, 40, 41, 43, 46; death of, 96, 98–99, 127; Emerson's expansion of, 35–36, 37–38; expansion by the road, 162–63; liminality and, 95–96; made by place, 176–78, 179; made monumental, 176; mocked by Miller, 181; multiplicity of, 25–26; re-formed by pilgrimage, 190–91; religious expansion of, 51; stability of, through others, 72–73; as stranger, 124, 125; travel as alternative to death of, 98; unconscious, 105
September 11, 108, 175
Sexson, Lynda, 52
seeing, 53
sex, 152–54; and strangers, 125–28, 132–36; trade, 152
Shakespeare, William, 36
shamans, 90
Shango, 150–51, 158
Sheltering Sky, The (Bowles), 7, 66, 97, 100, 105, 123–28
ships, 84
sites, 175–82; as anchor to self, 179; cultural, 50, 52–53; touristic, 35. *See also* places
sleep, 62
"Song of the Open Road" (Whitman) 81, 137, 162
space, as sacred, 168–70
Spielberg, Steven, 60; *Close Encounters of the Third Kind*, 60
stories, 31

strangers, 30; appeal of, 126; extreme, 123–28; as lonely, 115; and love, 136–41; and pain, 129; and power, 115; religious role of, 110–11; and threat, 114
Strayed Reveler, The (Arnold), 39
streets, 162, 189; as belonging to travelers, 182; as contact, 183–84; as excluding travelers, 185; as kinetic, 183; as physical, 184–85
stupor, 93. *See also* trance
subconscious, the. *See* unconscious, the
suffering, of strangers, 131
suicide, 98, 100
surfaces, 17, 42, 53; accepted, 18; body as, 131, 186; edge of, 71, 79–80; extended, 35, 50–51; guides and, 148, 158; left or lost, 17, 19–20, 24, 25, 27, 152; multiplicity of, 25–26; and orientation, 61; and pleasure, 188; ruptured, 18, 153; scrutinized, 150; sexual, 150–52; travel with, 18; unbroken, 110
surrealism, 104, 105, 149
survival, 29
Switzerland, 13
Syria, 155–56

Tangier: accosted in, 130; dreamed of, 104–5; ferry to, 112–13; and hotel, 174; as strange to Bowles, 99, 101; vulnerability in, 61, 77
Theroux, Paul, 177
Thoreau, Henry David, 30, 88–89, 161
threshold anxiety, 69
Tillich, Paul, 25
tourists: and anxiety, 70; defended, 57–58, 59–65; envied, 63; to oneself, 186; as ordinary, 60, 141; in religion, 56–57; scorned, 23, 57, 58–59; sites of, 35, 49–50; vs. travelers, 55–56; in *Wise Blood*, 117–18
trance: benefits of, 86–87; as dreaming, 101; and loss of self, 95–96; in passage, 82, 93, 97, 98; in religion, 106; sought, 102; in writing, 104
transcendence, 117

Studies in Religion and Culture